Mindful Prevention of Burnout in Workplace Health Management

Ingrid Pirker-Binder
Editor

Mindful Prevention of Burnout in Workplace Health Management

Workplace Health Management, Interdisciplinary Concepts, Biofeedback

Springer

Editor
Ingrid Pirker-Binder
Health-Consulting, Psychotherapy, Biofeedback
Vienna
Austria

Translation by
Andrea Zimpernik
Linguaserv–Translations
Business English
Vienna
Austria

ISBN 978-3-319-61336-9 ISBN 978-3-319-61337-6 (eBook)
https://doi.org/10.1007/978-3-319-61337-6

Library of Congress Control Number: 2017958605

Translated from German original "*Prävention von Erschöpfung in der Arbeitswelt. Betriebliches Gesundheitsmanagement, interdisziplinäre Konzepte, Biofeedback.*" Springer Berlin, Heidelberg, 2016

Enriched and updated

Printed on acid-free paper

This Springer imprint is published by Springer Nature
The registered company is Springer International Publishing AG
The registered company address is: Gewerbestrasse 11, 6330 Cham, Switzerland

I want to dedicate this book to all those people who pursue life and work in flow

To my sons

Foreword I

Do we really need another book that tells us that the modern work environment is the reason for burnout, is detrimental to people's health and reduces employees' productivity? The answer is yes, and Ingrid Pirker-Binder's book provides a great rationale for that answer. Global competition and technological advancement, especially the "freedom to work from anywhere, anytime" seem to have turned against us. And so, the prospect of ever higher salaries or faster careers is no longer enough to cover up that employees worldwide experience some degree of disillusionment and even burnout and that we are facing a talent and people crisis in organizations.

For instance, a recent and widely publicized study by Gallup has shown that 49.5% of employees are "not engaged" and 16.5% are "actively disengaged" in their work. On the flip side, another study by Dale Carnegie showed that companies with engaged employees outperform others by 202%. Shouldn't this alone be reason enough to address the issue?

Naturally, there are societal trends that are difficult to address by individuals or by organizations. But there are practices and strategies that we can control, including how we create meaningful work experiences and how we integrate them with our personal lives. Ingrid Pirker-Binder addresses these questions from the angle of occupational and business psychotherapy and provides great insight and wonderful, practical solutions. But she takes it even further. All too often, the relevant literature does little more than to suggest alternatives. Based on a profound understanding of the literature, Ingrid Pirker-Binder actually provides scientific insights into how our physical selves are impacted by the work environment and how a focus on our physical health can improve productivity and satisfaction in the workplace. In this book, she takes us on a journey from psychotherapy to occupational health and from nutrition to strategic management in organizations.

I truly hope not only that employees suffering from stress or threatened by looming burnout will read this book, but that it will also find a wide audience among top decision-makers who care for their employees and the long-term viability of their companies.

Gerhard Apfelthaler, Ph.D.
Dean and Professor
School of Management
California Lutheran University
Thousand Oaks, USA

Foreword II

This book ranges from the phenomenon of exhaustion to methods, which revive and support creativity in people.

In a time, which subjectively feels to be passing ever faster, during which the social and economic pressures are increasing, it is crucial to understand the connections.

Our understanding must be directed towards the true nature and culture of human beings. However, nature and culture can only be understood in dialogue, and the understanding thereof does not arise by itself.

This book examines the conditions in which there is a risk that people's life energy keeps diminishing to a point where it almost completely vanishes.

The editor is a specialist in the diagnostics and therapy of diminished or dwindling life energy. Her biofeedback procedure, refined in many facets and up-to-date, helps her to recognize the blockages and release them. This requires an understanding of the authenticity of each individual. This book provides all the details and leaves you truly enriched.

Univ.Prof.Dr.Dr.h.c mult Alfred Pritz
SFU Sigmund Freud Private University
Vienna Linz Paris Berlin Milano Ljubljana

Preface

Dear readers,

In my work as an occupational and business psychotherapist and psychotherapeutic expert on (in) ability to work due to exhaustion, I have become familiar with the everyday crises, problems, work and time pressure of my clients and patients and their stress and work-related complaints. This has spurred my inspiration and motivation for this book.

Technological progress makes it possible—unfortunately or fortunately:

Work anytime and anywhere.

People must not forget about themselves and get lost in the daily time pressure and ruminating. Work needs to be integrated meaningfully into life; a mindful way of life may also take place during work time to facilitate life and work in flow. Long gone are the days of work-life balance; the focus is much rather on *work-life integration* and *mindful interaction*; it is also no longer a question of relaxing but of preserving active regeneration.

From the perspective of a meaning-oriented occupational and business psychotherapy, I will show in this book ways to sustainably preserve human resources, performance capability and motivation, for the benefit of the working people and the economic success of their businesses.

To keep fit at work, a holistic view of humans, their needs, desires, strive for meaning, personality and work environment is required. The topics discussed in this book range from the company to the needs of the cell and from the importance of a meaning-oriented occupational and business psychotherapy and its integration into company health management as an internal or external Health Assistance Program to new holistic approaches for early detection of exhaustion. *LifeSkript-, WorkSkript- and LifeEnergyAnalysis*, which I developed, should serve as a guide.

The chapters of this book throw a spotlight on businesses and management, on the working people and their energy and on new measurement and training methods offered by biofeedback in the workplace; in particular, the importance of heart-rate variability for the prevention of exhaustion and for specific training to preserve health will be addressed; additionally, an expanded image of stress and strain will be presented.

I would like to sincerely thank my clients and patients for their trust and also my co-authors who have contributed much to the success of this book. Also, I wish to thank the employees of the publishing house who supported me and always provided assistance. Last but not least, I am indebted to my friends who have helped me with proofreading and creating graphics.

My co-authors and I hope you will find this book full of useful ideas and that you will enjoy reading it!

Vienna, Austria Ingrid Pirker-Binder

Contents

Editor and Contributors

About the Editor

MMag. Dr. Ingrid Pirker-Binder studied international business and educational sciences in Vienna and subsequently completed a psychotherapeutic training in Existential Analysis and Logotherapy by Viktor Frankl. She qualified in value-oriented imagination by Böschemeyer, EMDR, Bio-/Neurofeedback (aapb.org) and earned her doctorate at the Sigmund Freud University in Vienna. She is a sworn and judicially certified expert for psychotherapy. Her professional focus is on workplace health management, management training, and occupational and business psychotherapy. Besides her work as a psychotherapist in private practice, Dr. Pirker-Binder acts as a coach and consultant for capacity to work in the case of a fatigue syndrome, works as a business mediator and offers supervision. She applies methods such as bio-/neurofeedback, heart-rate variability measurement and training within stress and prevention management. Additionally, she is a lecturer and textbook author and holds lectures, seminars and workshops.

Contact
office@pirker-binder.at
www.pirker-binder.at
++43 (0) 676 70 47 668
RETREAT R^4—the adventure week in addition to the book:
Outpatient prevention of exhaustion at selected hotels
Reset * Reflection * Regeneration * Restart
Work and life in flow, preservation of performance capability and vitality
www.betriebliche-gesundheit.at
office@betriebliche-gesundheit.at

Contributors

Heinrich Anker Lyss, Switzerland

Bohdana Fialová DAP Services a.S, Ostrava, Czech Republic

Gerhard Moser Vigaun, Austria

Ingrid Pirker-Binder Vienna, Austria

Martin Reich Vienna, Austria

Jiří Šimonek DAP Services a.S, Ostrava, Czech Republic

Ingrid Spona Vitalogic Dr. Spona VertriebsgmbH, Vienna, Austria

Marie Šťastná DAP Services a.S, Ostrava, Czech Republic

Part I
Human Resources in the Work and Economic World

Chapter 1
Prevention of Exhaustion of Human Resources in Workplace Health Management

Ingrid Pirker-Binder

Humans have two tasks,
Creating the world through action,
and maturing on the inner path.

(K. F. Graf Dürckheim)

Contents

I. Pirker-Binder (✉)
Vienna, Austria
e-mail: office@pirker-binder.at

I. Pirker-Binder (ed.), *Mindful Prevention of Burnout in Workplace Health Management*, https://doi.org/10.1007/978-3-319-61337-6_1

Work-life-integration is replacing work-life-balance.

Global economic crises, the dynamics of our technological development, the loss of power of money, the reorganization of working environments (decentralized and flexible workplaces, home office, permanent reachability, etc.) call for a restructuring of economic and educational ways of thinking. The exclusive focus of the economy on financial success without regard to the environment is passé; a new way of thinking is arising from the crises. Humans and the preservation of their resources are being focused on more than ever. New media make it possible: **work has become omnipresent**! Humans have to learn to integrate work and their private life into the day and to distance themselves at the same time—it is an integration process and has long ceased to be a balancing act.

1.1 Initial Situation

Global economic crises, the dynamics of our technological development, the loss of power of money, the reorganization of working environments (decentralized and flexible workplaces, home office, permanent reachability, etc.) call for a restructuring of economic, educational and humanistic ways of thinking. The exclusive focus of the economy on financial success without regard to the environment is passé; a new way of thinking is arising from the crises, and the time has come to seek the preservation of human resources. Only if the individual can keep up his/her performance capability, can a company be successful and achieve positive long-term health results. Businesses are social and living systems.

Workplace health management deals with the human resources of the employees. Before any meaningful steps in health promotion can be taken in a company, a workplace health management needs to be put in place. Meaning-oriented occupational and business psychotherapy can make a significant contribution both, through business consulting of strategic management, as well as through consulting and designing policies and interventions for employees. Its purpose is the preservation of human resources and their performance and readiness potential.

The analysis aims at the individual in the social network at work, the basics of fatigue and prevention, leadership concepts and Viktor Frankl's concept of meaning as a motivating factor.

The word Burnout[1] (fatigue syndrome), with its wide terminology reflects today's zeitgeist. Numerous studies analyze the burnout status of various professional groups and describe the hazards associated with a psychological and/or physical collapse. Not to be neglected are the significant economic costs incurred by the temporary or permanent loss of capacity to work. According to a publication

---

[1]Here burnout is referred to as a condition of mental and/or physical exhaustion that can upset the internal and external balance if it is not recognized in time. If the balance cannot be reestablished, a complete mental and/or physical collapse may result. The term burnout will subsequently be replaced by exhaustion or fatigue syndrome.

of the European Community at least 40 million employees in the EU countries are affected and cause annual costs of at least 20 million euros, apart from the negative impact on production and competitiveness (European Commission 2000).

While technological progress has remained a permanent focus of attention and machines require, and are subject to, constant maintenance, the human resources have largely been neglected; humans with their needs and necessities have, so to speak, been subordinated to technical and economic success.

However, machines cannot replace the human factor. The "individual as a whole" and his/her resources are slowly being put into perspective, which is called human capital;[2] ways to make this human capital measured and displayable are being looked for.

The rising number of sick days caused by psychological and physical stress, the high rate of burnout cases shows that it is time to make the people and their needs the focus of interest so as to secure future economic survival. In this respect Souba (2014) pointedly quotes Wiener (1988),

> We have modified our environment so radically that we must now modify ourselves in order to exist in this new environment. We can no longer live in an old one. Progress imposes not only new possibilities for the future but new restrictions.[3]

Exhaustion at the workplace has to do with people, their performance capability, their achievement motivation and their ability to work; it concerns their communication, interactions, their physical and mental abilities and skills and the place where work takes place that provides the framework for their economic activities.

At the beginning of the technological explosion, it was assumed that the new technologies would facilitate the existing work and that human labor could subsequently be saved. Meanwhile technological progress has overtaken us. Dascal and Dror, professors of cognitive psychology in Tel-Aviv and London, write in this respect:

> Viewed from this perspective, we think that technological innovations have not necessarily reduced the amount of work but rather significantly changed the type of work performed by humans …These innovations did not replace human labour but introduced deep changes in its environment, which led to the requirement and development of new cognitive competences …We will not be able to describe the work environment by blunt physical and psychosocial factors. We will need a new vocabulary that describes the work by e.g. declarative, procedural, executive, memory capacities, implicit/explicit, etc. functions with relation to brain function. (Dascal and Dror 2005)

Now what does the technological progress mean for the working people, the society? First of all, certainly lifelong learning, followed by the willingness to change and a lot of flexibility, which concerns both the work and the activity per se. It almost looks as if the technological development were much faster than humans

---

[2]Human Capital, definition: The performance potential of the employees (work capacity) based on training and education (Gabler Wirtschaftslexikon 2014).

[3]Wiener (1988).
Souba (2014).

can take it. They lag behind. For the requirements of this time to be met, willingness to change and personality development are demanded from all people. This applies not only to dealing with oneself, but in future also the orientation towards the community and the communal taking of responsibility for ecology and nature will move more and more in the foreground: from the "I" to "you" to "we."

1.1.1 The Eternal Topic of Burnout and Stress

It is a fact that the word burnout is an often-used term, which is not yet clearly defined. It is imprecise and very often used incorrectly. In Austria it is allowed to stay at a rehabilitation health spa (so-called "Burnout clinics") because of burnout (usually diagnosed as exhaustion depression). In the Manual ICD-10 for the classification of mental disorders (2012) strain is classified with the number Z73.3 and fatigue syndrome (being burnt out, burnout) with the number Z73.0. Complaints that fall under these numbers do not entitle to compensation of costs in the case of psychotherapy. Burnout is thus only an additional diagnosis, not a treatment diagnosis. The term burnout has become a buzzword. In fact, however, burnout is a serious diagnosis when a person is suffering from it.

Burnout as a fatigue syndrome is a state of mental and/or physical exhaustion, which, if not diagnosed and the internal and external balance being restored, results in a complete mental and/or physical breakdown of the organism. The occurring complaints are complex, sometimes diffuse. For this reason, the term burnout is replaced by the terms exhaustion or fatigue syndrome in this section.

Long-lasting mental and/or physical stress and strain cause chronic stress, which may result in a fatigue syndrome. From the manifold definitions of burnout I would like to summarize based on Nelting (2010) and Ahola et al. (2005) as shown in the box below.

Exhaustion at the Workplace

Exhaustion at work is defined as a process-like illness, as a system excitation from a persistent, gradually-reinforcing or chronically existing workplace-related, emotional, mental or physical activation. This initiates a process of dissolution of the psychophysical self-regulation, with the cardinal symptom of exhaustion.

The more severe the exhaustion, the higher is the probability of a depression.

Stress
The word stress is used to characterize a state of activation. The organism does not know any difference between negative and positive stress, but only activation or different level of activation.

1.1.2 The Beloved Eustress as Savior?

Eustress (used for positive stress) is usually understood as a challenge, the person concerned has sufficient coping strategies for in order to take up this challenge and to cope with the task positively. However, prolonged eustress also results in exhaustion just as Distress does (e.g. "I love my work", "It does not bother me to work twelve hours every day"). Loving one's work, having a high level of motivation, do not suffice to keep people healthy, only life and work in flow, in accordance with the individual resources, does.

If one refers to this understanding of eustress as positive stress, all those should not suffer from exhaustion, who love their work and have sufficient skills and competences to complete the tasks at hand. Yet, this is not true anymore.

It's no longer merely a matter of cognitive coping strategies, but rather whether the organism of the working human has sufficient recovery times and mechanisms. As is known from the biofeedback research, it is assumed according to a new approach in active stress management that, for the preservation of health, the resonance ability of the organ systems within the body must not be disturbed or unsettled by prolonged strain (heart rate variability). So, it's not about relaxation, which means as much as reduction of tension starting at a given level, but rather the strengthening of the regeneration system, i.e. the parasympathetic part of the autonomic nervous system (specifically the vagus nerve) and preservation of the resonance ability of the heart rate. This is done in a harmonious and resource-oriented interplay between various degrees of alertness on the one hand and relaxed letting-go and deep regeneration on the other hand.

Basically it's about the answer to the question how much the working human is aware of his/her performance capability, resources and resilience and in how far he/she can bring life and work into a state of coherence or how he/she integrates recovery in work time (regenerative micro breaks).

It's not a matter of balance between work and life (work-life balance), but of integration of work in life. Integration is demanded even more, the more workplaces change; the home office can serve as one of many examples.

Work-Life Integration Replaces Work-Life Balance
It is no longer a question of two opposites, which are to be brought into balance, but of life with meaningful integration of times of activity and times of recovery and regeneration. The body cannot distinguish whether the person is working out of duty or for pleasure. Strain remains strain, no matter where it takes place. Hence, for quite some time it has not been merely about stress but regenerative capacity.

If people neglect the needs of the body and, in particular, its ability to recover, exhaustion or illness will not fail to appear. The solution is active energy management, awareness and a sense of using only as much energy as is necessary for the work at hand and not more: one can be all tense in front of the PC or work in a comfortable position. High muscle tension as a result of concentration is not necessary.

1.2 Successful Prevention in the Work and Economic World

If timely appropriate prevention, intervention and training measures are taken, longer-term sickness-induced absences, sick leave and, in the worst case, complete inability to work can be prevented. This raises the question of appropriate measures. It is, therefore, not surprising that almost feverish attempts are being made to influence this process of rising cases of burnout (see Footnote 3)[4] in various ways. In Austria the clearest reaction was the entry into force of the Worker Protection Law amendment (ASchG-Novelle; Federal Law Gazette BGBl 118/2012) on 1.1.2013, which places more emphasis on the importance of mental health and prevention of work-related psychological stress, which leads to inappropriate strain, and incorporates into law measures to assess psychological stress in the workplace.

With the Worker Protection Law amendment the duty to evaluate psychological stress at work has become required by law. Psychological stress, leading to inappropriate strain, and also strain on the musculoskeletal apparatus, are a common cause of work-related ailments and illnesses (physical requirements/mental requirements). They cause much human suffering, but also enormous business and economic costs (Federal Ministry of Labor, Social and Consumer Affairs 2015).

[4]Nil et al. (2010) speak of burnout as a labor psychological concept and not a psychiatric diagnosis: "As a concept it may easily be linked to existing stress models in the field of work physiology and psychology and their postulated, predictive health consequences. These extend, according to empirical findings, not only to psychiatric disorders such as depression, but with increasing evidence, also to somatic illnesses such as those of the cardiovascular system."

Psychological stress includes psychosocial, psycho-emotional and psycho-mental stress.

Psychological Stress from the Point of View of Occupational Science
"Psychological stress is the totality of all detectable influences that come to the people **from the outside** and influence them mentally" (Federal Ministry of Labor, Social and Consumer Affairs 2015). Reactions to psychological strain are understood as psychological stress at work.

Psychological Stress from the Perspective of Occupational and Business Psychotherapy
Psychological stress is the totality of all detectable influences that act **from outside and inside** on the people and have an impact on their emotional experience, emotions and reactions; because psychological stress at work and the reactions to it are individual and closely connected with the personality, the world of experience of the working people and the environmental factors.

1.2.1 Aspects of Successful Prevention

Hence, successful workplace prevention will increasingly need to be oriented towards the person and his/her world of experience. In the future companies should regard the term "success" in terms of health success, as market-based success follows resource-oriented work.

Prevention and intervention are areas of workplace health management, whose responsibilities include two questions:

A. **What role and what objective** shall the issue of health and commitment of employees have within workplace health management and as an integrated part of corporate thinking?

Answering this question is a strategic management decision. New concepts that are based on people are required here; the implementation of strategic decisions takes place within workplace health promotion (education, training, further training).

B. **What meaningful preventive measures** can be used to avoid health crises and what actions should be taken when they have occurred?

To answer this question interventions and concrete measures are necessary (consulting, coaching, brief therapy, various methods from the portfolio of therapeutic methods, emergency and crisis intervention, anonymous point of contact within the company or outside the company for all employees).[5]

The meaning-oriented **occupational and business psychotherapy** can make a significant contribution to answering both questions. Its contribution to question A lies in the business consulting function of strategic management and in project management; with regard to question B it provides consulting, designing measures and interventions for employees of a company. Its task is to maintain the specific human resources and their performance and readiness potential.

Successful prevention of exhaustion at the workplace refers to two aspects:

1. **Individual**: prevention based on the individual employee, his/her inner work experience, his/her attitude and evaluation system, his/her life story.
2. **Collective**: prevention based on groups, teams, and all employees of a company. Collective health ensures the company's success.

Collective prevention includes all employees of a company and is a basic precondition for commercial success. In a macroeconomic perspective, the understanding of collective health is extended to all working people of a society and the respectful use of all available resources.

If the individual employee is thriving, so is the team and the group as well. Healthy groups and teams have positive interaction patterns among themselves and in upstream or downstream teams. Even executives are employees, even though they are in a sandwich position between the top management/the company owner and its employees.

The basis of any prevention initiative should be the question about the currently lived corporate culture, because it provides the framework and the breeding ground for economic activity in an organization. A guideline for such consideration is provided through the LifeScriptAnalysis for companies.

The reductionist view claiming that health could be guaranteed by means of good nutrition, exercise and relaxation alone, is giving way to a holistic view of lifestyle. The human being is more than a functioning machine with inexhaustible physical and mental resources. The way the pendulum between health and illness swings, which pole it tends to move to, depends on the individual person. If the workplace is included, the community of working people in the company and the framework conditions also determine the swing of the pendulum.

- **Prevention should not merely be understood as a package of measures but as a process, as opening the awareness for the significance of human resources, for the individual person, a team, a company, for a resource-oriented economic way of thinking and acting**.

[5]Internal or external "health assistance program" (www.betriebliche-gesundheit.at).

If a company's success is considered health success, reasonable prevention viewed from a future perspective can be aligned along three areas:

1. Area of the company, that serves as a common place for a group of working people at their workplaces and offers a living and working framework. In the future, the health of a company will be determined by these factors:
    1. in how far it nourishes its roots, provides the employees with the framework to maintain their performance capability and achievement motivation,
    2. how it keeps the eye on the market and responds to changes quickly and flexibly. Thereby it should not constantly be hungry for higher returns, but also consider periods of regeneration.
    3. how much it respects nature, i.e. how it deals with its corporate social responsibility.
2. Area of the workplace as the location where work takes place, where most of people's lifetime is spent and culture is lived.
3. Area of the individual working individual: his/her psychological performance, his/her work experience, his/her life script, his/her meaning and value orientation. This is about the responsibility for the body and the individual's awareness of its needs for maintaining the mental and physical performance capacity.

1.3 Meaning-Oriented Occupational and Business Psychotherapy as Part of the Human Resources Department

The roots of the meaning-oriented occupational and business psychotherapy are in the research of Antonovsky (1997) on coherence, Csikszentmihalyi (2000, 2004) on the flow and Frankl on meaning (1969, 2002, 2004).

Antonovsky abandoned the pathogenic search for why someone falls ill and researched why people stay healthy. For success prevention this health-oriented approach is groundbreaking. He realized that stressors are challenges, which must be addressed. They are lifelong influences.

> The confrontation with a stressor … results in a state of tension one has to be able to handle. Whether the result will be pathological, neutral or healthy, depends on the adequacy of processing tension. (Antonovsky 1997, p. 16)

Antonovsky examined whether there may be predictions about tension processing and developed the concept of generalized resistance resources.

> … My fundamental philosophical assumption is that the river is the stream of life. Nobody goes safely along the banks. Furthermore, it is clear to me that a large part of the river is contaminated, both literally and figuratively. There are forks in the river resulting in a light current or in dangerous rapids and swirls. My work is dedicated to dealing with the following question: How do you become a good swimmer, regardless of the river's condition, the nature of which is determined by historical, socio-cultural and physical environmental conditions? (Antonovsky 1997, p. 92)

He noted that good swimmers possess three major components or resistance resources:

- understandability: life's challenges can be explained and are thus comprehensible.
- manageability: there is the belief that enough resources are available to master these challenges.
- significance: the challenges hold significance, a deeper meaning. This is about recognizing that the challenges have an inherent significance, a deeper meaning.

Depending on the distinctive relationship (coherence) of these three beliefs—generalized resistance resources—i.e. the higher the SOC ("sense of coherence"), the better the person concerned is equipped to master dangerous rapids in the river of life. However, Antonovsky's concept does not provide an explanation, why also people with high SOC scores may suffer from exhaustion at the workplace.[6] One explanation could be that obviously those people, who show high psychosomatic intelligence, do not suffer from exhaustion because of their good feeling for themselves and practice good energy management with and for themselves. Antonovsky's discussion about meaningfulness also led him to Viktor Frankl's philosophy and his concept of unconditional meaning in and towards life.

1.3.1 Frankl's Meaning Oriented Concept as a Motivating Factor

Viktor Frankl's fundamental belief system is built on the pursuit of meaning and values.

He founded the Third Viennese School of Psychotherapy, Existential Analysis and Logotherapy, after Sigmund Freud's Psychoanalysis, i.e. the First Viennese School and Alfred Adler's Individual Psychology, the Second Viennese School.

The **existential analytical approach** allows exploring the personal character of each individual.

---

[6] According to my hypothesis high eustress and high SOC scores are in a close relationship. Overwhelmingly high SOC scores indicate an overestimation of one's own resources.

The findings of Neuropsychotherapy (Grawe 2004) and the neurosciences offer theories for understanding the importance of basic human needs and allow hypotheses about which distortions of thought patterns, actions and attitudes and thus also strain might result if deficits or micro-traumas appeared during the fulfillment of basic needs during childhood, the impact of which extend into the here and now.

The **existential analytical approach** provides the rational basis for the individual living and work concept and explores the unconscious gaps. When unconscious experience becomes conscious, the individual is able to understand, to change and to build new coping mechanisms. Logotherapy focuses on the implementation of these findings and with the opening up of possibilities of meaning.

1.3.2 Exhaustion and the Question of Meaning at the Workplace

From a logotherapeutic point of view burnout or exhaustion can be seen as a **distortion in one's meaning of life**. The individual does not live what he/she could be, but what he/she has to live or believes he/she has to live. He/she does not recognize his/her own space and ignores the needs of his/her body. He/she is not aware of his/her wholeness and lives only individual aspects. Then the aspect of meaningfulness moves into the background in favor of gratification of needs. Work is more and more being reduced to fulfillment of purpose.

This is when the working people live in discord

- with themselves, their intuition, their purpose, their sense of life
- with their mental, physical and emotional resources
- with their working environment
- with the companies they work for

If open and respectful interaction at the workplace no longer exists, the individual poses the question, "Why am I still doing this?" Even Nietzsche wrote, "If one has one's Why of life, one gets along with almost anyone" (Nietzsche 2014). However, if there is no "why", "what for" or "for whom" any more, the individual starts to question the meaningfulness of his/her activity and dedication.

Questioning their own activities also affects those who have had a brilliant career, who have achieved something. Sometimes, in their career pursuit, they have become so distanced to their actual core business that they plunge into a crisis because the horizon of meaning of their job performance has changed and greatly departed from the original basis. Sometimes, though, these people face a crisis because they have simply lost their sense of meaning. They have forgotten to live the essence of life; they have lost the "what for". In this case one generally speaks of "midlife crisis". Crises of meaning associated with the workplace, are closely related to the lived culture, mission and vision, leadership, work contents and timelines.

Dichotomy Between Mission/Vision and Individual Concepts of Meaning and Values

Mr. X, a young man just over 30 years old, contacts me in my practice. He is close to tears and makes a very depressive impression. His wife had sent him because of burnout, he says. During the diagnostic interview it becomes clear that it is neither a case of burnout nor depression, but a question of meaning and values and the feeling of not having any freedom of choice.

Background: The young man was department head in a medium-sized company. He was known as very efficient and had good opportunities for advancement. Nevertheless, he himself had an ever-increasing identification problem with the mission and vision of the company. His work, the mission and future vision of the company were becoming less and less compatible with his attitude. He plunged into a crisis when he did not dare to quit. He had two small children, lived in a small town where he had also taken on various tasks such as working as a volunteer firefighter. He did not see any way out. After graduation from university he had already worked in 3 different companies, and he was of the opinion that changing jobs frequently would be a hindrance during the job search. In the existential analysis of his crisis it turned out that for a long time Mr. X had already been carrying a wish within himself, namely to become self-employed in the special area of the future-oriented field of environmentally friendly construction. He blossomed visibly as soon as he delved into that matter; his depressed mood had disappeared. He slowly began to recognize and to feel where his path would take him and that he had to leave his company if he wanted to recover. He eventually did so, although the company management tried everything to persuade him to stay.

A business as a living, social system offers people a place of individual growth by successfully managing challenging tasks. It takes a reflective person to perceive situations, be able to recognize relationships and act sensibly and purposefully. A balanced ratio of will to take action and activity requirements results in enthusiasm for the work and a sense of coherence (Bauer and Brown 2014, p. 17).

Another phenomenon is the crisis of meaning in the middle years of a person's life, which is generally known as "midlife crisis". It is the time when all the material and ideological objectives have been achieved, the house is built, the family is founded, and the children are grown up. At that point, frequently, the question "Why am I doing all this?" arises. In this case it is an existential crisis, which entails deep thought "What am I here for, what do I live for?" The finite nature of existence and the awareness of the terminal nature of earthly life cause an emotional shock. This is not a burnout, but the realization that there is an end to everything. The crisis contains the invitation to deal with one's own meaning of life or reorient oneself. The meaning must be found anew. Another aspect involves the fear of the loss of one's job.

1.3.3 The Theory of Meaning in Workplace Health Management

The logotherapeutic assessment concentrates on the distortion, i.e. what blocks people's experience of meaningfulness.

Frankl's theory of meaning has proven to be the motivation concept par excellence in today's management. Human activity is based on a causal strive towards meaningfulness. This pursuit, or determination, can be divided into two aspects, namely

- the inner aspect, which exists inside every individual and
- the outer aspect, which includes the offered concepts of meaning and options for the realization of meaning.

This primal force of wanting to do something truly meaningful, which is located inside every human, is neither diminished by illness nor by immaturity or senility. Willingness to perform and capacity to work originate here.

Coherence between internal and external aspects results in willingness to perform and psychological capacity to work. Work, as quest for meaning and realization of meaning, has an effect on psychological health or illness.

- **Exhaustion as a result of a distortion of realization of meaning**

If the realization of meaning becomes distorted, disruptive factors become active that may result in emotional and/or physical exhaustion.

Once a person no longer feels connected to his/her physical resources, ignores or denies all somatic indications, his/her resources may fail, any reserves are exploited —this results in a physical and/or psychological breakdown. Whether first a psychological or physical breakdown happens, depends on individual personality factors, primarily on where the person affected has hidden his/her blind spots and deficits. Disruptive factors may be rooted in the people themselves, for example, if work serves as a substitute for unsatisfied basic needs, or in the environment at work:

- lack of modes of meaning at the workplace,
- a conflict of values, which arises through a mismatch between the demands of work and individual attitudes and principles (Maslach and Leitner 2001, p. 17),
- onerous working conditions.

The basic needs are the same for all people; they merely differ in severity. In his consistency theoretical view of psychological functioning Grawe (2004, p. 190) states two influencing factors, namely

- the pursuit of congruence (fulfillment of all basic needs) and
- the pursuit of consistency (basic principle of psychological functioning)

In his opinion:

> Psychological processes are continually focused on perceiving in the sense of activated motivational goals.
>
> Behind the motivational goals are the basic needs … goals and behavior are, in contrast to basic needs, related to concrete situations or classes of situations. With regard to goals and behavior people differ due to their life experience, in their basic needs, however, they do not. (Grawe 2004, p. 190)

Elger (2009, Pos. 1459) describes from the point of view of "neuroleadership" four vital needs as the cornerstones, which are closely interwoven and ensure psychological wellbeing in life and working life:

- establishing, shaping and maintaining social relations,
- understanding the world—being curious and learning,
- preserving the existing and avoiding losses,
- developing and growing.

- **According to Frankl striving for realization of meaning is the elemental force per se, which is anchored in every human being.**

Looking now at this concept of motivation and Grawe's consistency theory, the roots of (in-) ability to work due to exhaustion can already be guessed here. If there are shortcomings in the basic needs, the quintessential realization of meaning is primarily directed towards overcoming those shortcomings, and only secondarily towards the actual finding of meaning in work life. An example would be if work served as a love substitute or boost of self-appreciation.

1.3.4 Meaning and Values—From the Concept of Meaning to Modern Management

Based on the human striving for realization of meaning work is meaningful. Here Frankl's existential analysis and logotherapy extend to modern management. In this sense, logotherapeutic expert opinions for the evaluation of psychological capacity to work can fill a gap between aspects of humanistic psychotherapy and modern leadership. Renowned business experts (Malik, Anker, Corvey etc.) are dealing with Frankl's logotherapy and describe his concept of meaning as the contemporary concept of motivation per se.

Corvey (1992) bases his model of Pro-activity (Fig. 1.1) on Frankl's theory of the inner freedom to decide for or against something and the ability to choose between stimulus and response.

Thereby Corvey understands the ability of humans to subordinate an impulse to a value. He distinguishes between reactive people, who are driven by their feelings, the circumstances or their environment, and pro-active people, who receive motivation from their values. So,

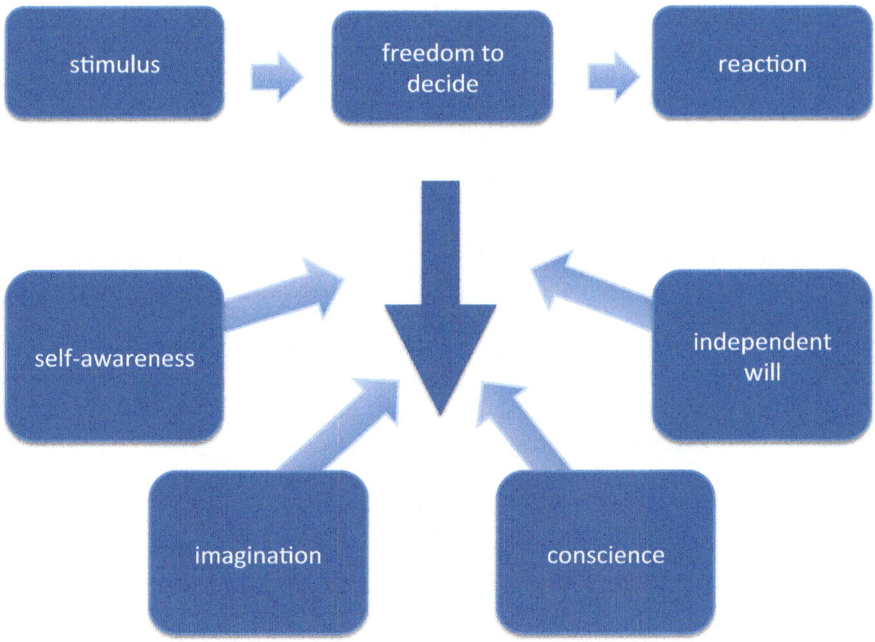

Fig. 1.1 Proactive model. Modified according to Corvey (1992)

> … Frankl utilized the gift of self-awareness to discover a fundamental principle: the individual has the freedom to choose between stimulus and response. In the freedom of choice lie the talents that make us unique as human beings. In addition to self-awareness, we have the imagination - the ability to mentally create something beyond our present reality. We have conscience - a deep inner awareness of right and wrong, of the principles that determine our behavior, and a sense for the degree to which our thoughts and actions are in accordance with them. And we have the independent will - the ability to act independently from all other influences on the basis of our self-awareness. (Corvey 1992, p. 69 ff.)

Anker uses Frankl's concept of meaning as a model of thinking for his book *Balanced Valuecard*; performance instead of egoism:

> Meaning-centered self-motivation mobilizes forces and creativity, which are completely neglected in neoliberal economics: professional circles estimate that employees under a utilitarian-neoliberal regime (can) only bring 30 to 50% of their potential to their work – an immense waste of resources, not taking into account the disregard of humans as beings with a profound need for meaning, for an answer to the "why" and "what for" of their actions and existence …
>
> Böckmann with recourse to Frankl: With meaning to profit - for the people, businesses and the economy … Our brain rewards cooperation, and it responds positively to appreciation, which we receive, - Contemporary research speaks a language very different from the utilitarianism of the 19th century. (Anker 2010, p. 237)

1.4 Prevention as Workplace Health Management of the Future

> It is interesting that the English words whole and health have the same roots (the Old English hal, as in unhurt or whole). Thus, it should not come as a surprise that the hopeless state of our world is in direct proportion to our inability to perceive it holistically. (Senge 2001, p. 88)

A future workplace health management deals with the questions: How healthy is the company, and not only from the perspective of economic indicators, but especially from the perspective of human resources? How can health be maintained in the company?

A future workplace health management will have to be oriented towards a holistic view and bear three aspects in mind:

- the health success of a company expressed as economic success
- the health success of its human resources—the performance capability and commitment of its employees, which is substantially influenced by the personality and social competence of the managers
- the livability of its mission and vision—corporate culture

In this context health success is understood as the future economic performance capacity of a company and is synonymous with the corporate success.

It will depend largely on the extent the management is able to shift its attention towards a holistic understanding of economic activity, towards meaning and value dimensions and sustainability in the future; it means a rethinking from ever-increasing growth figures towards the preservation of what already exists, of existing success and learning from nature. Without a healthy environment, there is no existence. Corporate Social Responsibility will be a guarantee of future survival; not only for the company itself, but also as an aspect of meaning and motivation for the people who work in such companies, because in this way the "What for and Why" of the effort made becomes clear.

88% of the working population in Switzerland express a strong preference for employers with social responsibility and ethical behavior. "Companies with social responsibility and environmental awareness are the most attractive employers" (Kelly study in Anker 2010).

The stronger staff retention, the less absenteeism and turnover of staff; according to a Gallup Study conducted in 2009, in Germany a company with 500 employees can achieve cost savings of nearly 1 million euros a year through staff retention, companies with 2000 employees, can save almost 4 million euros (Gallup Study in Anker 2010).

This suggests planning changes in terms of a future vision. How food for thought for changes can be found, is described by Scharmer (2009) in his book *Theory U—leading from the future*.

For the preservation of health and prevention of depletion of human resources both, on a small or big scale, the kind of change is crucial, which can be described as follows:

1. qualitative long-term or
2. short-term snapshot

- **Ad 1: qualitative long term**

Qualitative long-term changes are directed towards a future qualitative improvement—change processes are considered from a future point of view (Scharmer 2009).

- **Ad 2: short-term snapshot**

Short-term snapshots denote changes that are meant for the purpose of a correction of the current state. In case there is a problem, it is attempted to restore the previous condition in the sense of a homeostasis (Otto et al. 2007, p. 79). On the corporate level, they are comparable to the legal obligation to evaluate psychological stress in the workplace in Austria. With regard to its basic idea, this is a milestone for the appreciation of human resources in the work world. In practice, however, this is little efficient. Selected external parties interfere in companies for evaluation purposes. For now this is sufficient in terms of the law. However, change processes in a company require an impetus from the inside, the core of the system.

On a personal level such a procedure could mean that employees who are diagnosed with exhaustion are granted a dispensation from work and sent to a rehabilitation center. Once back in the work world, the old patterns start creeping into everyday life. Everything starts again. In this case the next sick leave is already pre-programmed. To illustrate this link, the story of the carpet dealer seems appropriate.

Story of the Carpet Dealer

Once there was a carpet dealer who discovered a large bump in the middle of his most beautiful carpet. He tried to smoothen it with his feet—with success. But it appeared again at a spot close to the first one. Again the carpet dealer jumped on the bump, and it disappeared—only to reappear immediately afterwards at a new spot. Angrily the man pursued the cheeky bump crisscrossing all over the carpet. He jumped and stomped, stomped and jumped, and was ruining the beautiful fabric until he finally lifted the carpet in a corner, and, behold—an angry snake darted out (Shah 1982 courtesy of Herder publishing house).

Conclusion: "Often the causes of our problems are a mystery to us, even though we would only need to look more closely at the solutions we arrived at yesterday." (Senge 2001).

1.4.1 System Thinking as Preventive Factor

Peter Senge is a pioneer in new disciplines of a learning organization. His book *The Fifth Discipline* (2001) is considered one of the standard reference works for new economic thinking, for system thinking.

In today's discussion of the preservation of human resources, this book together with the *Fieldbook for the Fifth Discipline* (Senge et al. 2000) a wealth of thought-provoking ideas not only for a learning organization, but also for successful prevention, or for an active workplace health management, for one of the key factors in a company is the personal qualities of its managers. Their attitudes, thinking and behavior models considerably determine the corporate culture and employee satisfaction.

The background is framed by abandoning the fixation on the present and a turning towards an active way of shaping the economic future; He calls this focus on a new way of perception system thinking—the fifth discipline.

System thinking focuses

- on a holistic approach
- on the perception of interrelations rather than a simple cause-effect causality
- on the perception of change processes

> The discipline of system thinking aims at being able to recognize wholes. This discipline creates preconditions so that we perceive interrelations instead of immovable things and change patterns instead of static snapshots … after all, system thinking is also a form of sensitivity for the subtle interconnectedness, which adds their unique character to living systems. (Senge 2001, p. 91 ff)

System thinking shows two components:

1. Detail complexity
2. Dynamic complexity

Ad 1 Detail complexity provides a very narrow change frame. The view of the higher-level whole missing; the employed instruments do not facilitate sustainable, new, future effective changes. According to its content detail complexity is equal to short-term snapshots.

Ad 2 According to Senge dynamic complexity exists when the same action has completely different effects in the short term than in the long term. Also, an action might have a specific effect in a particular system, but a completely different one in another system. To achieve long-term change, it is important to consider the leverage effect of individual instruments and strategies. Doing the obvious does not lead to the apparently obvious, desired result (Senge 2001, p. 91).

Prevention of exhaustion requires system thinking and raises the question of the right levers. Including the current situation on the labor market with the increasing number of psychological and physical exhaustion of working people, a sixth discipline can be added: the psychological and physical health for the health success of a company.

- **Workplace Health Management must be allowed to develop individually in companies and should be oriented towards the following question: What position in the company must be the starting point in order to bring about what long-term change in the future in terms of conservation of human resources?**

As a basis for system thinking Senge outlines the need for a change of learning and thinking in four core disciplines such as

1. Personal Mastery
2. Mental models
3. A shared vision
4. Team Learning

Ad 1: Personal Mastery The central content of personal mastery is the principle of creative tension. It arises when vision and current reality diverge. On the one hand creative tension allows development and growth, on the other hand, it can lead to emotional stress resulting in feelings like anxiety, tension, discouragement, hopelessness and helplessness. Personal mastery means committing oneself to the truth, that is, remaining faithful to one's visions and tracing one's negative beliefs and fears and undergoing a liberating change process (cited in Senge 2001, p. 190 et seq.).

Ad 2: Mental Models Mental models are understood to be deadlocked beliefs and ideas, which develop into theories and entail specific actions and behavior. Undetected mental models block system thinking, learning and change stagnate.

Ad 3: Shared Vision The shared vision, creating something together, is the greatest shared force and energy of a living, social system (Fig. 1.2).

If the visions of the individuals in a team diverge with respect to the corporate goal or how to get there (meaning, working conditions, climate, etc.), it does not only weaken the health success of the organization concerned, but also results in decreased commitment of the people working in it and may lead to frustration and illness.

Ad 4: Team-Learning Team-learning could also be understood as relationship learning. All members of a team have the same goal and thereby increase their energies and skills. Then they work in coherence with each other. According to Otto et al. (2007, p. 54) this can also be called swarm intelligence. Schools of fish or bird migration can serve as models. The movement of each individual member is carried out in perfect harmony with the other flock members. In nature this coordination happens intuitively, biologically. To achieve this a living social system needs

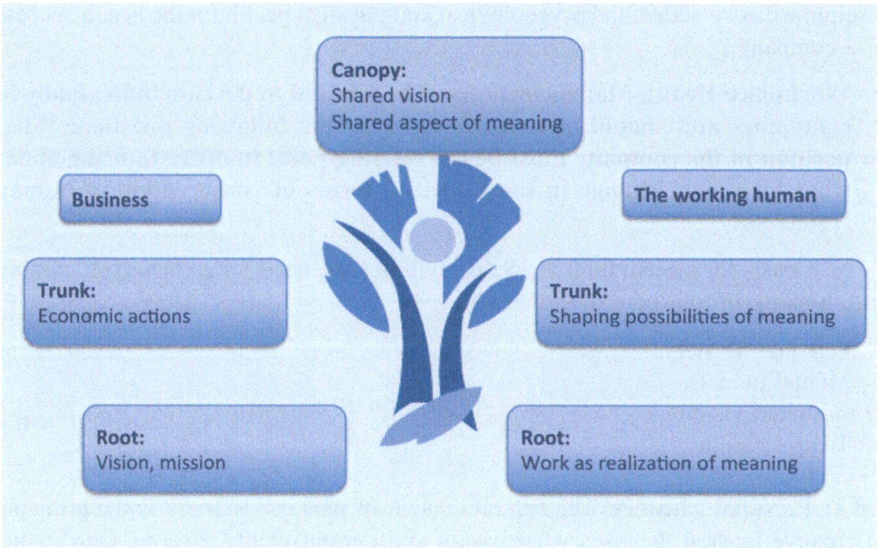

Fig. 1.2 Tree model (Pirker-Binder)

- flexibility in terms of the changing conditions
- robustness when one or more members are absent
- self-organization: the team organizes itself
- self-regulation: specific rules are set up or existing ones are further developed as needed.

The quality of the coherence of team members requires a high degree of social competence, empathy and willingness to learn and communicate. Dialog[7] provides an aid to efficient mutual understanding. In a dialogue different viewpoints are opened up and explored through professional, unbiased asking. In a dialogue, the parties become observers of their own thinking (Senge 2001, p. 294).

David Bohm, a quantum physicist and philosopher, was the pioneer of dialogue in the sense of free flowing group conversation. According to Bohm "our thoughts are incoherent and the resulting counter-productivity is the origin of our biggest problems … The dialogue aims to uncover the incoherence of our thinking" (Senge 2001, p. 294).

For a successful dialogue three conditions are necessary:

1. Assumptions and hypotheses must be presented and allow reflection.
2. Participants must consider themselves equal partners.
3. A neutral helper moderates the dialogue.

[7]Greek: "dialogos": "dia" = through; "logos" = the word, the meaning.

In his "Theory U" Scharmer (Fig. 1.3) addresses holistic thinking and refines it for learning and change processes, "Whenever a process stagnates on an action level, it is important to tackle the same problem differently, rather than do more of the same" (Scharmer 2009, p. 239). He expands Jaworski's thoughts, who points out that it is not enough to merely perceive the world superficially. Only those who succeed in delving more deeply into the nature of relationships, can detect new options:

> … It's about a shift from seeing a world made up of things to seeing a world that's open and primarily made up of relationships, where whatever is manifest, whatever we see, touch, feel, taste, and hear, whatever seems most real to us, is actually nonsubstantial. A deeper level of reality exists beyond anything we can articulate. Once we understand this, we begin to see that the future is not fixed, that we live in a world of possibilities … through this shift of mind, we begin to realize that the sense of despair we've been feeling arises out of a fundamentally naïve view of the world. In fact, absolutely everything around us is in continual motion …when we start to accept this fundamental shift of mind, we begin to see ourselves as part of the unfolding. We also see that's actually impossible for our lives not to have meaning (Jaworski 1998, S. 10 ff).

Similar to a psychotherapy process Scharmer describes four steps to capture social reality, wherein between steps a logical movement, opening and change process takes place.

"Downloading" denotes a first step in the disclosure of topics, aims, problems and visions.

Transition 1: **Opening of thinking:** pausing and opening. "Seeing" (taking a look) denotes a process of initial perception, of seeing different thinking and behavior patterns.

Transition 2: **Opening of feeling:** redirecting and immersion in perception. "Sensing" (feeling): Scharmer calls it delving into relevant contexts, also intuitively grasping relationships, which might result in a new perception, redirecting or refocusing of attention.

Transition 3: **Opening of the will**: letting go, letting come. "Presencing" describes a new quality of perception, which emerges from the creative source point (blind spot); a new perception, which enables new action from the resulting whole (Scharmer 2009, p. 236.). For the ability to go through this development or change process, courage is necessary to engage in the blind spot and to overcome the voices of resistance:

- **voice of judgment** (VOJ): letting go of fixed opinions and thought patterns
- **voice of cynicism** (VoC): letting go of negative emotions and language
- **voice of fear** (VoF): letting go of fear of change, of the future

Both Senge and Scharmer consider businesses living, social systems. To keep them healthy, a holistic approach and the promotion of personal development of employees and executives are the most important preventive measures. Thereby major focal points are dealing with rigid patterns of thinking and acting and emotions, because they give economic activity action input and an aspect of meaning. Scharmer describes the experience of Presencing:

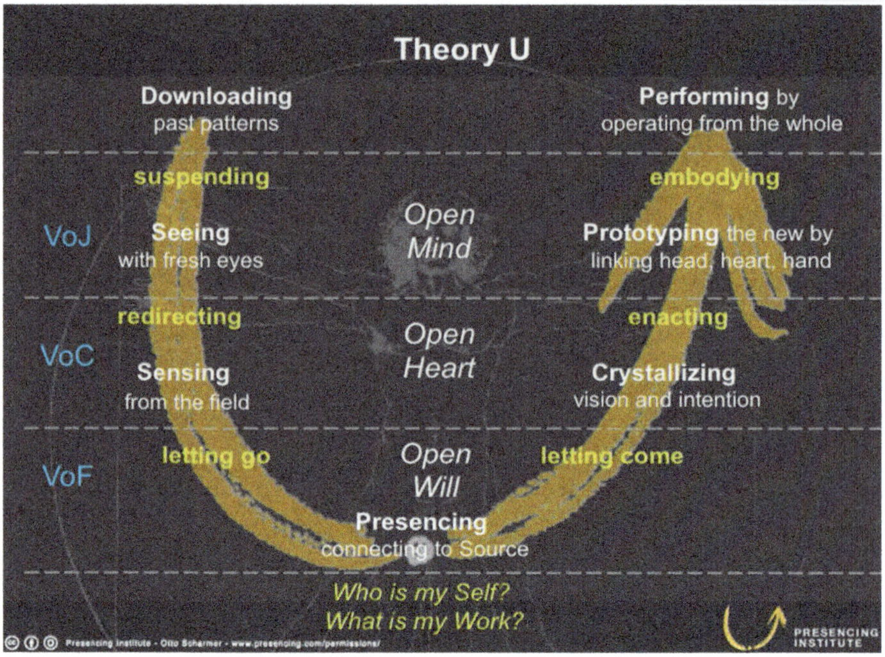

Fig. 1.3 Theory U. Image copyright: Presencing Institute, Otto Scharmer, www.presencing.com/permissions

> The state of the bottom of the U is presencing – seeing from the deepest source and becoming a vehicle for that source. When we suspend and redirect our attention, perception starts to arise from within the living process of the whole. 'When we are presencing, it moves further, to arise from the highest future possibility that connects self and whole. The real challenge in understanding presencing lies not in its abstractness but in the subtlety of experience.' (Senge et al. 2004, S. 89)

- **Meaning oriented occupational and business psychotherapy takes up Senge and Scharmer's ideas and promotes prevention management, humane change management and offers psychotherapeutic knowledge through consulting, projects and interventions.**

1.5 Management in Transition

The way interactions between people in companies happen and are performed is mainly determined by the corporate culture and in particular by executives. At present a paradigm shift is happening: away from a pure production society to a knowledge and service society. This change in values significantly influences the understanding of what it means to be human and management behavior in businesses and thus sets new challenges to social competences.

In the traditional approach executives have the right to control employees by integrating management tools.

This is contrasted with a new understanding of management, which is understood "as mutual interpersonal influence, interaction and permanent shaping of a corporate reality for the common achievement of aims." (Franken 2007).

Work is set in relation to meaningfulness, self-fulfillment, independence, accountability and participation. The transformation from a production to a knowledge society together with a change in the human image significantly influences the topic of management. The quest for realization of meaning and values changes the image of work, work and life quality. Rational values such as hard work, productivity and monetary incentives have changed in favor of a holistic perspective. Aspects of meaningfulness, self-fulfillment, autonomy and self-organization are new objectives and motives.

- **The paradigm and value change and the development of the people not only requires new business structures, such as new places of work (home office), working hours, work experience and mindsets (towards greater corporate social responsibility), but also a new understanding of management.**

An essential aspect of the paradigm shift is the appreciation of performance, respect of the personality of employees, error culture, flat hierarchies, involving instead of marginalizing and monitoring. Acting together instead of hierarchically against each other. Only together and with due respect for each other, is there a successful and healthy future for all.

1.5.1 Management Style in Transition—Transformational Management

One possible management model is called **transformational management**; it is a holistic model, evolved from the delegative management style, which gives the employees a high degree of personal decision, and adds a value dimension. Transformational or value-oriented management integrates the aspect of meaning into entrepreneurial actions. Anker (2010) speaks of three main roads on the way to the aspect of meaning in a company (Fig. 1.4):

- Individual action shall be orientated towards social values.
- Our objective and our actions should not just be an end in itself, but directed towards a "what for", something that goes beyond us.
- Social readiness for other people should exist.

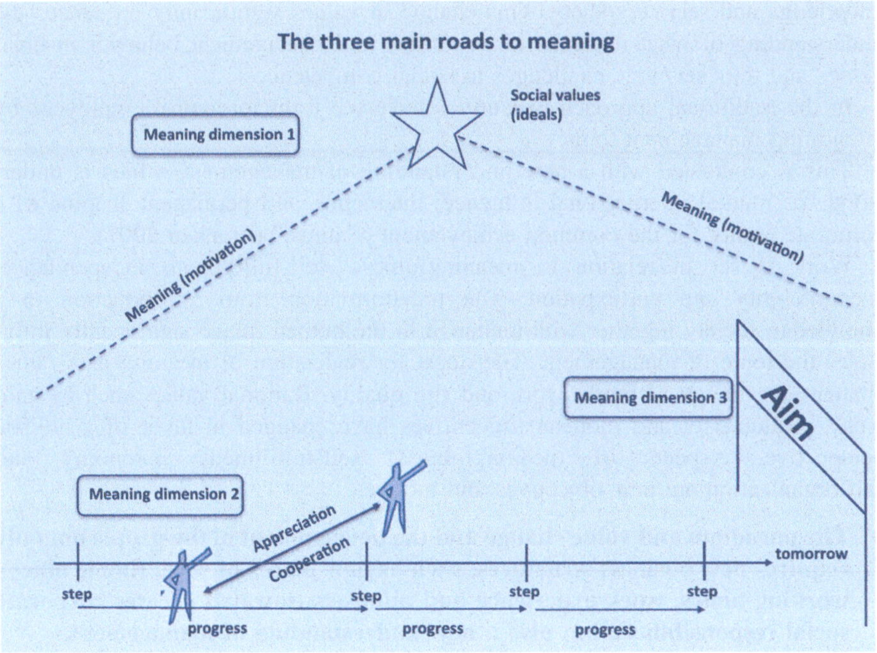

Fig. 1.4 The three main roads to meaning (Anker 2010)

The questions of "why" and "what for" may be asked. The motivation of employees happens through the aspect of meaning and intrinsic motives. Transformational Leadership does not only demand a high social competence from the executives—also the employees are expected to play an active part, participate, think proactively and also change and practice lifelong learning.

Transformational leadership requires a high degree of humanity and being human from executives—despite high economic demands and a success-oriented way of thinking. It may also be called the **4 i-skills** according to Bass (Franken 2007, p. 272):

1. **Individual**: employees are individually guided and developed.
2. **Intellectual**: There is mental stimulation; new ways of thinking.
3. **Inspiring**: objectives and tasks must be significant; the vision and mission should be appealing.
4. **Identifying**: the manager must be authentic and exemplary.

"Being human means being aware and being responsible", that's how Viktor Frankl (1986) phrased it.

1.5.2 Management and Its Effect on the Work Environment and the Emotional State of Employees

The results of the INQA 2005 survey (Franken 2007, p. 277) emphasize the importance of management for the mood of employees. About 50% of respondents complained about lack of support and 61% lack about lack of appreciation. Bad working atmosphere leads to physical and psychological reactions of those affected. Those who do not feel comfortable are not focused or stay at home; sick leave and underperformance are the results (Fig. 1.5).

Fear of losing one's job results in underperformance through presenteeism (presence at work despite illness). The Stanford University California has created a formula for calculating the downtime costs through underperformance of

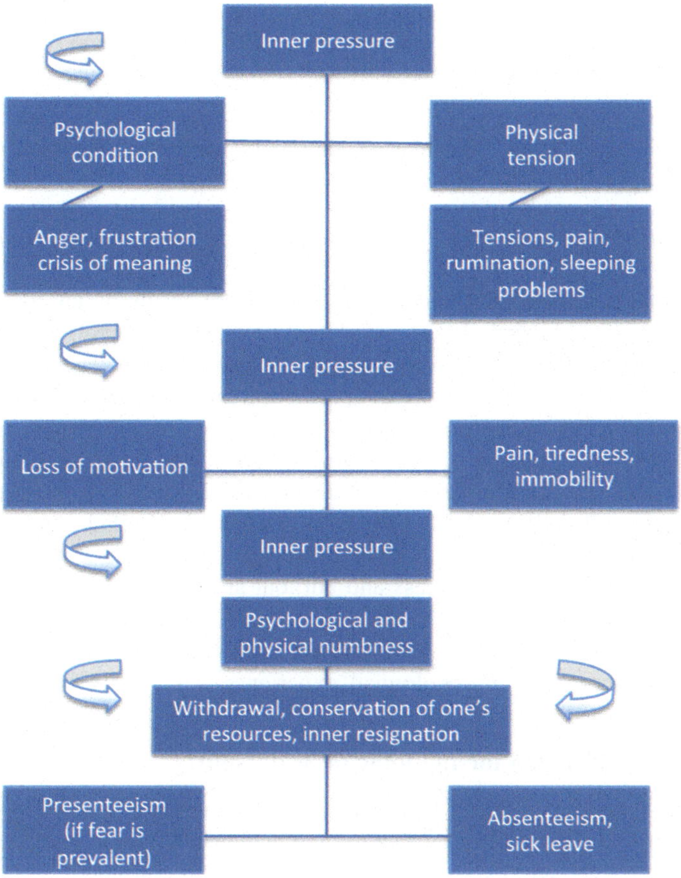

Fig. 1.5 Corporate culture, management deficiencies, fear, crisis of meaning, mobbingCorporate culture and sick leave (Pirker-Binder)

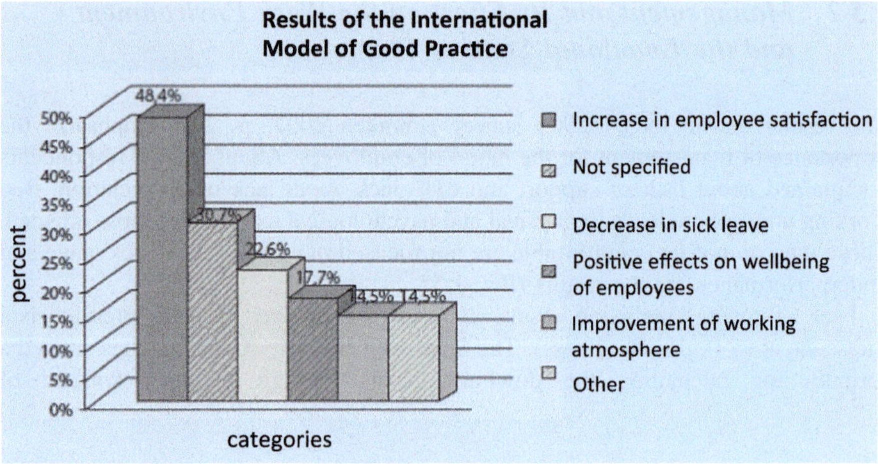

Fig. 1.6 Best practice models in the EU-27 area; concepts for the reduction of stress at work and promotion of health and wellbeing. *Image source* Jimenez et al. (2012), with kind permission

employees and executives, which were caused by problems like worries, stress, crises, bullying, addiction etc.

$$\textit{Number of employees}(NE) \times 20\% = \textit{Number of affected employees}$$

Poor managers make employees sick; this is the result of an EU study by Jimenez, occupational psychologist at the Karl Franzens University (Jimenez et al. 2012; Fig. 1.6). A boss with good management qualities, however, has healthier employees. The study proves that health promoting measures for stress and burnout prevention in companies are worthwhile:

In 48.4% of the companies the satisfaction, trust, loyalty and motivation of the employees increased. 22.6% showed a reduction in sick leave. 17.7% stated positive effects on staff welfare. 4.5% showed an improvement of the working atmosphere and environment. 14.5% noticed a sensitization of the employees for the issues of psychological health, stress and burnout and a reduction in staff turnover rates.

The reduction of the human being and his/her actions to reason, and the separation from his/her inner psychological experience has clearly been refuted by neuroscience.

- **What does this mean for the topic of leadership?**

The forecast rising numbers of absenteeism and underperformance, which are caused by stress or psychological factors, the ageing population and the resulting longer working lives require new motivation and health concepts.

A new set of meaning and values arises, which has to be incorporated more and more into corporate management.

The workplace is considered a place of realization of meaning—those who want performance, must provide meaning (Böckmann 1989, p. 87). The discussion about the questions, what should/has to be done to offer people meaning in their work, and thus preserve long-term willingness to work and performance, and which work and workplace concepts will exist for an ageing society, has occupied scientists and economists worldwide.

"Every affect status determines the immune status" (Frankl 1999, p. 74). This sentence clearly indicates that not only the individual access to thought and action patterns, learning, work and performance, but also the motivation and culture, which are decisively determined by managers, have an influence on the psychological health and performance capability of people and thus also on the survival of our society. Managers, wherever they might be active (Kindergarten, school, business, NPOs) bear this responsibility.

Siebert (in Neuberger 2002, p. 53) writes on the topic of emotions, "Emotions are not only the basis for learning motives and learning resistances, but our reality constructions themselves are caused and tinted emotionally. Emotions are—consciously or unconsciously—intentional motivations for action and also the gateway to health or sickness, depending on how they are lived, denied and/or processed."[8]

Takeover, Continuation of Business

Mr. Y started with a small company, which he had taken over from his father, and over time has established a globally highly successful business. Now he is considering passing the business on to his son. However, his son develops various kinds of psychosomatic complaints. The responsibility of taking over his father's beloved business crushes him. Several consulting companies are involved in the takeover, without taking care of the father's and the son's emotions and unvoiced wishes. Obviously, the father would like his son to continue the family business. The son basically feels pressured into this role; he has never had the option of a free decision whether he really wants take over the business, and if so, in which way.

Only after the father has withdrawn and the son realizes his creative and decision-making possibilities, can the burden, which rests on both of them, be eased.

Conclusion: in any kind of business takeover the emotions and needs of the involved people have to be considered and addressed respectfully. In addition to support in factual and legal matters also emotional support should be provided, e.g. by occupational and business psychotherapists.

Transformational leadership entails a wider debate on the meaning of social competence of managers. People, who successfully lead other people into the future, need a high degree of social competence. Competency enhancement within the meaning of healthy and resource-oriented management expands to management responsibilities in many areas, not only in the economy. On the contrary, it is

[8]Here emotions are defined as emotional states, which entail visible or invisible, noticeable physiological changes depending on their intensity.

always appropriate where people are involved in working, learning and training. Particularly important are healthy and resource-oriented leadership skills of people who educate children and adolescents.

Salovey and Mayer (1990, pp. 185–211) discussed for the first time the concept of emotional intelligence, which was popularized by Goleman (1996). People, who can lead themselves well and handle their emotions, aggression and frustration well, are successful.

Yet, in the discussion about healthy and resource-oriented leadership these capabilities alone are not sufficient. A new research approach is successfully presented by Fazekas (2006, p. 185 et seq.) including "psychosomatic intelligence"; he correlates thinking and feeling. A high psychosomatic intelligence implies a sensitive perception of one's own body:

Through the deliberate inclusion of bodily perceptions and emotions in a symbolized way, PI (psychosomatic intelligence) leads to a deliberate relatedness of thought processes to the whole organism. This relatedness to the whole organism is brought about by the fact that the thought processes are also based on comprehensive information which is relevant and thus comprehensive for the whole organism. Hence, these thought processes show particular relevance for the whole organism and its efforts to achieve an adequate individual-environment match.

PI includes five areas:

1. PI promotes sentience.
2. PI encourages thought processes oriented towards the whole organism.
3. PI deepens the understanding of one's own corporeal being.
4. PI extends the ability to regulate psychosomatic processes.
5. PI facilitates the recognition of inconsistencies and their use as information.

1.5.3 Leadership, Motivation and Emotional State

If we understand leadership as a tool for motivation of commitment and willingness to work towards a common aim, it is clear that there has to be a close relationship between emotional states and motivation. Just as students are only able to provide learning performance in a pleasant, positive environment, the employees are only motivated to provide their full performance capability to the company if they perceive the general conditions positively.

Intrinsic motivation (motivation from the inside out) creates a dynamic tension towards an action. In this respect a link to Eustress can be established, because then work brings joy, provides self-realization and fulfillment of meaning for a larger whole.

On the one hand an executive has to fulfill management tasks in the field of economic thinking and in the implementation of strategic goals, on the other hand, as the leader of a group of people, he/she has the task of motivating, promoting and challenging them.

If a negative state of stress arises between the executive and the employees, this results in a negative emotional state and the commitment decreases. Emotions do not only play a big role in decision and action processes, but also with regard to commitment. Emotions such as constant inner tension, emotional conflicts, anxiety or fear accelerate the exploitation of vital energy in the cells.

The reasons for a negative state of stress in the company can be diverse:

- strategic objectives, processes etc.
- incompetent leadership style and/or a personality disorder of the executives (e.g. narcissistic or histrionic personality disorder)
- work order, work allocation and working hours
- corporate culture

With regard to coherence the cooperation between managers and employees would be disturbed; the flow at the workplace, synchronous oscillation would be interrupted. If this occurs, resource-oriented work is no longer possible; exploitation of human resources occurs resulting in a decline in the company's health success.

Interaction between management and commitment according to Maslach and Leitner

Maslach and Leitner (2001, p. 111) describe the following interdependent areas:

1. **Input of management**. This includes:
    1. Mission and objectives
    2. Centralized management
    3. Control
    4. Communication
    5. Performance assessment
    6. Health and safety. These factors are responsible for the way in which work is lived in the company.
2. **How work is lived, how** human resources are used. This includes the factors
    1. Scope of work
    2. Control
    3. Reward
    4. Community
    5. Fairness
    6. Values

Area 1 and area 2 being in coherence leads to identification conducive with work, and the employees are motivated to perform.

3. **Degree of identification** with work, promotes individual use of human resources:

    1. Energy use
    2. Dedication
    3. Performance capability

Maslach and Leitner see the main challenges in a company in the definition of target agreements and value structures in the management field so that the greatest possible coherence of work and company life is reached, or as little misunderstanding and conflicts as possible arise.

Concerning these objectives there are two challenges according to Maslach and Leitner (2001):

- Creating harmony between people and their work in a way that
- leads to a change in both the working environment and the people (Maslach and Leitner 2001, p. 154).

In their view the following tasks for the management can be formulated as a solution:

- The scope of work must be bearable and feasible.
- The employee needs freedom to make decisions and for self-control.
- Performance must not only be recognized but remunerated accordingly.
- A living community is important.
- Fairness, mutual appreciation and respect, as well as justice must exist.
- The aspect of meaning and value of work must be given.

Mr. Z is a manager in a big company. He is an excellent strategist, and he has had a storybook career. However, in his department the number of sick leave days and absences due to "burnout" is increasing. The fact that the sickness rates might be connected to him is beyond him. Mr. Z is a power seeker, narcissistic and choleric. His employees complain that they never know what mood he is in at any particular moment. He might scream and shout at the slightest little thing, and in this case his choice of words also leaves much to be desired. For his employees his behavior means pure stress. They are afraid of his outbursts of rage and humiliations.

Quite often managers become executives, even though they are not suitable for human resources management.

They may be good strategists, but lack of emotion control and social competence should be a reason for exclusion from leadership positions. Leadership cannot be studied from a course book but only acquired through reflection and self-experience; leadership is a value based on experience. Primarily this value demands a great understanding of one's own emotions—only those who are able to understand their own life story, their motives for thinking and acting and impulses for action, have the appropriate basic knowledge in order to grasp their counterpart in his/her own life. Soube demands in his article "The phenomenology of leadership" a phenomenological approach to leadership. "A phenomenlogical inquiry[9] into leadership does not study the attributes of leaders, but rather the fundamental structures of human beings that make it possible to be a leader in the first place."

In terms of successful prevention the selection of appropriate executives should be a priority in a company; executives with a lack of social competence should be referred to an occupational and business psychotherapist for self-experience purposes. The coaching framework is not sufficient for this.

References

Ahola K, Honkonen T, Isometsä E, Kalimo R, Nykyri E, Aromaa A, Lönnqvist J (2005) The relationship between job-related burnout and depressive disorders-results from the Finnish Health 2000 Study. J Affect Disord 88:55–62

ASchG-Novelle. BGBl. I Nr. 118/2012. http://www.arbeitsinspektion.gv.at/AI/Gesundheit/Belastungen/default.htm. Last access on 9 Sept 2013

Anker H (2010) Balanced Valuecard; Leistung statt Egoismus. Haupt, Bern

Antonovsky A (1997) Salutogenese; zur Entmystifizierung der Gesundheit. DGVT Verlag, Forum, Tübingen

Bauer W, Braun M (2014) Zukunftsforschung: wie werden wir in 20 Jahren arbeiten? In: Badura B et al (2014) Fehlzeiten-Report 2014:17 ff

Böckmann (1989) Sinnorientierte Leistungsmotivation und Mitarbeiterführung. Ein Beitrag zur Humanistischen Psychologie, insbesondere der Logotherapie nach Viktor E Frankl zum Sinn-Problem der Arbeit. Enke, Stuttgart

Bundesministerium für Arbeit, Soziales und Konsumentenschutz (2015) Arbeitsplatzevaluierung psychischer Belastungen. URL: www.arbeitsinspektion.gv.at/AI/Gesundheit/Belastungen/default.htm. Last access on 28 Oct 2015

Corvey SR (1992) Die sieben Wege zur Effektivität. Campus, Frankfurt am Main

Csikszentmihalyi M (2000) Das Flow-Erlebnis. 8. Aufl. Klett-Cotta, Stuttgart

Csikszentmihalyi M (2004) Flow im Beruf; Das Geheimnis des Glücks am Arbeitsplatz

Dascal M, Dror IE (2005) The impact of cognitive technologies. Towards a pragmatic approach. Pragmatics Cogn 13(3):451–457, John Benjamins Publishing Company. URL: http://cognitiveconsultantsinternational.com/Dror_CT_pragmatics_cognitive_technologies.pdf

Elger Ch (2009) Neuroleadership: Erkenntnisse der Hirnforschung für die Führung von Mitarbeitern. Kindle Ed, Rehm, Heidelberg

Europäische Kommission (2000) Streß am Arbeitsplatz ein Leitfaden. Würze des Lebens oder Gifthauch des Todes. Amt für amtliche Veröffentlichungen, Luxemburg. URL: https://menschenrechtsverfahren.files.wordpress.com/2013/10/wc3bcrze-des-lebens-e28094-oder-gifthauch-des-todes.pdf. Last access on 16 Dec 2015

Fazekas CH (2006) Psychosomatische Intelligenz; Spüren und Denken – ein Doppelleben. Springer, Wien, New York

---

[9]A phenomenon (from Greek phainomenon meaning "that which appears or is seen") could be defined as any occurrence entity or situation known through the senses rather than by deduction or reasoning (Burns 1978 in Souba ...Phenomenology is the study of phenomenon and the way in which they are experienced from the first person point of view. Smith 2013 in Souba (2014).

Franken S (2007) Verhaltensorientierte Führung: Handeln, Lernen und Ethik in Unternehmen. 2 Auf, Gabler Wiesbaden
Frankl V (1969) The will to meaning, New American Library, NY, quoted in Frankl V (1986) Die Psychotherapie in der Praxis, Piper München, p. 61
Frankl V (1986) Die Psychotherapie in der Praxis. Piper, München
Frankl V (2002) Logotherapie und Existenzanalyse, Texte aus sechs Jahrzehnten. Beltz, Weinheim Basel 1
Frankl V (2004) Der unbewusste Gott. Psychotherapie und Religion. 7 Aufl dtv, München
Gabler Wirtschaftslexikon (2014) Springer Gabler Verlag (Hrsg) Stichwort: Humankapital. URL: http://wirtschaftslexikon.gabler.de/Archiv/54658/humankapital-v8.html. Last access on 3 Aug 2014
Goleman D (1996) Emotionale Intelligenz. dtv München
Grawe K (2004) Neuropsychotherapie. Hogrefe, Göttingen Bern
Jaworski J (1998) Synchronicity; the inner path of leadership. Berrett-Koehler, San Francisco
Jimenez P, Eibel K, Schaffer C, Šarotar Žižek S, Treven U (2012) Best Practice Modelle im Raum EU-27 – Konzepte zur Reduktion von Stress bei der Arbeit und zur Förderung von Gesundheit und Wohlbefinden. http://www.chanceforchange.eu/uploads/9/8/2/6/9826663/eu27.pdf. Last access on 07 Jan 2016
Maslach C, Leitner MP (2001) Die Wahrheit über Burnout. Stress am Arbeitsplatz und was Sie dagegen tun können. Springer, Wien New York
Nelting M (2010) Burn-out – wenn die Maske zerbricht. Wie man Überbelastung erkennt und neue Wege geht. Mosaik, München
Nil et al (2010) Burnout – Eine Standortbestimmung. URL:http://www.sanp.ch/docs/2010/2010-02/2010-02-053.pdf. Last access on 10 Aug 2014
Neuberger O (2002) Führen und Führen lassen, Lucius und Lucius, Stuttgart
Nietzsche F (2014) Der Fall Wagner. Götzen-Dämmerung. Der Antichrist. Ecce homo. Dionysos-Dithyramben. Nietzsche contra Wagner. Kritische Studienausgabe. 12. Aufl, dtv, München
OSHA in figures: stress at work – facts and figures; European observatory report 9, European Agency for Safety and Health at work. https://osha.europa.eu/de/tools-and-publications/publications/reports/TE-81-08-478-EN-C_OSH_in_figures_stress_at_work. Last access: 15 October 2016
Otto KS, Nolting U, Bässler C (2007) Evolutionsmanagement. Von der Natur lernen: Unternehmen entwickeln und langfristig steuern. Carl Hanser, München Wien
Salovey P, Mayer JD (1990) Emotional intelligence. Imagin Cognit Pers 9:185–211
Scharmer CO (2009) Theorie U – von der Zukunft her führen. Carl-Auer, Heidelberg
Senge PM (2001) Die fünfte Disziplin: Kunst und Praxis der lernenden Organisation. 8. Aufl. Klett-Cotta, Stuttgart
Senge PM, Kleiner A, Smith B, Roberts C, Ross R (2000) Das Fieldbook zur Fünften Disziplin (Systemisches Management). 4. Aufl, Klett Cotta, Stuttgart
Senge PM, Scharmer O, Jaworski J, Flowers BS (2004) Presence, human purpose and the field of the future. Society for Organizational Learning. Crown Business, New York
Shah I (1982) Das Geheimnis der Derwische, Herder Freiburg
Souba W (2014) The phenomenology of leadership. Open J Leadersh 3. http://dx.doi.org/10.4236/ojh.2014.34008
Wiener N (1988) The human use of human beings. Cybernetics and Society, Da Capo, Boston MA

Chapter 2
Leadership from the Perspective of a Commercial Executive

Martin Reich

Contents

This chapter includes four components that need to be taken care of. The starting point is the point of view of a controller of a health institution, who is directly assigned to the management due to his function as a department head. The first component is leadership. Anglicisms have to be understood, and therefore, the term is to be defined. The second component is vision, because the roles and responsibilities directly determine the orientation of the point of view. The "vision" has two dimensions, as it follows commercial management. The commercial aspects form their own system, with business literature applying to it. Here the view of the executive is shown. The commercial component is visualized by the controlling process. The fourth component—and that is the most important—is the executive as this is the person that has to bring together all parts. The main focus is on the personal aspect, dealing with changes, strain and the energy balance that has to be controlled. It starts with the component of leadership.

M. Reich (✉)
Lacknergasse 106/1/2, Vienna 1180, Austria
e-mail: martin.reich@a1.net

I. Pirker-Binder (ed.), *Mindful Prevention of Burnout in Workplace Health Management*, https://doi.org/10.1007/978-3-319-61337-6_2

2.1 Leadership

Leadership no longer essentially consists of the distribution of work and coordination of daily operations but has as the core task to "create conditions, which enable average intelligent staff to complete their tasks independently and efficiently."

(Doppler and Lauterburg 1994, p. 54). The previous boss or dynamic leader and top manager does not only have to get used to the role of the trainer, coach or highly qualified service provider, but also master and fulfill this role.

The traditional concept of leadership (attempt to control the employees, regulations and detailed instructions as to what has to be done by whom and when) is management under false pretenses. It is about giving freedom and space to act to teams and individuals (Pflägig 2009, p. 64). In addition to comprehensive expertise in the respective field (i.e. in-depth business management knowledge, detailed knowledge of the controlling tools) also not so easily measurable factors are required, which I would like to describe as "instinct/gut feeling". Gut feeling and experience bring security and calm, even in turbulent times when it comes to change and its management. Being calm and having the courage to listen to your gut feeling or allow it to exist are an art that must be learned. What is more, the individual has to want it and allow it. Then, a path evolves, which is marked by consistency and continuity, which is very significant not only for the respective person, but also for the employees. However, the employees in this environment must also meet certain characteristics, which are marked by natural curiosity, a spirit of independence and the perception regarding the delegated competence and responsibility. The relatively old Harzburger model (Hoehn and Böhne 1969) appears again here and is integrated. Employees, who do job-oriented work and need instructions for individual steps, must be regarded as a chance for further development on the part of the executive—provided that the potential exists. According to Malik (2000, p. 171–264) the prevalent tasks are:

Ensure goals:

- organize,
- decide
- control.

Tools used (Malik 2000, S. 277–373), are:

- sessions,
- reports,
- job design,
- budgets
- and performance reviews, but also systematic garbage disposal.

The latter is a difficult discipline. Only systematic releasing permits selective access. A timely withdrawal creates the opportunity for a new beginning. Simply adding projects with the target of growth are not conducive to the development.

It is a great skill to master the sequence of letting go, opening options, focusing, accessing, letting go, etc. (Risak 2003, p. 89).

Special attention has to be given to behaviour patterns that seem to contradict the change process. In The Robber Hotzenplotz Ottfried Preußler describes Kasperl's behavior, who—dressed up as "Seppl"—makes the great magician Petrusilius Zwackelmann let him off of numerous tasks "due to inanity". (Preußler 2012, p. 56). The great magician being glad to have a stupid service messenger, who does not figure out his spells, at best fits into the ancient definition of management, but not at all into any modern requirements. However, such statements clearly shape from childhood on. In organizations it is the executives' task to recognize these patterns and change them. This requires calm and a lot of endurance; it is often faster to complete tasks (seen in the short term) instead of delegating them to others, which prevents learning. Following key issues are central (Doppler and Lauterbourg, 1994, p. 54 f.):

- What qualifications do the employees need?
- Who needs to learn what, so that the required performance level is achieved and can also be kept in the long run?
- What information, resources and personal support do the employees need so that the pending tasks can be tackled independently and successfully?
- What can/must be changed in terms of optimization of costs and benefits in the operation?

It needs not be explained here that these are long-term, multi-year processes. It is about "step for step thinking" and actually taking the steps; just like Nordic walking. The poles only help when they are properly used with the right technique.

- It is about step-for-step thinking and actually taking the steps.

In the change process the executive is mentally a few steps ahead, but must not lose the reference to reality and to the employees. The magic words are communication and targeted consistent information. This is easier said than done. It is an art to find the right balance between too much and too little. Too much creates "over-filling", too little creates uncertainty. In any case, it takes time to prepare information and time again to give information. Here, the executive is greatly challenged. Not every single person can be informed.

The art is to bring the team consistently and transparently on the right level of information and to keep it. The time required for this has to be planned. The basis for a functioning process is trust, which is formed through feedback loops incorporated in decision-making processes. This must be addressed in communication at eye-level with employees (Henckel von Donnersmarck 2014, p. 63). The controlled handling of important information is one of the taboos. There must not be a circle of "better informed". Information cascades distort messages. Stakeholders and involved parties should obtain all information directly (Lenz 1998, p. 142).

Tips[1]

- ask yourself and also your manager the key issues.
- delegate skills and responsibility and thus create trust.
- take time for feedback and in turn demand feedback.

2.2 Commercial Component

The classical controlling process that is usually the central process of management begins with the target agreement/planning. Based on that the degree of target achievement is measured during the year (quarterly/monthly) by means of a planned/actual or plan/projection comparison. The first shows a snapshot for example of the last day of the month; the second shows the expected result involving measures taken (implemented) and thus evaluated up to the end of the year. Depending on how projection is defined, the effect on all those involved in the process is different. If, for example, by the end of June of the current budget year overruns are determined and the projection assumes reaching the targets in compliance with specifications, massive pressure to implement the measures results. The time frame for countermeasures is shrinking. The process is completed with the result of the year (Fig. 2.1).

A fund-financed hospital in Austria (BMG 2014) faces the challenge to run three controlling processes parallel, because settlement through the provincial fund will only be completed in October of the following year. One controlling process is in the planning stages, one in the control phase, and one in the settlement phase. The executive faces multiple challenges at the same time. In the planning phase, the plans of the departments have to be integrated into an overall plan taking the objectives of the owner into account. This requires skills such as scheduling and adherence to schedules, stress management, reporting, as well as stamina and especially trustworthiness.

The controller team stands for values (not only budgeted figures in euro) and reliability. Only in this way, can the responsible profession be exercised. The management of amounts in euro, the booking of plans on cost centres and cost categories is the result of agreements that are comprehensibly documented with the accounting document in the planned cost calculation. Business expertise is assumed; living through trustworthiness is the style. This, and only this, creates a positive image towards customers and attracts people who also possess this virtue (Henckel von Donnersmarck 2014, p. 45).

---

[1]Regarding the tips I give at the end of each section, one should be aware that the implementation must be matched to the respective person and situation. Also experiences both in dealing with signals of the body and from the professional environment play a large role.

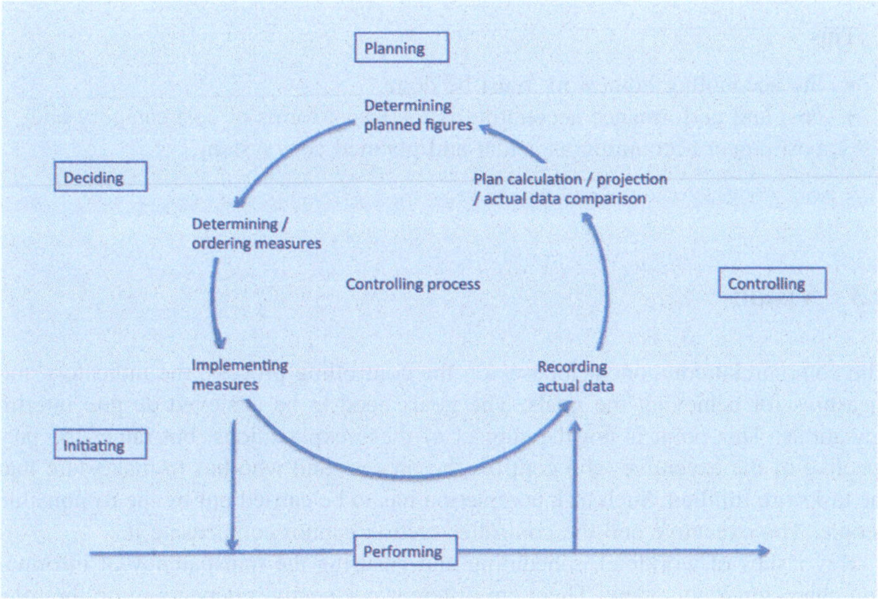

Fig. 2.1 Controlling process. Modified according to Eisl et al. (2008, p. 779)

The controller section has a difficult task to tackle—representing and communicating corporate goals to the departments (in the hospital these are the clinical areas as well as the specialist directorates) as well as the consolidation of the departmental plans but also a comprehensive coaching function. This is to set out the planning method, but also to explain the planning premises together with the corporate management and to ensure that no pure requirement plans are submitted. Planning has to be in line with the corporate management. Receiving only requirement plans means substantial additional effort for the controller section. Each department must be streamlined (=additional effort in times of tight schedules).

A compensation of the activities of the departments through the central controller-section must not happen, because otherwise no learning effect is obtained and the identification with the plans is not given (see Petrusilius Zwackelmann). For the controller and therefore, the executive, the main task is to keep the process going.

This requires much endurance, experience and the correct tempo (Sect. 2.4.1 energy usage).

Tips

- the accounting homework must be done.
- cost and performance accounting is the basis; forms of cost category and cost center accounting as actual and planned cost system.

2.3 Vision

The commercial component focuses on the controlling process, the indicators and measures for achieving the goals. The goals need to be achieved despite interim deviations. This point is not the subject of these explanations, but rather the perspective of the executive who controls the process and who has to make sure that the tasks are fulfilled. Such task completion has to be carried out by the responsible people. The executive and the controller section cannot compensate it.

Key issues of workload, scheduling and ensuring the transparency of information characterize this view. There are different perspectives depending on the role. As a controller, the sandwich position between controller section, the departments within the company (such as hospitals) and the company management is pre-programmed. The business management literature describes controlling as an activity at the intersection between management and controller section (Fig. 2.2).

Figure 2.2 clearly represents the intersection. In practice, the situation looks different. For the controllers as the providers of this service function, the roles in the

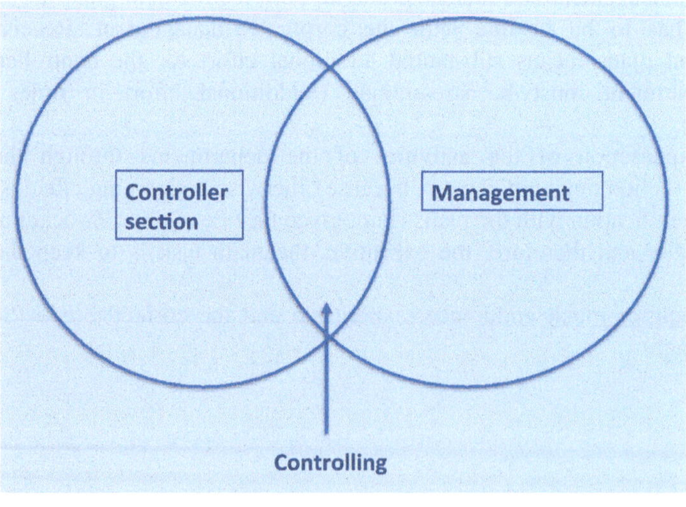

Fig. 2.2 Controlling as intersection. Modified according to Dehyle (1996), p. 177

controlling process, the management position in their division, and the coordination with corporate management converge. The tasks and views are different depending on the role and not easy to juggle. Regarding coordination with management, there are again two dimensions—management and the departments (i.e. clinical areas) that need to be brought together. Taking into account the own management function, this means first and foremost, to cope with the complexity, to structure and go a consistent way. The prerequisites are only partly inherited or can only be learnt to some extent during university education.

Tips

- When at the intersection do not allow being crushed!
- Remain true to yourself!

2.4 Executive

In the sections leadership, commercial component and vision the subject matter and the complexity that has to be coped with were explained. This section is about the executive, about dealing with pressure, emotions, peak workloads, different interests, but also compensation and prevention.

2.4.1 Use of Energy

In the section commercial component the controlling process was represented, which must be kept running. It is clear that this energy is necessary, but also the correct gear ratio if one imagines the moving (rotating) process as the rear wheel of a bicycle.

This ratio must not be too large, because otherwise the energy is not sufficient to cope with the long haul. It shouldn't be too small either, as then sprinting may be possible, but the pace for an endurance track is far too high. The example of the bicycle has specifically been chosen as the overall ratio determines the pace or the resistance, which have to be overcome, as well as the expected performance. Grade, headwind and road conditions are excluded from the model. Also that in practice it is never just one person who provides the energy, and thereby keeps the process running, must be clear.

- The executives are in the unique position to be able to integrate the theme of energy management in their own target agreement, and in those of the employees. Thus, it is subject to corporate planning.

The art to manage this energy management is sophisticated, but it is hardly the subject of management literature or of controlling curricula. My extensive experience and intensive dealing with both subjects have shown that energy management is essential. It is the executive's responsibility but also that of every individual.

Tips

- Accept that energy is not freely available and therefore the control of the energy balance is an important task.
- Endurance gets you further than a succession of sprints.

2.4.2 *Schedule and Task Planning*

Day-to-day operations concern the integration of schedule and task planning in the processes. If correctly applied, computer programs such as Outlook can help to create work appointments, and thus scheduled times for activities in the office (such as cost category and cost centre planning), and thereby to incorporate that as well as meeting dates in the organization of work.

Meeting deadlines should also carefully be dealt with. It is essential to decide who attends what appointments, or whether the meetings are necessary at all. The meeting itself has to be planned and the agenda has to be set up. The literature in this respect (Malik 2000, p. 280 ff.) is impressive, but practical application often greatly differs. Here it depends on the self-discipline and the learning performance of the executives (I include myself here), but also on all stakeholders whether improvements are achieved.

The main function of executives is to be a role model, and to go all the way.

This way is by no means even. Interim uphill and downhill passages may happen, but should not discourage you. Exact ideas and goals help here quite a bit. For the employees, the executive should schedule as much time as for sessions and work schedules. It does not only include a monthly jour-fixe, but the planned possibility to talk to each other during the week without having to check if this is even time even allows it.

- Good scheduling becomes evident when unforeseen tasks come up.

The implementation of this scheduling is the duty of the administration and must be closely coordinated. The administrative staff must support the schedule and communicate it in a suitable form. Otherwise conflicts arise quickly, as appointments arrive at administration first. "No" must be said here; this is where priorities are communicated. The executive has to coordinate these priorities with the general management. Saying no supports organized working. It is clear, however, that this is not always possible in the case of deadlines. Good scheduling becomes evident only when unplanned tasks come up. Here, also, the step-for-step process and consistent implementation is coupled with communication for best practice.

Tips

- all appointments have to be put into a calendar.
- defend your appointment and task plans.
- set your priorities and coordinate them with superiors and co-workers.

2.4.3 Dealing with Signals

This topic is discussed in the business literature, but rather in terms of the signals from the environment of the company, i.e. regarding the signals concerning the market (Ansoff 1976, p. 129–152). Due to the financial crisis the market signals are also evident in the Austrian healthcare system. In the health sector, the market does not collapse; the patient volume rather continues to grow. The revenue side, which is provided by the public budgets and provincial funds (linked to the VAT tax revenue), will become lower. Hence, company management is under considerable pressure to reduce costs.

In this context signals refer to the reactions of the body in relation to the energy management and how to manage it. "The body has a far better sense of time than the brain; it does not miscount and knows when to stop" (Tammet 2014, p. 294 ff.).

- The body has a far better sense of time than the brain; it does not miscount and knows when to stop.

It is a must for every person, not only to be informed, but also have a targeted personal strategy to see the signals, so as not to succumb to the phenomenon of rushing permanently. (Seiwert 2005, p. 23–29). It is caused by the mistaken belief that, if we do everything faster, we can achieve everything. What is missing out in this case is our personal rhythm, which is derived from our physical, mental and emotional condition and is crucial for our wellbeing.

If we do not listen to our body and ignore the personal rhythm, we cannot tackle our tasks in the long term. Here, the "step-for-step method" is expedient. Should this not suffice, the body shows very clearly what is not good for it. What lessons are learnt from these experiences and whether there is the opportunity to make and utilize any changes, remains to be considered in each individual case. The personal willingness to deal with the issue and to learn how to handle the signals, as well as their assessment is vital for steps toward energy management and dealing with stressful situations. There is no general recipe.

I must listen to the signals and practice what I have learned, which assists and helps in stress situations. These tools (e.g. relaxation techniques, specific regeneration, learned breathing techniques while maintaining the body tension) should be integrated into everyday life.

A measure for me was, for example, selling my moped and replacing the drive to work with a daily walk to and from work. This allows for plenty of air and helps get your head free, which should not be underestimated. Also, realizing that there are many books apart from the business literature can be valuable. People, who like to read, can integrate their own preferences.

People should not strive for complete relaxation everyday. This goal should not be set, as otherwise it generates reverse pressure. But the tools help to achieve a never previously thought of sustainability, which maintains the energy balance. The art is to integrate downtime even in times of heavy workload. In times of change, the executive is particularly challenged. Nevertheless, it is rarely discussed that the executives also undergo the process of change, which means that they have to deal with their own emotions as well. It is a fine art to direct the change, to think about the goals and to understand one's own signals that accompany this process. The executives must be alert and willing to learn. They must be grounded to be able to maintain the ground, because stability is essential for survival in uncertain times.

Tips

- Allow yourself to hear signals timely, so that they do not have to scream at you.
- Take time and space for processing and training.
- Find your own way.

2.4.4 The Role of Sports

Sport is essential in the field of energy management. People who are good with numbers should not do sports with objectives. There were times I did cycling with an annual total kilometer goal. That matched my job beautifully, but not the human body. Now I have a new goal, which is called wellbeing, where conditions are determined by medical examinations. The optimal training area was set. Only by doing so could I succeed in bringing together training and recreation.

- Sport in the nature has many advantages. It helps to get the head free and ground yourself.

Also an important experience for me was that with sport, Nordic walking sticks can be used and that nature can be experienced. By walking—also on paths without concrete—it is possible to experience the nature more intensively, to feel the bumps, to smell, to see. As I can very easily remember images, I can again take the impressions from nature as relaxing images. Especially in times of intense preoccupation with numbers and in the course of the change processes, this option is very helpful—in the sense of clearing one's head. Nature also greatly helps with grounding. Ultimately, work benefits from this time and again. Leisure is never unproductive but reproductive and equally important for success as working time (Henckel von Donnersmarck 2014, p. 15).

Tips

- Sport is important, but please do not rate it with numbers and targets.
- Step by step has great effect and leads to sustainable success.
- The nature experience is fun. It helps when dealing with emotions.

2.4.5 Handling Emotions

Never forget, "The controller is a person!" The experiences on a daily basis do not leave you indifferent. They touch; they affect you in various degrees. Here, the personal value system plays a big role. Whenever this is affected, the energy balance is involved as well.

- The controller is a person! Work experiences leave no one indifferent.

The personal handling of attacks on the value system also has to be learned. It does not have to happen every day, but a personal calendar with entries based on demand helps here. For sport there should be a personal booklet, in which beautiful tours should be entered. Dealing with emotions is always a matter of personal concern and dissociation. The numbers person tries to reach a factual level by communication through and about numbers, where emotions are largely avoided. Each number, especially in a comparison of planned/actual data, is pure emotion.

Self-image and external image come together, trustworthiness is evident or dissolves into nothing, and measures are effective or are counteracted by effects. Here it becomes evident whether values are lived or are mere lip service (Hlinka 2014, p. 2 f.). These phenomena need to be processed and a way, which is comprehensible, and also documented, should be found. This way decisions are made transparent and differences are explained. The controller must be able to realize that the deviation is the rule, not the exception. Of course, the private environment that acts as a backbone in all situations and is irreplaceable helps when dealing with emotions.

Tips

- Do not take everything personally.
- Emotions are allowed and should be felt.
- Take time for and space for processing and training.

2.4.6 *Consequence*

The "step-for-step method" means that a continuous development takes place - such as when going on a Nordic walking tour. If you proceed like this, the 4-h tour is not the goal, but each step, and at the end comes the surprise about how far the way was. Working life is, of course, not so haphazard, but knowing the target should facilitate proceeding in manageable portions with a sense of achievement built into the process. With a walking tour planning and also realizing it is one's own responsibility—except depending on weather conditions. In the controlling process step 1 is done, but at the same time three more steps are required. The art is to stop and briefly review a completed task item (such as planning). Also, the emptiness, which is formed emotionally, must be felt and processed before proceeding. Consequence allows such moments and is equally necessary when dealing with employees. Thereby, it is important to note the following points (Mesnaric 2010, pp. 72–74):

- Support your employees to feel their inner impulses. This requires relaxation instead of great pressure, and silence instead of perpetual background noise and meeting marathons, as well as listening to the inner voice.
- Train their capacity of reason.
- Analyze the skills and abilities of your employees before determining their fields of activity.
- Give real, serious appreciation and recognition.
- If potential and talents show, which do not match with the corporate goals, check whether the company can be changed as a living system.

Then there is the chance to associate positive feelings with work and to achieve job satisfaction on the way to target completion. (Camelli and Rosenstiel 2009, p. 63) Only then do "whiners, distrust monster, know-it-all villain, leviathan impatience, abstract rip-off, digital idiot and routine grubber—all the good mood thieves" not have a chance anymore. (Püttjer and Schnierda 2009, pp. 24 ff.)

- The art is to stop and briefly review a completed task item. Also, the emptiness, which is formed emotionally, must be felt and processed before proceeding.

Tip

- You should walk step by step, and continue walking.

2.4.7 *Meaning*

"The job has to be fun", is a popular saying—in my opinion, it must be **meaningful**.

The meaning of the tasks of the controller in a hospital ranges from cost transparency to support in achieving the company's goals, but ultimately it is always for the benefit of the patient. Everyday life is often dry and sometimes the question of meaning arises. Particularly in this role, this question must be permitted, even wanted; however it must not permanently become a topic.

The tightrope walk between reflecting one's doing, making sure to be in the present moment and being able to look into the future, is the main point of the controller profession. From this, you can develop an inner drive, which should be used to continue in a focused manner. The same applies to your own work, whose place in society and its mission must be clearly defined, to exactly create this meaning. The self broadcast stand with the talents and interests accordingly. Only then do you achieve the lightness (Henckel von Donnersmarck, 2014, p. 25 ff.) for your head to be clear and thinking freely. "Dream your goal before you realize it!" (Maxwald 2002, p. 70).

Tips

- Dare to ask the question of meaning, and take time to answer.
- As an executive, convey meaning and also demand it.

References

Ansoff HI (1976) Managing surprise and discontinuity—strategic response to weak signals. zfbf 3:129–152

BMG (Bundesministerium für Gesundheit). Modell der leistungsorientierten Krankenanstaltenfinanzierung in der geltenden Fassung. URL: http://bmg.gv.at/home/Schwerpunkte/Krankenanstalten/LKF_Modell_2014/. Last access on 9.11.2014

Camelli G, Rosenstiel LV (2009) Führung durch Motivation. Vahlen, München

Deyhle A (1996) Controller Praxis Band II. 11. Aufl, Verlag Controlling Wissen AG

Doppler K, Lauterburg C (1994) Change Management. Campus, Frankfurt

Eisl C, Hangl C, Losbichler H, Mayr A (2008) Grundlagen der finanziellen Unternehmensführung. Linde, Wien
Henckel von Donnersmarck F (2014) Reich werden auf die gute Art. Edition a, Wien
Hlinka A (2014) Rettung für die Unternehmenswerte. Kurier 19.7.2014, Karrieren
Höhn R, Böhne G (1969) Führungsbrevier der Wirtschaft, Bad Harzburg
Lenz G, Ellabracht H, Osterhold G (1998) Vom Chef zum Coach. Gabler, Wiesbaden
Malik F (2000) Führen, Leisten, Leben, 3rd edn. Deutsche Verlagsanstalt, Stuttgart
Maxwald F (2002) Struwelpeter für Manager. Gerling Akademie Verlag
Mesnaric C (2010) Aristoteles für Manager. Campus, Frankfurt
Pflägig N (2009) Die 12 neuen Gesetze der Führung. Campus, Frankfurt
Preußler O (2012) Der Räuber Hotzenplotz. Thieneman, Stuttgart/Wien
Püttjer C, Schnierda U (2009) Keine Macht den gute Laune Dieben. Campus, Frankfurt
Risak J (2003) Der Impact Manager. Linde, Wien
Seiwert LJ (2005) Wenn du es eilig hast, gehe langsam, 9th edn. Campus, Frankfurt
Tammet T (2014) Die Poesie der Primzahlen. Carl Hanser, München

Chapter 3
Work Areas, Concepts and Methods or Meaning Oriented Occupational and Business Psychotherapy

Ingrid Pirker-Binder

Contents

Meaning oriented occupational and business psychotherapy understands businesses as living, social systems. They provide a framework, a structure and a space in which people do their work. The founders, whose visions are thereby transformed from a possibility into reality, sow the seed. A vision and a mission provide the framework for the structures, processes and the culture.

If preventive measures are to be taken in the field of human resources, it is necessary to install an appropriate office within the company or externally. Also a combination there of may be useful. It is crucial that there is a properly defined framework, which allows answers to questions regarding health and the reintegration after an illness, measures of personality development and individual emo-

I. Pirker-Binder (✉)
Saileräckergasse 43/26, 1190 Vienna, Austria
e-mail: office@pirker-binder.at

I. Pirker-Binder (ed.), *Mindful Prevention of Burnout in Workplace Health Management*, https://doi.org/10.1007/978-3-319-61337-6_3

tional crisis counseling. Establishing a department for occupational and business psychotherapy as an "internal assistance health program" (IAHP) or as an "external assistance health program" (EAHP) is highly recommended.

In the case an employee is indefinitely written off sick with a "stress-induced depression" or any other disease, there is often great helplessness about the proper therapeutic procedure and the time frame for convalescence and recovery of performance capability on both sides, i.e. the person himself or herself as well as in the company. Many unanswered questions arise. The psychotherapeutic expert can provide help answering questions about (in)ability to work, treatment recommendations and reintegration, and advise and support managers as well as affected employees. The expert report may be issued by an external psychotherapeutic expert or within the company, as part of occupational and business psychotherapy.

Other focal points include the description of two motivational concepts from the meaning oriented psychotherapy by Frankl. These concepts serve as a preventive measure, tasks, objectives and tool kit of occupational and business psychotherapy in workplace health management. The tree model of the LifeScriptAnalysis is applied for psychological health in a company from the perspective of human resources. It is intended as a guide and facilitates the detection of structures, interactions and lived culture in a company.

3.1 Freedom of Decision: A Thought Concept Taken from Existential Analysis and Logotherapy

3.1.1 Freedom of Decision—The Power of the Noetic Dimension

Frankl (2004) extends the two-dimensional consideration of being human, which represents the psyche and the soma (physicality), with a third dimension, i.e. the noetic (spiritual) dimension, named after the Greek word "nous" for "spirit". All three dimensions are always active in the human being, but in different forms:

- The **somatic** dimension comprises assigned corporeality, emotions and instincts in existential analysis and logotherapy.
- The **psychological** dimension is made up of assigned thought concepts, cognitions, emotions and skills.

The third dimension is the most significant level of being human. It allows **free opinion through a free decision** concerning oneself, physicality, psychological condition, includes "conscience as a sense organ" according to Frankl and acts as the highest moral authority, intuition, creative and artistic designing, meaning orientation, understanding of values and love. Even though all three dimensions are anchored within a human being, they interact differently (Fig. 3.1).

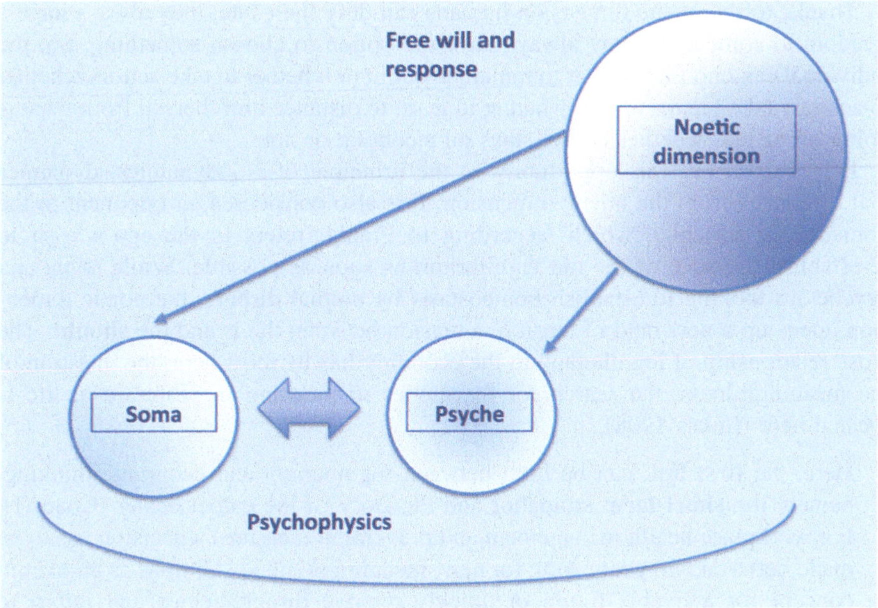

Fig. 3.1 Free space for decision (Pirker-Binder)

While soma and psyche constantly interact and mutually influence each other, the mental-spiritual, or noetic dimension rises above them[1] (Fig. 3.1, example a). Should the person tremble with fear (emotion) (soma), the noetic dimension still allows an opinion. It provides a free space; the individual can decide how he or she wants to deal with fear and trembling. Thus, the individual is **no longer simply stuck** in his/her fear and trembling.

The individual can emerge from his/her helplessness, act again, develop a new attitude and/or set an action (Fig. 3.1, example b). Even if the work pressure is very high, the individual decides how to deal with it, how much energy he/she applies, when he/she needs a regenerative break and also takes it, or allows it.[2]

The noetic dimension calls on the individual

- to gain in knowledge (through his/her feelings, thought concepts, cognitions) and
- to formulate an opinion about it (e.g. how do I deal with this insight, which actions do I want to take?).

[1]Noetic, or mental-noetic dimension is in no way related to spirituality in terms of esoterism, but is to be understood as an expansion of consciousness which facilitates a distanced perspective, i.e. response to internal and external conditions.

[2]Logotherapy depicts the human being as an active being, contrary to behavioral therapy, which regards the human being as a reacting being, and psychoanalysis, which presents humans as venting beings (Lukas 1998, p. 15 ff.).

Thanks to the noetic dimension humans can defy their fate; they always have a freedom to something, they always have the option to choose something. So, the individual can choose whether to remain a victim or whether to take action, whether to actively take breaks or not, whether to learn to distance him-/herself from what is going on or not, whether he/she stays an alcoholic or not.

Frankl describes this opportunity as the principle of Noodynamics, dynamics that originates from the noetic dimension. It is also considered an opponent to the homeostasis principle, which, according to Frankl, refers to the ego's wish to re-establish the state of the old equilibrium as soon as possible. While soma and psyche are looking to establish homeostasis by mutual dispute, the noetic dimension opens up a new field of tension, a tension between the **is** and the **should**. The close relationship of logotherapy to the economy has its roots here; the question of the meaningfulness, the search for the modes of meaning in professional life is located here (Lukas 1998).

1. Here, the **first link** can be built between logotherapy and economic thinking, namely the **short-term snapshot** and the story of the carpet dealer (Chap. 1). For workplace health management and prevention measures a decision has to be made between two goals: look for new, meaning oriented solutions as an overall concept for a livable future or quickly remove disagreements and return to homeostasis.
2. The **second link** is established by the principle of noodynamics, the search for realization of meaning, value sets and structures in working life. It is about the contrast between is and should. If the aspect of meaning of work and/or work life or experience shifts, or an imbalance develops between mission, business objectives, corporate culture and/or leadership styles and the employees' attitudes and experience of meaning, this tension affects the commitment and the health of the employees. In case a person or a group feel restricted in their freedom to design modes of meaning, the intrinsic motivation changes and thus the will to common creation (Fig. 3.2).

- **Common will is the strongest force within living social systems. It is the will, which originates in the intention stemming from intrinsic motivation that leads to realization of meaning, an action, a process or a deed.**

The **third link** can be established as a contribution to the concepts of Senge (2001, 2004, 2008) and Scharmer (2009). Both deal in their theories with the blind spot in living, social systems with a simultaneous view to the overall whole. For a resource- and meaning oriented workplace health and prevention management this can mean a **three-stage program of change**:

a. An existential analytical consideration of the company in terms of analyzing **what is**. Scharmer transforms this question into a process of downloading, the unbiased realization of **what is**. An existential assessment of the current state explores what should be preserved and looks for what needs to be changed.

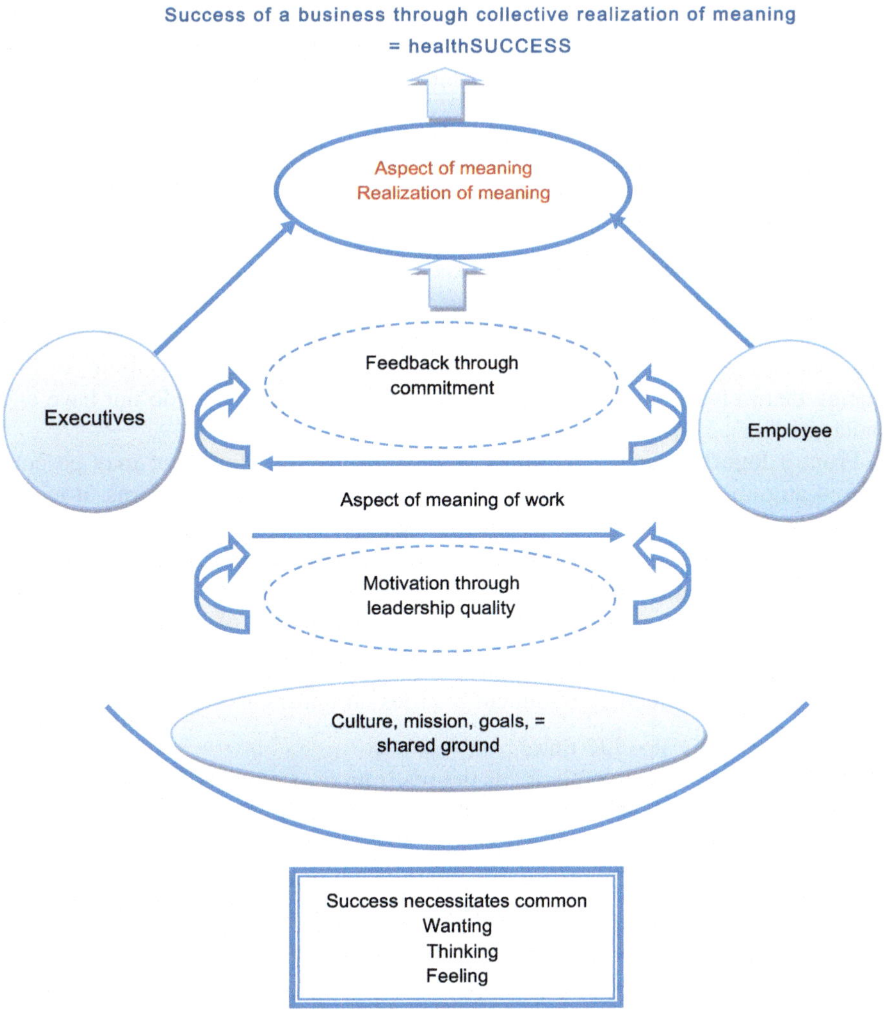

Fig. 3.2 Success through collective realization of meaning (Pirker-Binder)

b. **Locating the blind spot** and an enquiry into the modes of meaning and understanding of values. The relevant question could be: how should work be lived and understood in the future. **What for** and **how** do we create a common "we" in the company. "**What are the inner sources from which individuals or groups become active when they perceive, communicate and act?**" (Scharmer 2009, p. 28). This raises the question: "How can health success be carried into the future?"

From the recognition of the blind spot, from the experience of a non-judgmental inner stillness that Scharmer calls "presencing" for tapping the deepest source, new models for workplace health management and prevention as well as intervention measures can be developed.

- **To initiate the process, the promotion of personal development of executives is required. After all it is them who must produce the results that are generated from processes and decisions.**

The **success of an intervention** depends on the internal condition of the intervening party. It is about the source, which constitutes the basis of acting; it is all about the bare screen that is to be written on (Scharmer 2009, p. 28). In practice, this means: if the executives have lost their quality of life or their ability of distancing themselves or are not aware of their own resources, they do not have any understanding of their employees.

From a **logotherapeutic perspective** recognizing the blind spot may be considered an unbiased stepping back from old attitudes or thought patterns. It means checking the goals, the mission, the lived culture, etc. One allows taking a step outside to perceive and recognize from the noetic dimension, the superordinate context, what is good, what should be preserved and which structures and values should be changed in terms of prevention and preservation of health success.

c. Preservation and further development of mission and vision in the corporate culture for a common commitment requires an understanding that
    - work time is also life time,
    - work must provide options for the realization of meaning and
    - long-term survival is only possible under consideration of the great superior whole.

3.1.2 Two Motivational Incentives from Meaning Oriented Occupational and Business Psychotherapy

According to logotherapy workplace health management as prevention management includes two motivational incentives (Fig. 3.3):

- the willingness **to something**: motivational incentive for the individual
- the willingness **for something**: motivational incentive for a group, a team

The willingness **to something** in a living, social system requires personality characteristics, which I summarize under the German acronym **ASTI**:

- A "awareness" = mindfulness, respect, appreciation of others
- S "social competence" = social thinking and feeling

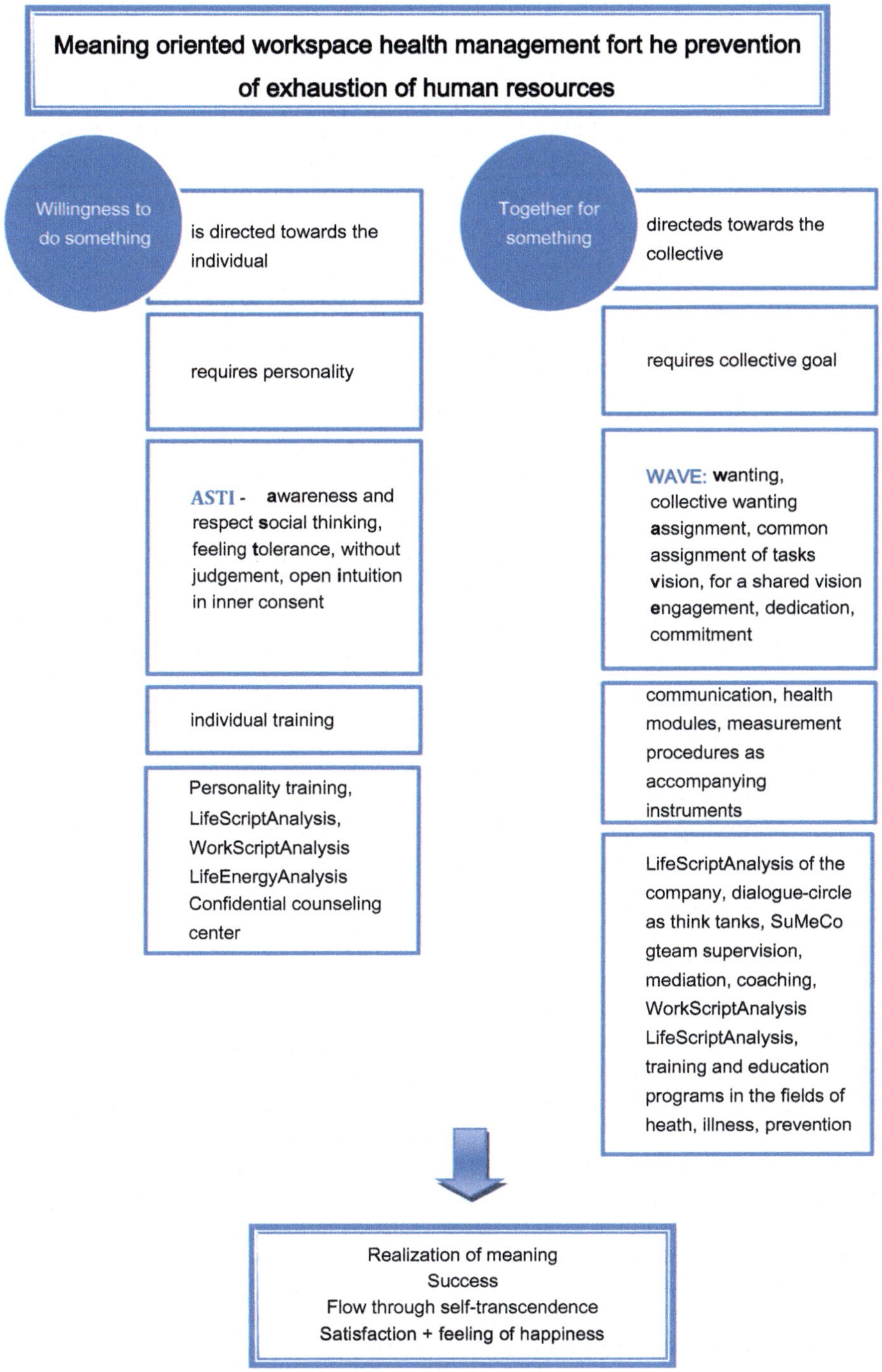

Fig. 3.3 Meaning oriented workplace health management (Pirker-Binder)

- T "tolerance" = tolerance for errors, flexibility towards one's own attitudes, learning ability
- I "intuition" = intuition: the inner consent of thinking, feeling, acting

The willingness **for something** in a living, social system requires a collective pursuit of the same goals. Everyone involved therein pulls together and in the same direction. I would like to sum up this collective pursuit with the acronym WAVE:

- W "want": collective wanting
- A "assignment": common assignment of tasks, mission
- V "vision": for a shared vision—as a specific destination, an image of a desired future (Senge 2001, p. 182)
- E "engagement": commitment of the group

The acronym **WAVE** also represents the economic process, which cannot lead straight upwards to continuously growing success, but moves in waves like the tides.

Two ways become apparent as preventive measures against the exhaustion of human resources at the workplace (Fig. 3.3):

- measures for the support of individuals (employees and executives),
- measures for the support of the collective.

3.1.3 Meaning Oriented Occupational and Business Psychotherapy as a Key Point Within the Human Resources Department

Meaning oriented occupational and business psychotherapy understands businesses as living, social systems. They provide a framework, a structure and a place where people do their jobs. The seed is sown by the founders, whose visions thereby evolve from a possibility to reality. Vision and mission frame the structures, processes and the culture.

Living, social systems are, if they want to survive successfully, dependent on each other and coordinated; they constantly develop and change. Their survival ensures the ability of both, keeping an eye on and realizing the changing needs and necessities within the system and keeping in sight the future whole, the aspired goal and the influence of external factors.

- **Living, social systems are learning systems. They are not rigid, but always moving, adapting to internal and external factors.**

- **Living, social systems are about interactions and fine-tuning between the individual parts of the system—interactions between people.**

Considering organizational structures in companies, a human resources department can be found in all of them.

It is usually entrusted with legal, organizational and professional training measures. The company doctor or occupational health professional deals with health matters. So far the works council has more or less been available as the contact point for conflicts and also emotional problems. If prevention of human resources is to be taken seriously, it is necessary and useful for the future to establish a suitable office in the company or outside, or both. A confidential health and crisis counseling office for individual psychological problems, reintegration after sickness and measures for personal development should be offered. The creation of a department for occupational and business psychotherapy as an "internal assistance health program" (IAHP) seems to provide a suitable option.

For small and medium-sized enterprises, the cooperation with external occupational and business psychotherapists providing an "external assistance health program" (EAHP) might be more cost effective; they are available externally or only come to the companies at certain times.

External (EAHP)/Internal Assistance Health Program (IAHP)
Due to the increasing number of cases of psychological illness, it is useful to allocate this field of activity to professionals, such as occupational and business psychotherapists, who are not only familiar with the company as a system with its processes and structures, but also have therapeutic expertise and diagnostic capabilities (psychological problems, stress due to disease, personality disorders, psychological emergencies, bullying, stalking, crises etc.) and skills for personality development and conflict resolution. An important focal point in this respect is the obligation of confidentiality of occupational and business psychotherapists.

Active prevention always means a change of attitudes, habits, thought patterns, rituals and more. People's life stories, fears and micro traumas can be obstacles for such processes.

"In seminars, coaching sessions and through questionnaires I have been told again and again that I should change myself, my attitude and behavior—but no one has told me so far, how to tackle this," are remarks I frequently hear in my practice. Personal change and responsibility management interfere with the individual life script and require a cautious and trusting approach. Occupational and business psychotherapists are trained in this respect and deal with issues of people that concern their work, work culture, work experience, but also the individual in his/her life story; plus, they have economic knowledge.

In addition to the departments already installed, i.e. human resources, works council, occupational medicine, work and organizational psychology (which is responsible for the work on the system, structures and processes) occupational and business psychotherapy is responsible for the work with people.

- **The scope of activities of occupational and business psychotherapy includes the preservation of human resources in businesses and addresses both, the individual and the collective.**

3.2 Psychotherapeutic Services at a Glance

Based on the Psychotherapy Act, Austrian Federal Gazette BGBL. No. 361/1990 psychotherapeutic activity comprises the following areas:

- psychotherapeutic treatment including diagnosis and indication
- psychotherapeutic counseling and care
- psychotherapeutic training activity pursuant to §§ 3 et seq. and 6 et seq. Psychotherapy Act
- measures of personal development:
  - self-awareness
  - coaching
  - training of psychotherapeutic intervention techniques
  - supervision[3]
  - further training of psychotherapists
  - measures of health promotion, prevention and rehabilitation
  - psychotherapeutic findings and expert reports
  - psychotherapeutic research.

3.2.1 Area of Responsibility of Meaning Oriented Occupational and Business Psychotherapy

Occupational and business psychotherapy combines psychotherapeutic knowledge and economic thinking and builds a bridge between the prevention of depletion of human resources and corporate goals. Thereby this work may focus on individual employees, but also on groups. Hence, the field of activity goes beyond ordinary psychotherapeutic services.

[3]Supervision is a form of counseling for people working in psychosocial professions.

The scope of work of meaning oriented occupational and business psychotherapy comprises

- **in workplace health management**
  - Advising the management,
  - Project Management in the field of health
  - Action plans for prevention
  - Crisis intervention, bullying, addiction, conflicts etc.
  - Diagnosis of inability to work due to psychological exhaustion
  - Psychotherapeutic expert reports for performance capability
  - Short-term therapy
  - Support of employees during reintegration after sickness
  - Therapeutic interventions and advice of employees
  - Work-life supervision or preventive business mediation
  - SuMeCo: think tank for a value-oriented team culture and change processes
  - ASTI & WAVE © Personal Mastery Concepts
- **in workplace health promotion**
  - Measures for health awareness
  - Education and further training on health issues

The contracting authority of an occupational and business psychotherapist is the company. The therapists are bound by a duty of confidentiality in the individual work with the relevant people.

3.3 Measures and Promotion of the Collective in Terms of the WAVE Process

Before preventive measures can be taken, it is useful to get a general impression of a company. How intense or detailed this should be done depends on the particular task, goal setting and target design. A first impression can be gained through a LifeScriptAnalysis of the company. It serves to understand structures, interactions and the lived culture of the system. Based on that the first steps and action packages can be worked out. Figure 3.1 shows the four areas and their impact on the health success of a company.

In addition to being a counseling center and a contact point for mental problems, conflicts, bullying, the department of occupational and business psychotherapy should also design and offer lectures and training measures, which relate to joint action in terms of a healthy working environment as a living space, work experience, culture and interaction. With regard to structural developments dialogues, discussion groups or think tanks (idea workshops) according to Scharmer (development of concepts from a future perspective) seem to be appropriate for executives.

An overview of possible measures:

- **Work-Life supervision** or preventive business **mediation** as an accompanying service in the company
- **SuMeCo** in conflicts (Pirker-Binder 2016) includes content from supervision, mediation,[4] coaching[5] and psychotherapeutic knowledge. SuMeCo is a prevention and intervention concept of logotherapeutic occupational and business psychotherapy for personal development and the preservation of psychological health. The aim is to provide within the company an open framework for personal development and neutral interaction for a healthy and beneficial working culture, which is oriented towards a common **what for** in order to overcome disharmony as soon as possible. SuMeCo is understood as a think-tank for a value-oriented team culture and change processes with the aim not to lose sight of the common vision and aspects of meaning, as well as to promote consistency in the common work: creates space for change processes.
- **ASTI & WAVE Personal Mastery Concepts®** include:
  - ASTI: promotion of the individual (Fig. 3.3).
  - WAVE: Promotion of teams (Fig. 3.3).
  - LifeScriptAnalysis. (Table 3.1) of the company as an initial analysis for a holistic approach to health promotion in workplace health management.
  - WorkScriptAnalysis (Chap. 2): explores—similar to the LifeScriptAnalysis for the working people—the working culture, the work experience of the group, the team. The goal is the timely detection of conflicts, bullying, loss of motivation, management errors.
- **LifeEnergyAnalysis** (Chap. 12) describes the possibility to record through vegetative functional diagnostics both, the individual psychological and physical stress and the stress within a group or a team early on. The new technology of biofeedback devices (Pirker-Binder 2008) and evaluation procedures—they will be explained in detail in Chap. 12—allows reporting back the gathered information to the employees as a health tool and increasing the responsibility for their own health. This can result in preventive measures for the individual employee, but also for a group. Possible measures could be more health information for shift workers, compliance with rest periods or a survey of the strain on frequent flyers.

---

[4]Mediation is a form of out-of-court conflict management (http://wirtschaftslexikon.gabler.de/Definition/mediation.html?referenceKeywordName=Mediator, last access 11 April 2015).

[5]Coaching is an interactive person-centered advice and support process in the context of work (http://www.coachingdachverband.at/index_html?sc=285962687, last access 11 April 2015).

Table 3.1 The four areas of LifeScriptAnalysis for psychological health of the company

Areas	Who/what is involved?	What does it influence?	Who causes it?	"Tree of success"
Mission, vision	Founder's vision	Type of company, company style	Culture: internal and external impact	"the seed"
Management	Executives	Leadership style	Work atmosphere	"the trunk"
Employee	Human resources	Interaction and communication	Human capital	
Collective wanting	Understanding of meaning and values	Commitment	Success	"the treetop"
Corporate-Social-Responsibility			Sustainability	Quality of life
Health success				

Case study shiftwork

Mr. X is a shift worker in the construction industry; his workplace is about 800 km away from his home. This means that every Friday after his shift has ended he drives home as fast as possible. A 24-hour heart rate variability analysis shows great tiredness after his shift, between 10 and 11 o'clock. Even though he felt it, he was not aware of its significance regarding the risk for the journey back home. On the basis of the measurement Mr. X realizes that it is irresponsible of him to drive home immediately after the shift. Thereby he puts himself and the colleagues who are riding with him in danger. He becomes aware of how irresponsible his behavior is. The risk of micro-sleep is incredibly high. Through the measurement he can understand the needs of his body, in this case, for urgently required recovery after working a shift and before driving home. Even during the week he rarely slept after his shift, but stayed online, his phone was never put to silent mode. He was basically always alert, suffering from related health issues.

- **A perception and sensitization training** with biofeedback in order to increase self-management, self-competence and inner peace and to prevent hyper-activation as well as enhance the individual stress tolerance and strengthen the regeneration potential of the organism by means of a training of the heart rate variability.
- **Further training measures** for personal development, information from the field of psychotherapy, psychology, medicine and nutrition
- **Health certificate** for employees in which health-promoting courses, regeneration training, tips on healthy physical activity are documented. Not only the yearly turnover success should be celebrated, but there should also be a bonus system for health-conscious employees or managers.
- Creation of a **psychotherapeutic expert report** on the ability to work.

The aim of the measures is

1. to develop increasing responsibility for health and, particularly, for the preservation of psychological and physical performance capability of both, each employee in a team and the executive, in terms of their duty of care for their employees, to reflect on themselves and their individual leadership style and social competence.
2. to improve the team culture and the interaction with each other and with other teams. The better the working and interaction culture, the higher the commitment within the company, the greater the health success in the company.
3. to support the diagnosis and preparation of a set of measures for the employee and the company with a psychotherapeutic report in the case of suspected exhaustion and to give suggestions for preventive measures that arise from the questions for a report.
4. to promote the understanding of the risk of exhaustion and a culture of open dialogue about it.

3.4 Answer to Questions on the Ability or Inability to Work in the Case of Exhaustion

A psychotherapeutic expert report in business consulting can answer questions on ability or inability to work in the case of exhaustion. If an employee is indefinitely written off sick with a "stress-induced depression" (or any other disease), there is often great helplessness about the proper procedures and the time frame for convalescence and recovery of performance capability on both sides, i.e. the person himself or herself as well as in the company.

The most frequently asked questions are:

- Who makes the diagnosis of emotional distress and/or strain?
- Who gives a treatment recommendation?
- What should be considered?
- What can I do as an executive?
- How long will the employee be absent?
- Should there be changes in the working time (home-office, part time), if so, what changes?
- Does the employee have to be taken out of the company (sick leave), or can he/she continue to work with support?
- Will he/she be completely fit after sick leave again? Or is a convalescence period needed during rehabilitation?
- Who supports the affected colleague during rehabilitation?

The psychotherapeutic expert can answer these questions and advise and support executives and affected employees. The expert report may be issued by an external psychotherapeutic expert, or as a part of occupational and business psychotherapy in the company.

A psychotherapeutic expert report about the ability to work includes:

1. Psychotherapeutic diagnostics about the mental condition, ability to work, work experience (psychotherapeutic conversation for the analysis of the current situation, LifeScriptAnalysis, WorkScriptAnalysis, questionnaires). It provides information on the current emotional distress, stress and ability to work.
2. A vegetative functional diagnostics by means of a 24-hour heart rate variability analysis (Chap. 12). It provides information about the current strain on the organism and its performance capacity (vegetative functional diagnostics) and about a possible risk of physical collapse.
3. Recommendation for a set of interventions and measures; sick leave, home office, short-time work, etc.
4. Psychotherapeutic reports within the scope of meaning oriented occupational and business psychotherapy deal with issues concerning the topics work, resilience, rehabilitation after sickness, reduction of working hours, sick leave, indication of interventions and measures.

3.4.1 Content of Psychotherapeutic Expert Reports

Expert reports can provide clarification in all areas in which psychotherapeutic questions arise (economy, industry, art, technology, medicine, psychology) (Lankse and Pritz 2002).

Definition

Psychotherapeutic expert reports examine and assess, on a psychotherapeutic-scientific basis, psychosocially or psychosomatically caused behavioral disorders and states of suffering that do not only include disease treatment but also health care and promotion.

Logotherapeutic expert reports are psychotherapeutic reports, which draw upon Viktor Frankl's teaching and image of humanity as well as his existential analysis and logotherapy in their diagnosis and logical structure.

It is noted that "also in the healthcare sector either parallel to or completely regardless of medical or clinical psychological or health-psychological assessment, psychotherapeutic expert reports have their own place, where the objective of the question induces the examination of psychotherapy-relevant facts" (Bartuska et al. 2005).

Consequently, the creation of psychotherapeutic expert reports on the subject of ability to work in the case of exhaustion is to be assigned high importance, not only as a support for companies and their employees, but also in the healthcare sector for the duration of sick leave, therapy measures, proposals for spa treatment and much more.

3.4.2 *Legal Foundations of Psychotherapeutic Expert Reports*

In 2002 the Federal Ministry of Health in Austria defined criteria for the creation of expert reports by psychotherapists for the first time. Paragraph 1 Psychotherapy Act, Austrian Federal Gazette BGBL No. 361/1990 describes the profession of a psychotherapist as follows:

> … comprehensive, conscious and planned treatment, which is preceded by a general and specific training, of psychosocially or psychosomatically caused behavioral disorders and states of suffering with scientific and psychotherapeutic methods in an interaction between one or more treated and one or more psychotherapists with the aim to alleviate or eliminate existing symptoms, to change dysfunctional behavior and promote personal maturity, development and the health of those treated (Bartuska 2005, p. 15).

Accordingly, the treatment is preceded by psychotherapeutic diagnostics. This diagnostics is described as findings in the expert report. The findings contain the individual information of the affected person and the diagnosis of the expert to clarify the issue (in this context about the seriousness of exhaustion or on ability or inability to work).

The diagnostics to be performed by the expert claims to be based on the latest psychotherapeutic-scientific methods. The findings are followed by the actual report, which contains the assessment of the expert and a clarification of the issue.

3.4.3 *Psychotherapeutic Diagnostics*

In the diagnostics guidelines for psychotherapists (Bundesministerium für Gesundheit 2004)

> psychotherapeutic diagnostics is regarded as an inherent part of psychotherapeutic treatment. The diagnosis is a snapshot within a diagnostic process, which can be perceived and assessed depending on the degree of possible differentiation… The object of psychotherapeutic diagnostics is the assessment of psychopathological matters in terms of the subjective suffering of one or more persons under the conditions of cultural and social norms as well as economic conditions.

There is a differentiation between the initial, development and final diagnosis. In my view the essential legal information is provided by the Supreme Court judgment of 18.8.1998, which, in the course of the 50th amendment to the General Social Insurance Act, ASVG, equates psychotherapeutic treatment with medical aid if, according to § 135 para. 12 sentence Z 3 ASVG, before or after the first, or in any event, before the second psychotherapeutic treatment a medical examination has been carried out. (Bartuska et al. 2005, p. 45). An interesting aspect can also be found in the Supreme Court judgment definition of psychological illness according to §§ 120 paragraph 1 and number 1 and 133, paragraph 2:

> Psychological illness is an anomalous (pathological) disorder caused by mental or physical factors, which necessitates medical treatment; through the medical treatment the health, ability to work and the ability to meet vital personal needs, should be restored as far as possible, strengthened or improved. Psychological illnesses are no longer or only partially subject to the volitional control of the patient; they are recognizable in emotional, physical symptoms or in pathological behavior (disorders of perception, behavior, processing of experience, social relations and the body functions). Disrupted social relations are only considered an indication of a psychological illness, if the relationship disorder is linked to an anomalous (pathological) change in the psychological or physical condition of a human being and medical treatment is required.

References

Bartuska H, Buchsbaumer M, Mehta G, Pawlowsky G, Wiesnagrotzki S (2005) Psychotherapeutische diagnostik. Leitlinien für einen neuen Standard, Springer Wien NY

Begriffsklärung und Grundlage eines Gutachtens des Psychotherapiebeirates vom 15.6.2004; URL: http:// www.bmg.gv.at/cms/home/attachments/6/8/3/CH1002/CMS1144348952885/diagnostikleitlinie_fuer_psychotherapeutinnen_und_psychotherapeuten_formatiert_fuer_homepage.pdf last access 24.9.2013)

Bundesministerium für Gesundheit (2004) Diagnostik-Leitlinie für Psychotherapeutinnen und Psychotherapeuten

Frankl V (2004) Der unbewusste Gott, Psychotherapie und Religion. 7 Aufl dtv, München

Lankse P, Pritz A (Hrsg) (2002) Das psychotherapeutische Gutachten. LexisNexis ARD Orac Wien, S 18

Lukas E (1998) Lehrbuch der Logotherapie. Profil, München Wien

Pirker-Binder I (2008) Biofeedback in der Praxis, vol II. Erwachsene, Springer, Wien NY

Pirker-Binder I (2016): SuMeCo, in Vorbereitung

Scharmer CO (2009) Theorie U – von der Zukunft her führen. Carl-Auer, Heidelberg

Senge PM (2001) Die fünfte Disziplin: Kunst und Praxis der lernenden Organisation 8. Aufl. Klett-Cotta Stuttgart

Senge PM, Scharmer O, Jaworski J, Flowers BS (2004) Presence, human purpose and the field of the future. Crown Business, New York

Senge PM, Kleiner A, Smith B, Roberts C, Ross R (2008) Das Fieldbook zur Fünften Disziplin (Systemisches Management). 5 Aufl, Schäffer Pöschel, Stuttgart

Chapter 4
The Value Balance in Business®—Healthy Corporate Culture, Healthy Employees

Heinrich Anker

Contents

H. Anker (✉)
Heilbachrain 26, 3250 Lyss, Switzerland
e-mail: anker@pop.agri.ch

I. Pirker-Binder (ed.), *Mindful Prevention of Burnout in Workplace Health Management*, https://doi.org/10.1007/978-3-319-61337-6_4

The Value Balance in Business® is on the one hand the reference model of a meaning- and performance-oriented corporate culture, and on the other hand an instrument for the analysis and diagnosis of existing cultures and their further development towards realization of meaning and commitment of the employees.[1] The core of the Value Balance in Business® is an ethical one: it is about the "condition humane" of the employees, about their health and quality of life as well as its resulting growing power and desire to do their best in their work—for their own benefit and that of the company, its customers, its shareholders and other important groups.

Hereinafter the Value Balance in Business® is introduced as a reference model for a meaning and performance-oriented corporate culture with a particular focus on its importance for health promotion.

4.1 A Company Is Struggling for Its Identity—To the Beginnings of the Value Balance in Business®

The beginning of the Value Balance in Business® is determined by the author's professional experiences: as a member of the management of a service provider he lived through the whole range of what a company can demand from and do to its employees when it loses its soul and breaks its stride: the fears of how to continue in one's professional and private life, tensions, arguments, intrigues, times of disorientation, uncertainty and the paralytic feeling of being stuck in the mud—all of these did not fail to leave their mark physically and psychologically on the employees: the sickness rate continued to increase.

The company's inner life was more and more reflected to the outside: its once excellent reputation suffered; the market shares slipped. The reason why the author himself did not consider quitting at that time is the conviction, which was formed through numerous personal discussions with colleagues and teams, that by far the largest part of the staff did not desire anything more than being able and allowed to work for a reputable company and "do a good job" for the customers.

In principle, everything required was there: above-average well-trained, committed and responsible, sincere employees, the necessary equipment and good wage and working conditions, as well as a still comfortable market position—what was wrong, completely wrong, was the "software ", the "mental program" or the culture of the company. In this company less and less was compatible internally. The symptoms were manifold: misunderstandings, conflicts, mutual recriminations,

[1]The Balanced Scorecard® is an instrument for the systematic development of company strategies; thereby, always the same four perspectives (the finance sector, customers, internal processes and learning and development perspective) are applied; similarly, the Value Balance in Business® is an instrument for the systematic development of corporate culture: here also certain perspectives are applied (a total of nine).

competence skirmishes, power games, intrigues, bullying, burnout, termination of work contracts.

Carried by the vision of what this once respected company and its many integral employees would actually be capable of and what joy and pleasure it would be for them, their relatives and the customers if only a sustainable corporate culture existed, the author started to promote the development of a mission statement.

Thanks to various favorable circumstances (more of this below) the new development of the "software", i.e. the development of a mission statement gained momentum. It was carried out cautiously and prudently, step by step: the company's internal situation analyzes were confronted with scientific foundations to test their plausibility and reliability. Then, practical implementation started. With this permanent exchange between theory and practice and the results of the corresponding implementation steps, the Value Balance in Business® had its beginning. The positive results of this concrete mission statement development ensured the energy to further develop this concept and refine it.

4.2 When Employees and Management Are Pulling Together—But in the Opposite Direction

We are in a company with approx. 1500 employees: the salaries, the holidays and leisure regulations are among the most generous of the industry, there is no lack of technical equipment, and the "workload" is in the comparison with the other companies of this industry sector demonstrably lower—and yet, at every step you will be confronted with complaints like "We are totally overloaded ", and complaints about bottlenecks regarding labor capacities. There is hardly any discussion with executives and employees that does not include the catchwords "stress" and "work life balance" or in the call for more employees.

Behind this, considerable tensions are hidden: the professional ethos, the knowledge of the importance of the company's services for the customers and society is highly developed; it even seems a bit excessive, but, on the other hand many employees including those in the middle management are haunted by big worries: if they look beyond their company, they find themselves in an industry with an extraordinarily intense transformation dynamics and at the same time they feel that nearly nothing is moving in their company. The fear of missing the boat is big and widely spread. What is going on inside the company is also found on the outside: according to studies, which are also picked up by the media, the customers and the wider public regard the company as "reliable", but increasingly also as "backward" and "dull", and their products are increasingly seen as "not current", "distanced", "not close to the customers" and "emotionally not very appealing". This is also reflected in the market shares of the company, which continuously decrease. Having this mirror held up before them adds to the employees' pain and confusion. From their point of view they see the image of a ship whose captain has gone off the course, but he stubbornly keeps going instead of changing the course to avoid the lurking danger.

The captain is not turning a blind eye to the slipping market shares, yet he does not have relevant exchange with employees and stifles change and innovation proposals from their side in the core. Probably not least because of the influence of a small but influential informal network of beneficiaries of the situation, he is explicitly not willing to accept the social change, which leads to new needs of customers, society and, "nota bene", employees in his industry sector as well. He refuses to steer the company to a new future oriented course.

As a result, an increasingly and deeper division between the employees (including the lower and even middle management) and the company's top management opens up. "You up there—us down here!" becomes the predominant view; with the participation of the superiors, the departments and teams isolate themselves from the top management. Communication becomes more and more precarious, and the top management finds it increasingly difficult to recruit suitable staff for leading positions. The suspicion on both sides grows, and the climate deteriorates. The management, in particular the CEO, cannot understand this: "What do you really want? Our wages and working conditions are among the best!" Hence, business management control mechanisms are developed, which the employees cannot but perceived as additional harassment; they reinforce the debilitating feeling of overload and lost motion even more.

These internal tensions make the company more and more concerned with itself, and those resources that should be transformed into services for customers and other stakeholders, are wasted within the organization. This damages the reputation and the assessment of its services even more, and the market shares continue to fall—a threatening downward spiral!

4.3 Salutogenesis—Link Between Health, Performance and Corporate Culture

What does all this mean for the health of the employees? As a first approach to this question the concept of salutogenesis according to Aaron Antonovsky provides a helpful concept. At the center of his social psychology model of health is the Sense of Coherence (SOC) (Schiffer 2011). Depending on the power of their characteristics, an individual is at a particular place within a health-disease-continuum. Antonovsky defines the Sense of Coherence as "... a global orientation... which expresses the extent to which one has a penetrating, persistent and lasting feeling of confidence that one's own internal and external environment is predictable and that it is highly likely that things develop in a way as is reasonably expected. " (Antonovsky 1997, p. 16) In the sense of (analytical) separation, Antonovsky distinguishes three Sense of Coherence-components:

A. **Comprehensibility**: Do I understand what is happening with my professional environment and me and what impact does this have on me?
B. **Manageability**: Do I myself have any influence on these events? Can I help shape the conditions and in what form?
C. **Significance** (Antonovsky 1997, pp. 34–38) or meaningfulness (Schwarz u. Wyssen 2013, p. 38): Can I attribute meaning to my job and to what is happening around me? Does my acting show a clear "for what" or "why" or "for whom"?

In the terminology of salutogenesis, the employees of the above mentioned company show very pronounced components of significance or meaningfulness, however, the component of manageability is hardly perceptible—a considerable stress and frustration potential, which keeps building up, with the corresponding consequences for the well-being and welfare of the employees and (in a figurative meaning) their company.

Antonovsky sees a close relationship between the Sense of Coherence factors of significance/meaningfulness and comprehensibility: their interaction not only includes a cognitive, but also an emotional and a motivational component (Antonovsky 1997, p. 110). With regard to the latter, in his salutogenetic model Antonovsky establishes a direct relationship between health as well as motivation, that is, performance capability and motivation. For the Value Balance in Business® as a model a meaning and performance oriented corporate culture Antonovsky's connection of meaning, motivation and health is crucial.

- It may be concluded that there is a link between "health" on the one hand and the Value Balance in Business® as a corporate culture model on the other hand, i.e. a relationship between corporate culture and health.

4.4 A New CEO or the Fear of Employees that a New Broom Might Clean Too Well

Back to "our" company: After the retirement of the previous general manager a new CEO was supposed to save the company from this downward swirl. A difficult legacy! When he starts to implement long overdue reform steps on business management level and in the product sector, the situation initially aggravated even more: the employees are gripped by the fear that due to economic reasons the new manager might turn to the reduction of benefits in the areas of salaries and holiday arrangements, etc. or even to laying off employees. In general, the fear spreads that he appreciates the importance of the company's services less than the employees and that for him, these services are merely economic products without any deeper meaning than achieving a higher sales rate as quickly as possible and recapturing market shares. These fears were supported by the network of the former CEO's beneficiaries. It was one of the first important steps for the new management to deprive this "informal clique" of power.

In the Antonovsky terminology this means that among the employees now no longer only the component of **manageability** was experienced as critical, but also that the two core components of the Sense of Coherence, meaningfulness and comprehensibility, were being questioned more and more; for the employees things were getting to the "core of the matter". Where this is the case, soon nothing will work anymore. The reason for this is that in times of high uncertainty a growing number of employees are in a panic mood and only thinking about themselves. They want to salvage their own job and turn more and more into lone wolves. This also happened in "our" company: the stress, conflict and frustration potential reached new heights and this had a direct and drastic effect on the health of the employees. Within two years the amount of colleagues being on sick leave increased by nearly 30%—an unpleasant situation.

That this company is still alive and that the threatening downhill swirl has turned into an upward spiral with many enthusiastic employees, a high social reputation, widely valued services and a growing market share—8% within three years—has not been achieved with business and organizational measures alone, but it involved initiatives in the field of corporate culture.

4.5 From Being a Swimmer in the Stream to an Oarsman in the Rowing Boat—Discovering the Independent Force of Cooperation

"Culture" is a genuinely social phenomenon with its own strength. Antonovsky himself speaks on many occasions about a "social SOC" and also explicitly focuses on the health aspects of the work situation. He mentions historical-cultural characteristics that lead to life experiences, which in turn strengthen or weaken the individual SOC. They are summarized below (Antonovsky 1997, p. 112):

1. Participation in socially valued decision-making processes; they provide fun and pride at work and discretionary power
2. Social respect for the company
3. Social respect for the work performed
4. Decision—making powers with regard to the work and the legitimacy of power distribution among the colleagues
5. Balance with regard to the resources for the individual and within groups; the extent in which existing potentials can be used in complex work situations
6. Consistency as a degree of clarity regarding the work environment and one's own position therein; confidence in the safety of one's job; communication and social feedback at work.

(Almost) all these factors have an impact on the health-promoting corporate culture; however, they do not provide its foundation: The power of the social and the culture lies in the people being rooted in a thought, feeling and behavioral community (Badura 2011). In it the essence of successful cooperation can be found. This is not adequately expressed in Antonovsky's analyses, which can possibly be explained with his paradigmatic concept: "…my fundamental philosophical assumption is that the river is the stream of life"—and we are the swimmers in this river. Antonovsky's view seems to remain centered on the individual ("individual fighters").

Consequently, the Value Balance in Business® as a model for corporate culture has to be based on a different image, i.e. not one of swimmers in the stream, but one of a rowing boat: if you start by placing yourself in a slim, sleek single-seater and forcefully start rowing, you might be under the impression of making quite some headway and are satisfied with yourself. Now, switch to an eight-seater and row in sync with the others—the force, the speed, and the dynamics that you experience in comparison to rowing in the skiff are incomparable. It will grasp and inspire you—you have the feeling you are flying over the water, you may even find real "flow".

This experience of community or co-operation is the symbol of sociocultural coherence (Sense of Coherence/SOC) of a group or a community, including a company.

- The sociocultural SOC will sustainably strengthen your personal SOC, that is, your trust in what you can accomplish, in what strength you have in you, your confidence in being able to achieve high goals as well.

David Packard, founder of HP, describes what is at stake here in simple yet powerful words. For him profit is an important aspect of entrepreneurial activity, yet he sees the meaning of an enterprise's existence elsewhere:

> We inevitably arrive at the recognition that a group of people get together and exist as an institution we call a company so they are able to accomplish something collectively that they could not accomplish separately – they make a contribution to society. (Collins and Porras 2005)

4.6 On the Interplay of Individual and Sociocultural Sense of Coherence

Before we can launch the eight-seater rowing boat, we have to make some more mental effort in advance. It is about working out the social dimension of the two Sense of Coherence components "meaningfulness" or "significance" on the one hand, and "comprehensibility" on the other hand, so as to make them fruitful for the social phenomenon "culture". It is about conceiving "meaningfulness" and "comprehensibility" not only from the perspective of individuals (individual Sense of Coherence), but also from the point of view of the community (sociocultural or collective, Sense of Coherence). This is important since the individual and communal feeling of coherence are in a synergy relationship with each other, as mentioned above: in the worst case they may weaken or neutralize each other, whereas in the positive case they mutually reinforce each other and bring employees and companies into an upward spiral.

4.6.1 The Concept of Meaning

Viktor Frankl, the founder of the meaning-centered psychology (a branch of humanistic psychology), works out the interplay between the individual and social dimension of the concept of meaning based upon the background of the theme "health". On the theme "psychological well-being" he writes:

> I would say what man really wants, is ultimately not happiness, but a **reason** to be happy. As soon as a reason for happiness is given, happiness ensues. (Frankl 1992, p. 15 ff).

Nevertheless, people do not find reasons for happiness in themselves; our personal wellbeing always has a social dimension. Decisive for our mental well-being is, according to Frankl, "solely and exclusively… the feeling of being there—for something or for someone." (Frankl 1992, p. 57) Frankl further elaborates on this idea:

> Happiness cannot be pursued, it must ensue and it only does so as the unintended side-effect of one's personal dedication to a cause greater than oneself or as the by-product of one's surrender to a person other than oneself. Happiness must happen …you have to let it happen by not caring about it. (Frankl 1985, p. 17).

The experience of being happy and having a meaningful and fulfilled life becomes possible when people do not focus on themselves and their own happiness, but by looking beyond, by serving a thing greater than themselves, or by intentionally approaching other people.

Applying one's energies to a bigger cause than we are means defending the interests of groups of people or letting one be inspired by their ideals and values.[2] An example is the doctor, who not only works for his fees, but also in the service of the ideal of the health and wellbeing—the life quality—of other people. The universe of ideals, which may provide us with orientation in our actions and give meaning to our lives is infinite: freedom, (self-) responsibility, democracy, education, health, justice, security, mobility, equality before the law, humanity, ecology, the service of life, free opinion, etc.

The second important source of meaning and happiness is the affection that we give other people or the affection that we receive from others—also in this case, we look beyond ourselves, to others, i.e. the "you".

[2]Ideals are considered to be the symbolic representation of the values of groups of people.

4.6.2 The Concept of Comprehensibility

Meaning orientated actions in a sense of giving attention to the “you”, or to a larger whole according to Viktor Frankl, requires mutual understanding. In various fields like philosophy and from anthropology to neurobiology surprisingly great accordance exists that during communication the ability to empathize emotionally and cognitively (the latter as a human specificity) plays a decisive role. Without them no successful social relations, no fruitful co-operation, no viable management and customer relationships can be imagined.[3] This means comprehensibility as a component of the Sense-of-Coherence presupposes empathic communication.

Our empathy is not only the key to comprehensibility, but it leads us back again to the experience of meaningfulness. Approaching groups of people or ideals helps us through our ability to empathize to experience **being good for something.**[4] Also based on our ability to empathize, paying attention to other individuals enables us to experience **being good for someone**. They both end in the experience and the certainty: “It is good that there is me, I have a place in life, I have a place in this world and I can actively participate in it. Sharing and shaping reality—my existence has meaning” (Frankl 1995, p. 29 f).

We conclude from this: the individual Sense of Coherence components “meaningfulness” and “comprehensibility” go back to one and the same existential need: to the need for insight into the meaning one’s own doing and the associated appreciation that we grant others and that is given to us.[5]

Ultimately they can only flourish through social interaction respectively or cooperation—“meaning” is always connected to culture. From this, the following can be derived:

- Health and health promotion can never be seen as a merely individual phenomenon; they always have their social and socio-cultural dimension—even and particularly where people are interacting in highly complex social structures such as companies.

In our modern era of the economic dogma of maximizing personal advantage and self-interest (and the associated individual competition) this is probably not “so easy” to accept for all company managers.

---

[3]See, for example, Marshall B. Rosenberg and his contributions to non-violent communication.

[4]Thanks to our ability to empathize, we are subject and object, the active and the suffering parts of our actions and omissions at the same time. The ability to feel empathy allows us to understand the consequences our actions have for others—we put ourselves in their shoes and comprehend their vision of the world. If we do something good, we will also comprehend it ourselves; if we face others in hatred, we experience this hatred within ourselves as well. Empathy might have more immediate and drastic, good and bad, consequences on our health than we are aware of.

[5]We may receive this appreciation directly as a result of our doing through the others, but we can also emphatically follow it. For example, if we in the wake of a disaster make a donation, we rarely receive the thanks of those directly concerned, however, we emphatically understand that their suffering is alleviated through our contribution (or we hope so, at least).

The insight into the meaning of our actions and the empathic experience to be valued as an individual, that is, being "good for someone" or "good for something" are for us humans, according to Viktor Frankl, linked inseparably. That is, they are not further questionable, i.e. constitutive of our human being. They are in a fundamental sense our elixir of life and thus the sources of vitality and life quality. Thus, the forces that we can mobilize for our tasks are correspondingly strong if, from our point of view, they are connected with the experience of meaning and appreciation. Their importance for health as well as successful cooperation is directly evident.

This means: "If you ask for performance, you have to offer the experience of meaning and appreciation to the people or the employees" (Anker 2012, p. 61). Nota bene: even above all instrumental health and motivational considerations this is a fundamental ethical duty: it is about being human itself.

- If you ask for performance, you have to offer the experience of meaning and appreciation to the people or the employees!

To illustrate the importance of meaning and appreciation, let's make a small thought experiment: imagine, you wake up one morning and suddenly the thought shoots through your head: "I see no sense in what I do, and no one is waiting for me!" Perhaps you physically feel your strength wane. Do not hang on to these thoughts too long, rather compare how it feels when you go to work and can say, "Well, someone is waiting for me there, I am welcome. My services are needed and I will also be appreciated as a person!" Or imagine how it feels when you are on the way home from work and you can say: "Great, today I could do a good job for someone, my efforts have paid off!" Obviously such healthy and motivating experiences remain hidden from many employees—and this can have serious consequences for them as well as for their companies:

- In the most important economies according to Gallup in 2008, 70 to around 90% of all employees only had a weak or no relationship with their work and their employer (Gallup 2009);—not even a critical relationship, which would still show interest in their own work and the that of the company.
- Around 50% of all employees worldwide would be happy to accept a lower salary or occupational status, if they could only do more meaningful work.[6]

Due to its existential nature the need for meaning and appreciation cannot be replaced by anything where it is unfulfilled, neither by material incentives nor by the prospect of pleasure and/or power.[7]

---

[6]The question was, "Would you take on a lesser role or lower wage if you felt that your work contributed something more important or meaningful to you or your organization?" (Kelly Services 2009a, b).

[7]According to Elisabeth Lukas, "people are willing to accept sacrifices, if need be, and to leave needs unsatisfied. The physical and mental wellbeing play a secondary role in the search for meaning. Compared to this, failure in the search for meaning cannot be balanced by any psychophysical well-being" (Lukas 1998, p. 39).

Meaning and appreciation are the main pillars of a meaning and performance-centered and at the same time salutogenetic corporate culture, i.e. they are at its heart. They are not only effective inside a company, but also against the outside, in dealing with the customers, the suppliers and many other stakeholders. Also for them is the experience of meaning and appreciation most important, and at the same time they are again a source of motivation for employees thanks to the experience of being able to "do a good job for someone", "being good for someone or something"—"Inside, like outside!"

4.7 If You Consider Your Employees to Be Good, You Create a "Healthy" Company

Until the top management of our company was ready to start tackling the development of a mission statement building on this concept of humans and the related motivation theory, there were hard struggles. Some representatives of the senior management level still represented a "selfish" concept of humans characterized by Darwinism and Taylorism: they interpreted the ongoing complaints of the employees about being overloaded as a tactical measure in the struggle for yet better salary and compensation conditions. Among other things, pointing to current findings of neurobiology enabled their colleagues to soften their position:

Joachim Bauer writes on the topic of meaning and appreciation from a neurobiological perspective, (Bauer 2007, p. 190/204): "If appreciation, attention and trust are the neurobiological fuel of the motivation systems: where does this fuel come from? It comes from only one source: the interpersonal relationship." Bauer further states: "Motivation as a basic attitude is greatly influenced by the extent to which people have the feeling that their work or, what they work for, is basically meaningful." An economic company is "meaningful" if it ultimately serves objectives that are beneficial for society. Where the managerial level keeps an eye on the question of a superior meaning of the economic activities, potentials can particularly be activated when crises or temporary difficult phases must be bridged in a company. If temporary unpleasant decisions are explained in a convincing and comprehensible manner, this can be a decisive motivation impulse."

Gerald Hüther, a neurobiologist like Joachim Bauer, describes what development and performance potentials are combined with human recognition and cooperation:

> Once we start thinking about what basic attitudes one would have to make his/her own to use one's brain more comprehensively, more complex and more networked than before, (alongside mindfulness and caution) a whole range of terms come to mind… meaningfulness, sincerity, modesty, prudence, truthfulness, reliability, commitment… The only thing, he/she needs is other people, who he/she can share his/her perceptions, feelings, experiences and knowledge with." According to Hüther, cooperation makes us intelligent, whereas self-interest makes us wither away. (Hüther 2006, p. 123 f.)

Not least thanks to Edgar Schein the "Darwinists" and "Taylorists" in the management gradually realized that the alleged selfishness of employees rarely stands at the beginning of a development, but instead it is the result of a corresponding concept of humans and its resulting leadership "philosophy":

> Executives who believe that people are fundamentally lazy, passive and not interested in the company, but merely in their own affairs, … train their employees to become lazy and selfish. Such arising control-oriented organizations might stay alive in stable situations, or even make progress, as soon as their environment becomes more turbulent; they go under… (Schein 2004, p. 396).

Against the background of the current state of the company with its continuously declining market shares, increasing sick leave, its established control-oriented management and wide-spread mistrust of the new CEO, facts explained by authors such as Bauer, Hüther and Schein, did not fail to be effective. The decision to start developing a mission statement according to the requirements of a meaning and performance centered culture, was ultimately made unanimously thanks to the new CEO's prudence.[8]

4.8 Substitution or Differentiation Strategy? A Weighty Decision

This basic decision led the company management to a second, also highly challenging corporate philosophical question: If it is true that who is calling for performance must provide experiences of meaning and appreciation, then for a company the question arises, how it can create meaning for the employees and give them appreciation. To anticipate it right here: the most effective way of doing this is being "good for someone" or "good for something", that means consistently serving the needs of the customers and society.

Fortunately, "our" company did not follow the currently prevalent reflex of short-term shareholder value or short-term profit maximization:

- It renounced entering into (self-) destructive cutthroat competition for the sake of short-term re-conquering of market shares; the company still had an impressive market position, and in this case hardly anything is more costly than a price war.
- Not least bearing in mind the concept of humans the management had previously decided to adopt, two key strengths of the company were refocused on: the still above-average high level of education of the employees, and the more or less latently available high professional ethos.

A price war with the aim of regaining short-term market share and the inevitably resulting redundancies and service reductions for customers would have massively

[8]Otherwise, the development of a mission statement would have caused even more damage.

compromised the existential need of the employees for meaning and appreciation, as well as the associated resources and motivation forces. Instead, the management decided to develop the company in the sense of a differentiation strategy into a service-oriented personality, which consistently meets the needs of customers and society with a distinctive face and thereby setting the benchmark for quality standards in the market. This according to Peter Drucker:

- Business enterprises—and public service institutions as well—are organs of society. They do not exist for their own sake, but to fulfill a specific social purpose and to satisfy a specific need of a society, a community, or individuals. They are not ends in themselves, but means. (Drucker 2007, p. 11)

In the terminology of salutogenesis this decision was about the "reanimation" of the SOC components of meaningfulness and comprehensibility. And the more intensely the management had the employees participate in the development of a mission statement, (a strong signal of the company's top management with regard to appreciation and trust in the employees) from their point of view, the more room was regained by the component of manageability—it became increasingly attractive to board the eight-seater rowing boat.

The self-image as a "service-oriented personality" led to a high, market-driven innovative power and to the already mentioned long-term increase in market shares—it proved to be as sustainable as the rediscovered joy and enthusiasm of many employees in their work and their appreciation for the company—the eight-seater rowing boat gradually found its rhythm and steadily took off.

This second philosophical decision took place only after intense discussions and recourse to a wide range of empiricism and theory. An important contribution were the following works:

- Peters TJ, Waterman RH (1982) In search of Excellence Lessons from America's Best Run Companies, New York
- Kotter JP, Heskett JL (1992) Corporate culture and performance. New York
- Collins JC, Porras JI (2002) Built to last. Successful habits of visionary companies. New York, (1994)
- Joyce W, Nohria N, Roberson B (2003) What (Really) works. The 4 + 2 formula for sustained Business success, New York

These studies are in a chronological sequence. Their research design was improved from one to the next. They all have one common denominator: In the long term[9] companies are particularly robust and financially sound,

1. if they look beyond themselves and their short-term self-interest, that is, if they are guided by the primacy of performance in favor of customers and society and not by the self-interest of short-term profit maximization and shareholder value.

---

[9]The observation periods differ according to the number of years: 10 (Joyce et al.), 11 (Kotter and Heskett), 20 (Peters Waterman) and 64 years (Collins & Porras). Apparently companies with a performance-oriented company culture have high life expectancy.

2. if they treat the staff appreciatively and value them as individuals, and enable their active participation in their work as such.

Important insight from a company perspective: the long-term income of companies with a performance primacy and appreciative treatment of the employees surpasses those with an egoistic primacy of profit or of maximizing shareholder value, though depending on the study and on the success criterion (total return to shareholders, growth of stock prices), six- to nine-fold in the long term.[10]

There are good reasons for this.

1. In companies that are self-consistent in the service of customers and society and in this sense "good for someone" or "good for something", the employees' experience of doing something meaningful and being valued, goes beyond the limits of the company. Their horizon of meaning seizes worlds beyond and expands in a decisive way. If a company follows this process, it increases its offer of meaning to the employees and thereby the performance potential by several orders of magnitude, whereas otherwise it is greatly reduced. The greater the contribution of a company to the benefit of customers, society and its greater environment, the more motivating and salutogenetic is its effect on the employees.
2. In this way companies acquire a sense of meaningful existence and appreciation, i.e. a valuable reputation among customers, responsible and dedicated shareholders and in the wider public—all these are important sources of economic resources that can contribute to a long life and a lasting high yield of the companies.

4.9 Mission, Vision and Values—The Corporate Culture Sources of Meaning and Appreciation

With these considerations, the path was free to develop the core of a mission statement. It consists of a mission, a vision, and societal values analogous to the (at least) three ways humans perceive meaning and appreciation. The latter are about the following three:

1. **Space and time transcending dimension of meaning**: the orientation towards an ideal, that is, to a high, very long-term or timeless value. Such an ideal has the function of a guiding or fixed star, which we can orientate ourselves both in calm and stormy times; such a star gives us support and orientation in every life situation.

[10]See Kotter and Heskett (1992), p. 11; Collins & Porras (2002), p. 5; Joyce et al. (2003), p. 14 f. Peters and Waterman (1982) focused on a sample of financially above-average successful companies of the respective industry; in contrast to the following studies this one did not contain a comparison between successful and less successful companies.

2. **Social Dimension of meaning**: the orientation towards values and related ways of acting and behaving, which ensure mutual appreciation.
3. **Time dimension of meaning**: the orientation towards a non-unachievable, but challenging, high-pitched goal. With such a goal in mind every step towards the goal makes "sense". The higher and the more desirable the goal, the more strength and will we invest in order to take the individual steps even if they are arduous.

The core of guiding images on the basis of a meaning centered and salutogenetic corporate culture—this is an important aspect of the Value Balance in Business®—is based on the same, previously discussed three dimensions of meaning. It is formed by:

1. a **mission** (in the sense of an ideal, that is, a high societal value transcending time and space)
2. **social or societal values** (social dimension)
3. a **vision** (long-term high-pitched goal as temporal dimension)

In Table 4.1 the individual and collective senses are connected.

Table 4.1 Individual and collective meaning dimensions

Ways to meaning for individuals	Ways to meaning for enterprises
What are the life maxims and ideals I want to hold on to in good and bad times? What ideals do I want to be guided by? Which are the highest values that give me support? (Time-transcending dimension of meaning, our lasting fixed star)	**Mission**, fixed star or ideal: which is the real meaning of the enterprise's existence? (David Packard). What or who is it good for? How do we want to put it in the service of customers and a larger group of people/society? (Peter Drucker) It is not about the range of products, but about their function: health, mobility, education, communication, beauty, security, belonging, pioneer spirit etc
High-pitched goal, at which an individual can grow and perhaps even outgrow him-/herself. (Temporal dimension of meaning)	**Vision**: a concrete, high-pitched goal that challenges the human mind, which it makes sense to give one's best for, together with the others
Specifically experienced appreciation or attention to the "YOU", to other people: How do I want to be good for someone or something in my life? How do I want to enrich people through my existence and my work? (Social dimension of meaning)	**External values:** **Benefit values:** How can we and how do we want to solve the problems of our customers? What purpose should our products have for them? **Relationship values:** How do we want to fashion our relationship with the customers (and, if necessary, also with the suppliers)? How can we appreciate them? **Internal values:** What values do we want to keep in the company in order to deal with each other in an **appreciative** way? What does it take to make our company successful?

These three dimensions of meaning develop their biggest strength when they are consistent among themselves. In the following, the mission, the vision and values will be illustrated through some concrete examples.

4.9.1 The Mission—The Fixed Star of Companies Serving Customers and Society

> We are driving the future of our country! (a school bus company)
>
> For Ricola, business success must not be an end in itself, but it should rather facilitate taking responsibility towards the employees, society and the environment… As Ricola is a nature-loving company, it places the greatest value on excellent quality of the raw materials. And so, the processed herbs strictly stem from controlled environmentally friendly cultivation. Such herbs are not only more aromatic but also possess an inner force: the strengthening power of nature. (Ricola 2015)

4.9.2 The Vision—High-Pitched Concrete Objectives Are Inspiring

- We are the BBC of Switzerland! (Swiss Radio DRS)

In every household a PC! (Bill Gates)

Authentic fidelity—sound experience like a live concert (Dynaudio loudspeakers)

4.9.3 Values: What Is Important Is Valuable, What Is Valuable, Is Meaningful

Example of internal values:

"Like the cylinder for the crane, the work basket for the stage, the lifting fork for the forklift, such are the employees for Palfinger.[11] (Palfinger 2015)

Examples of (external) benefit and relationship values:

- We Trisans are grateful to be able to produce, honest and meaningful products" (relationship value), which communicate health, joy and wellbeing (benefit values) to our fellow human beings. (Trisa 2015)
- The endeavor to serve our fellow human beings all over the world (relationship value) with practical, functional, efficient and inexpensive quality products (utility value) gives our lives a deeper meaning as well as joy and gratification at work."(Victorinox 2015)

---

[11] A probably somewhat "palpable" formulation, however, it has the advantage of great clarity: in the language of the industry each one immediately understands, what this entails.

In "our" company the company management developed the mission statement in an intensive dialogue with the employees. This process alone already created the foundations of a climate of mutual appreciation and confidence between top management and employees, but also among the employees: hardly anything is more thrilling, reassuring and motivating (and binding) than to see that the colleagues also do their best in the eight-seater rowing boat. The mission, a brilliant vision and clear-cut and consistently lived internal and external values worked like a catalyst or fountain of youth with regard to the employees' commitment and willingness to perform. In the sense of differentiation the company achieved strategically decisive innovation and the sickness rates were reduced again by a good 30% to the level before the outbreak of the crisis. At the same time also the claims of the employees for compensation of irregular or extraordinary work decreased.

Consequently, the company succeeded not only in consolidating its position in the market, but in strengthening it permanently (the market share increased by 8%). At the same time, also the perception by the customers and the general public turned positive—the company actually developed more and more into a successful, robust service personality with a distinctive and likeable face.

4.10 Excursus: Facets of a Salutogenetic Company Organization

Cultures, including corporate cultures, are closely connected with concepts of humans, that is, with ideas of the human being, of what moves people, what they strive after, whether and how they are embedded in a larger whole. Today's standard theory of economics still sees humans as intelligent animals, beings that utilize all their abilities merely to maximize their personal benefit. The fundamental question of the company organization is in this case: How can the actions of all employees be coordinated so that they facilitate the maximization of the company's benefits? This approach leads to a command and control structure—the company as a purely rational machine and the employees as replaceable at any time—as little cogwheels.

If we consider humans as beings with an existential need for meaning and appreciation, a completely different organization principle arises: a living organism. The two alternatives are compared ideal-typically in the following Table 4.2 (Anker 2012, p. 116 f).

The organization built on meaning and appreciation has a salutogenetic effect. It corresponds in various ways to the Sense of Coherence concept of salutogenesis and the associated health factors like manageability, the comprehensibility and meaningfulness.

Table 4.2 Facets of a salutogenetic company organization

The human as a selfish being—the company as a rational machine	Man in search of meaning and appreciation —a salutogenetic company organization
Self-interest creates mutual distrust	Striving for meaning and appreciation: climate of trust (Meaningfulness, comprehensibility, manageability)
Disciplining, coercion (command and control structure), no space concerning responsibility	Scope of responsibility for employees (Meaningfulness, comprehensibility, manageability)
Stiffness, "interfaces" ("machine")	Flexibility, "seams" ("living organism") (Manageability)
Fear, paralysis due to negative sanctions	Motivation, self-initiative, creativity (Meaningfulness)
High burden of control	Low burden of control (Manageability)
The company looks inside	The company looks outward, at customers, society, the environment (Meaningfulness)
Company not adaptable in turbulent times: danger	The 6-f company: fit, fast, flexible, focused, friendly (for customers), fulfilling (for employees): high adaptability (Comprehensibility, manageability, meaningfulness)

4.11 Value Balance in Business®—Corporate Culture as the Basis for Comprehensive and Sustainable Health Promotion

Returning to our initial question regarding the link between corporate culture and occupational health promotion we would like to state:

Workplace health promotion is gaining in effectiveness and sustainability and goes hand in hand with a growing willingness to perform in the company if it is borne by the knowledge of the existential importance of meaning and appreciation for the employees (of all levels!): health promotion becomes a sustainable comparative competitive advantage for a company from a cultural perspective, when it places itself in the service of customers and society through a responsible mission, corresponding values and a corresponding vision. In this way, horizons of meaning arise for the employees as well as sources of empathic appreciation, which are clearly beyond their actual work in the company: through their work they play an active part in the (co-) shaping of their reality and that of all others. Thereby it is all about a fundamental experience of participation, effectiveness, coherence, "value of life" and health.

If 80–90% of all workers in Europe, North America and Asia voiced preferences for employers who would be ethically and socially responsible and environmentally friendly (Kelly Services 2009a, b), this cannot be a temporary phenomenon but the existential need of people for meaning and appreciation.

A second essential contribution of a meaning and performance oriented corporate culture to the health promotion and enhancement of the company's performance potential is that it helps the employees grow closer together through a shared mission, shared values and a commonly pursued vision towards a community of thinking, feeling and behavior, i.e. a cooperative community.

Its performance potential is high because it is borne by a shared sense and mutual appreciation. That is, in the face of the synergetic link between individual and sociocultural SOC, health care has to regard people within their social relationships and from including them in its efforts. This concerns the social relationships in the company itself as well as those of the employees to the customers and other stakeholders of the company.

In the long term it is important for companies to understand which concept of humans, which motivation theory,—it is at the same time always a "health theory"—they want to be guided by in dealing with the employees, but also in dealing with the customers, suppliers and other stakeholders. Businesses are only efficient in the long term if human beings receive their space, if economic value and societal values are in a balance—hence the concept of the Value Balance in Business® and its credo:

- The increase in economic value of the company starts with the appreciation of the employee as whole, unique and irreplaceable person, as a being in search of meaning and appreciation.

Lack of meaning and appreciation cannot be compensated for—neither with regard to the health of the people or the employees, nor their motivation and their ability to perform.

With regard to occupational health promotion, we are confronted with an interesting finding: Antonovsky's concept of health, with its three components of comprehensibility, manageability, and meaningfulness, or the related existential categories of meaning and human appreciation easily applies to the corporate world, on two levels: that of the employees as individuals as well as that of the company as an organization or institution. These two levels are inextricably linked. Specifically, this means:

- Measures for health promotion can only have sustainable positive effect if they are not exclusively directed towards the employees as individuals, but also include their firm's culture and its organization.

The recourse to Antonovsky's salutogenesis is all the more important as his understanding of health is inextricably linked to the concept of resilience; the epitome of the will to live and the vitality of people and organizations, even in challenging times; never have they been more challenging than in today's global world.

The approach developed here does not stand alone: in the form of the so-called Meikirch-Modell (Bircher and Kuruvilla 2014) recently published a new, future-oriented health definition that is fully compatible with the concept developed here, i.e. a concept in accordance with Antonovsky's the Sense of Coherence:

- "Health is a dynamic state of well-being emergent from conducive interactions between an individual's potentials, life's demands, and social and environmental determinants. Health results throughout the life course when an individual's potentials—and social and environmental determinants—suffice to respond satisfactorily to the demands of life. Life's demands can be physiological, psychosocial, or environmental, and vary across individuals and contexts, but in every case unsatisfactory responses lead to disease."[12]

References

Anker H (2012) Ko-Evolution versus Eigennützigkeit. Creating Shared Value mit der Balanced Valuecard, Berlin
Antonovsky A (1997) Salutogenese. Zur Entmystifizierung der Gesundheit, DGVT, Tübingen
Badura B (2011) Entwicklung einer Kultur der Achtsamkeit für Gesundheit an Schulen. Vortrag, gehalten in Pforzheim, 4. Oktober 2011
Bauer J (2007) Prinzip Menschlichkeit. Warum wir von Natur aus kooperieren. 5. Aufl. Hoffmann und Campe, Hamburg
Bircher J, Kuruvilla S (2014) Defining health by addressing individual, social, and environmental determinants: new opportunities for health care and public health. J Pub Health Policy, Macmillan Publishers Ltd. www.palgrave-journals.com/jphp/
Collins J, Porras JI (2002) Built to last. Successful Habits of Visionary Companies, New York (1994)
Collins J, Porras JI (2005) Immer erfolgreich. Die Strategien der Topunternehmen, Dtv, München
Drucker PF (2007) The essential drucker. Selections from the Management Works of Peter F. Drucker, The Classic Drucker Collection, edn 2007
Frankl VE (1985) Man's Search for Meaning. Washington Square Press, New York
Frankl VE (1992) Psychotherapie für den Alltag. 4. Aufl, Freiburg
Frankl VE (1995) Die Psychotherapie in der Praxis. 5. Aufl, München
Gallup (2009) Engagement index Deutschland 2008. Pressegespräch Marco Nink, Potsdam, 14. Januar 2009
Hüther G (2006) Bedienungsanleitung für ein menschliches Gehirn. 6. Aufl, Vandenhoek und Rupprecht, Göttingen
Joyce W, Nohria N, Roberson B (2003) What (really) works. The 4 + 2 formula for sustained business success, New York
Kelly Services, Media release (2009a) Social responsibility key to attracting top talent. Troy, Mich. October 28
Kelly Services, Media release (2009b) Around the globe the desire for meaningful work triumphs over pay, promotion, and job choices. Troy, Mich., February 25

[12]Detailed information on the Meikirch model of health available at: http://f1000researchdata.s3.amazonaws.com/manuscripts/8450/9e8b9c61-f654-43b6-964d-771adaf9064f_7849_-_johannes_bircher.pdf.

Kotter JP, Heskett JL (1992) Corporate culture and performance. New York
Lukas E (1998) Lehrbuch der Logotherapie. München/Wien
Palfinger (2015) Media release. URL: www.palfinger.ag/de/karriere/arbeiten-bei-palfinger/palfinger-werte. Download 23.11.2015
Peters TJ, Waterman RH (1982) In search of excellence. Lessons from America's Best Run Companies, New York. Last access on 23.11.2015
Ricola (2015) Media release. URL: http://www.swiss-press.com/newsflashartikel.cfm?key=1057194. Last access on 23.11.2015
Schein EH (2004) Organizational culture and leadership. 3rd ed, San Francisco
Schiffer E (2011) Synergieeffekte durch salutogenetisches Denken und Handeln in der ärztlichen Praxis. Talk, held on 10 November 2011 at "Ärztekammer Hannover"
Schwarz S, Wyssen R (2013) Sinnorientierte Führung. Entwicklung der Wertekultur im Unternehmen. HRM-Dossier Nr. 62, Zürich, S 38
Trisa (2015) Media release. URL: http://archive-ch.com/ch/t/trisa.ch/2012-10-05_371773_2/Philosophie_Kultur_und_Mission/. Last access on 23.11.2015
Victorinox (2015) Media release. URL: http://www.victorinox.com/ch/de/Homepage/cms/home?lang=de, http://www.vic-torinox.com/ch/app/content/%3bjsessionid=0C5C2E4FA0EBF1766CEA54116. Last access on 23.11.2015

Chapter 5
On Diagnosis and Development of a Health—Promoting Corporate Culture with the Value Balance in Business®

Heinrich Anker

Contents

5.1 Introduction

Management and management instruments are never neutral and objective: they are based among other things on the more or less reflected basic assumptions of their authors. With the choice of instruments, their users determine to a certain extent also their procedure and the results of their interventions. This also applies to the Value Balance in Business® (VBB) as an instrument for the analysis and development of corporate cultures.

In theory, the VBB is based on the findings of meaning-centered psychology (Viktor Frankl), neurobiology, anthropology and medicine (salutogenesis). They all concede: humans are not primarily self-serving beings, as utilitarian economics still teaches, but they rather derive their vitality and their will for life and performance

H. Anker (✉)
Heilbachrain 26, 3250 Lyss, Switzerland
e-mail: anker@pop.agri.ch

I. Pirker-Binder (ed.), *Mindful Prevention of Burnout in Workplace Health Management*, https://doi.org/10.1007/978-3-319-61337-6_5

from the experience that their actions are meaningful and that they are valued as human beings—not least as a result of their realization of meaning.

Meaning and appreciation have a (socio-) cultural dimension: they occur in mutual understanding and cooperation on the basis of empathy. At the same time, these are elementary factors of our health according to salutogenesis. The motto is therefore, "if you want to strengthen the health and performance capability as well as the motivation of the employees, you must offer them the experience of meaning and appreciation."

- This motto is only sustainable if meaning and appreciation are alive in the culture of a company and not merely understood and implemented as an economic instrument—the VBB is opposed to any instrumentalization of employees.

Against this background the guiding questions of the VBB in its function as corporate culture audit are the following:

1. How far do the employees see and experience meaning in their work?
2. How far do they experience human appreciation in the company?
3. What is the resulting level of commitment of the employees?

To systematically record the perception and experience of meaning and appreciation by the employees in the company, the Value Balance in Business® audit uses a fixed grid with nine perspectives. They are the basis, with the help of which reliable information about the extent of the perception of meaning and appreciation by the employees (always of all management levels) and the associated performance potentials are collected.

From its basic conception the Value Balance in Business® (as a method of development and maintenance of company cultures) is similar to the design of the Balanced Scorecard (as a tool for the development of company strategies). The Balanced Scorecard (BSC) works on the basis of the four perspectives: customer perspective, internal process perspective, and learning and development perspective. They all contribute directly or indirectly to the financial perspective. The Value Balance in Business®, on the other hand, is based on nine perspectives, all of which can contribute to performance commitment. Every company has to adapt it to its situation.

The nine perspectives of the Value Balance in Business® result from the observation where sources of meaning and appreciation can be found in the company—always from the point of view of the employees. Each of these perspectives is operationalized through 8–12 interview questions to the employees. The scope of the survey and the wording stem from qualitative preliminary studies in the respective company (mostly semi-structured individual interviews with selected employees). Subsequently, the staff survey is mostly based on closed questions. Below the content of the nine perspectives is briefly outlined.

1. **Mission, vision and internal as well as external values** These are the central sources of meaning and appreciation in a company and form the core or the

uppermost reference point of a meaning and performance oriented, salutogenetic corporate culture. The most important questions in the assessment are whether they exist in a company, and in how far they are known to the employees, and how consistently they are lived according to their experience.
2. **Top Management/Leadership** Do the top company managers live the mission, the vision and the values in an exemplary way and can they demand it from the other employees as well? Have they earned the employees' confidence to facilitate a secure future for the company? Do they have an open ear for the concerns of the employees; is their "know how" and "know what" appreciated? Do the employees understand what important business matters specifically mean for them, what they have to be prepared for? How well do the processes in the company work, how well do the units/subunits cooperate with each other (processes)?
3. **Customers** Do the employees consider themselves capable of being able to solve the problems of the customers effectively and efficiently and to treat the customers as appreciatively as they themselves would like to be treated as customers? If this can be affirmed, the employees in turn emphatically anticipate the appreciation of their customers. The same can also happen when dealing with the company's suppliers and other groups involved.
4. **Products (services)** Are these a fair offer for the customers according to the point of view of the employees? Can they look the customers in the eye when selling or giving advice? Is the company fair? As with the question of the customer relationships, the question or experience here is mainly, "Am I good for someone or something?" "Can I do a good job for the customers?"
5. **Competitiveness of the company** Does the company provide the right products for the market? Is it forward-looking and innovative? Can it set standards? Does it have a good reputation in the industry, i.e. do the competitors respect the employees and the company? The clearer these questions can be affirmed, the more confident the employees are regarding their future and the more meaning they see in their commitment for the company.
6. **Reputation** Does the company have a good standing in the public? Do the customers and the society believe that, according to its mission statement (mission, vision, values), the company is good for someone or something? Is it considered a "good citizen", employees can commit to with conviction?
7. **Shareholders** Are the shareholders—always according to the employees' perception—entrepreneurially minded, that is, do they have the ambition to advance the company, or are they speculators whose sole interest is to suck out its substance as quickly as possible? Much of this creates distinctly different future and meaning perspectives of the employees and determines their commitment and loyalty to the company.
8. **Communication** The primary task of internal communication is not the mass of communicated content but ensuring the organization's information channels and information flow: it has to guarantee open and mutual exchange "top down–bottom up", as well as between the business units and functional areas.

Once this is the case, the communication partners will provide the relevant information content themselves. This means that the communication executives' duty is not gathering and disseminating information, but managing the communication channels. Good communication fulfills two functions: through the transmission of knowledge, it generates meaning, comprehensibility and manageability. At the same time, it creates mutual appreciation between employees and management and also between members of the various business and functional units (meta level communication). Internal communication plays a crucial role for the health and well being of the employees.

9. **The employees and their immediate environment** In this perspective, various topics come up such as the management relationship with the direct supervisors (communication of meaningfulness and appreciation), social integration (teams, working groups), work organization, personnel management (compensation and benefits, career planning, further training, work equipment), but the personal dispositions of the employees as well: in how far are they willing to take responsibility for the larger whole? How do they rate their own initiative and team spirit? How great is their personal work ethos, that is, to what extent are they prepared from their inner impulse to go "the last mile", so that they are satisfied with their own work? How well are they able to deal with challenges like failure and uncertainties? (Coping skills).
10. **Commitment as the target value** It is based on the self-assessment of the employees with regard to three questions. One of them captures the degree of emotional attachment to the company, another one asks directly for the commitment to the company (pragmatic dimension), a third one focuses on the employees' attitude towards the subject of "professional work" in general (work ethos, i.e. work as a social value). In the subsequent questionnaire, an index of "commitment" was formed from the answers to these three questions (the three variables were all of the same weight in the index).

In contrast to many other employee surveys, the Value Balance in Business® also systematically includes the aspects of the mission, the vision, as well as the internal and external values, the quality of the products, the quality of the customer contacts, the intentions of the shareholders as well as the internal communication. They are not only important with regard to the experience of meaning and appreciation but also from the perspective of the health and wellbeing of the employees.

Like many other audit tools, the Value Balance in Business® also works with a more or less predefined questionnaire (the nine perspectives). The evaluation, however, is different for each company, which is another special feature of the VBB. External benchmarking is therefore not possible; this would be a contradiction in terms of corporate culture: the culture of a company is what makes a company incomparable, lends it a distinctive face, its own "personality". External benchmarking, on the other hand, leads to standardization (and to substitution strategies) rather than to differentiation and self-determined development of the company due to its own special potential. (On the other hand, the VBB permits unlimited internal benchmarking between business units and subunits.)

5.2 The Value Balance in Business® in Practice—A Concrete Case Study

5.2.1 *On the Profile of the Audit*

What the Value Balance in Business® does as an audit tool, is illustrated below with reference to a case study. It is a company located in Switzerland's economic capital with almost 700 employees. It is the Swiss subsidiary of a globally operating IT company. The audit took place in a very exciting phase: one year before, a company unit was acquired from another company, and at the time of the audit itself the integration of another company was imminent. Therefore, we will be dealing with three business units (BU): BU 1 is the parent company, BU 2 is the unit that was acquired in the previous year, and BU 3 denotes the business unit whose takeover and integration was imminent at the time of the investigation.

The survey was aimed at all employees of BU 1, BU 2 and BU 3. It ran online and was fully completed by 425 employees. The return rate was almost 65%—a considerable figure for an average processing duration of 45 min.

5.2.2 *A Cause-and-Effect Model—References to Starting Points of the Development of a Company Culture*

In a first step, the data were reduced by a factor analysis and condensed into factors. A model with 10 factors proved to be the best solution in this case (see Table 5.1). These 10 factors are based on 27 variables or interview questions; for them a "grading" by the employees (on a scale from 1 to10) (see "Average value" in Table 5.1) was available.

In the next step, these 10 factors were related to the dependent variable "commitment/motivation" (see Fig. 5.1). Seven of the 10 factors have a directly quantifiable effect on the commitment. With a declared variance of 63% their influence is remarkable; this is an indication of the consistency and validity of the VBB model for this special company. Factor 1 "appreciation as a person" has the greatest effect on commitment followed by factor 2 "values" and factor 3 "customers". The strength of the impact of these factors is equally significant with their leverage when defining and implementing measures to strengthen the commitment.

In this company satisfaction does not precede but follow commitment, and even more: with every point that commitment increases, satisfaction even experiences an increase of 1.13 points. From the perspective of a company culture based on meaning and performance, this situation can be interpreted in such a way that the employees are satisfied when they learn that they are "doing a good job", i.e. providing meaningful performance.

Consequently, satisfaction is not a prerequisite for the employees to do perform well. In accordance with Viktor Frankl, feelings of happiness or satisfaction can

Table 5.1 Factors and their underlying variables *Source* Anker (2012)

Factor designation	Mean value factor	Interview questions or key performance indicators (KPI)
1. Appreciation as a person	7.3	Respect of employees as real people Quality of the working environment
2. Values	8.7	Striving for trustworthiness among colleagues Concern for the wellbeing of the colleagues Environmental protection
3. Customers	7.9	Degree of the presence of customers and their needs with the employees, even if they do not have direct customer contact (self-assessment) Assessment of the competitiveness of the company in the industry Value attitude with regard to customers
4. Market position	7.2	Company affiliation with the top companies regarding the state of development of its products Importance of belonging to a top company from the employees' perspective Assessment of the reputation of the products in the home market
5. Coping skills	7.9	Ability to bear insecurities Coping with failures
6. Teamwork	8.2	I am a motivator Teamwork above personal success Attitude to teamwork
7. Company	7.5	Future prospects for the company The mission thrills[a] Company perceived as leader in the industry Proud of their company
8. Compensation	6.9	Satisfaction with company services
9. Team leadership	8.0	Employees' opinions are asked by their superiors Support for employees, especially in difficult situations Loyalty to employees Employees feel perceived as people
10. Innovative inclination	8.5	Openness to innovation Willingness to take risks

[a]A provisional mission statement was queried for test purposes; a real mission did not exist at the time of the survey

result from meaningful action. For this reason, the VBB, in contrast to other assessment instruments, does not focus on the satisfaction of employees, but on their commitment.

There are two descriptions for these 10 factors: the degree of their effect on commitment (Table 5.1) as well as the employees' assessment of how well these factors are met in the company. Thanks to these two dimensions, a conventional four-field matrix can be formed (Fig. 5.2). On the ordinate axis, the degree of the

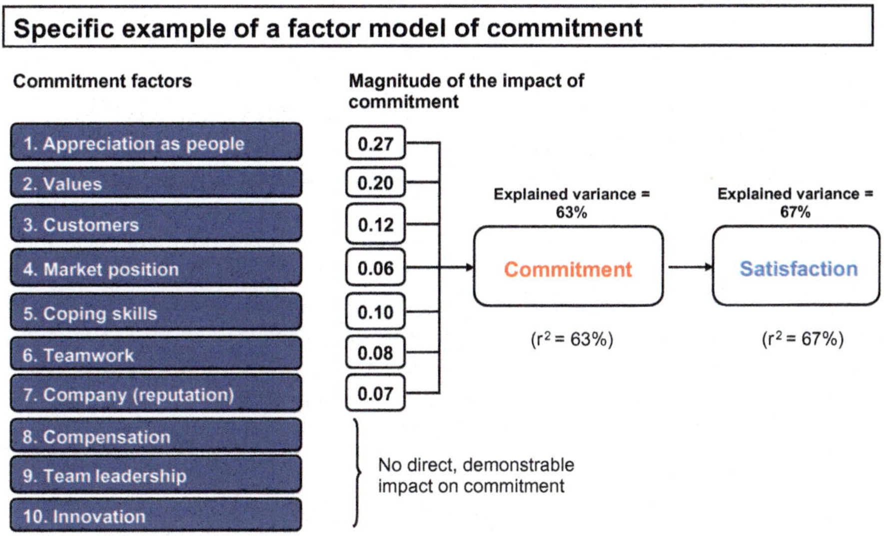

Fig. 5.1 Factor model of the survey in an IT company (n = 425). Legend: if the assessment of factor 1 ("Appreciation as people") rises by one point, the commitment increases by 0.27 points. *Source* Anker (2012), by courtesy of Erich Schmidt publisher, Berlin

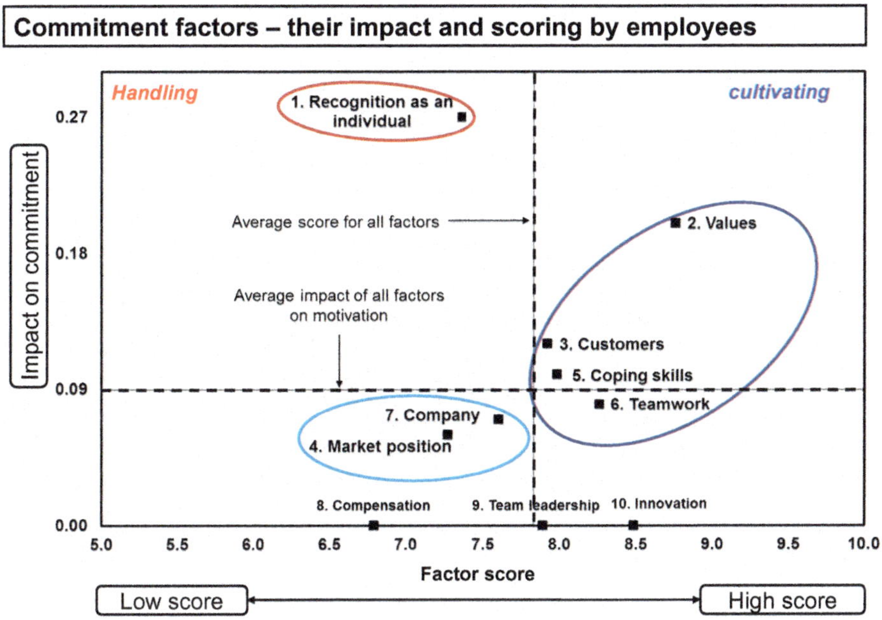

Fig. 5.2 Fourfold table: impact of the factors on commitment and their scoring. *Source* Anker (2012), by courtesy of Erich Schmidt publisher, Berlin

effect of the factors on commitment is represented, whereas the x-axis shows the assessment by the employees.

In a certain sense Fig. 5.2 reflects the “cultural landscape” of the company as perceived and experienced by the employees. What holds people together in this company are factor 2 “values”, factor 3 “customers” and factor 5 “coping skills” as well as factor 6 “teamwork”. They form the core of the current corporate culture. It can build on it.

The most critical factor is factor 1 “appreciation as a person”. This acts more efficiently than all other factors on commitment, but at the same time it is more critically assessed than the average of all factors—evidence of a clear deficit. It seems sensible to continue to cultivate and optimize the performance factors 2, 3, 5 and 6. However, an important key to greater commitment (and to more satisfaction) is also provided by factor 1: it has the strongest leverage effect in terms of commitment.

5.2.3 The Distribution of Commitment in the Company

How commitment is spread in the company is shown in Fig. 5.3. On a scale from 1 to 10 the average performance in this company is at 8.3, the internal benchmark, formed by the five units with the highest commitment, is 9.1. It is below average in the central services (human resources, finance and controlling as well as legal department). These are those units of the company, which were particularly challenged by the merger in the year preceding the survey and also by the imminent merger.

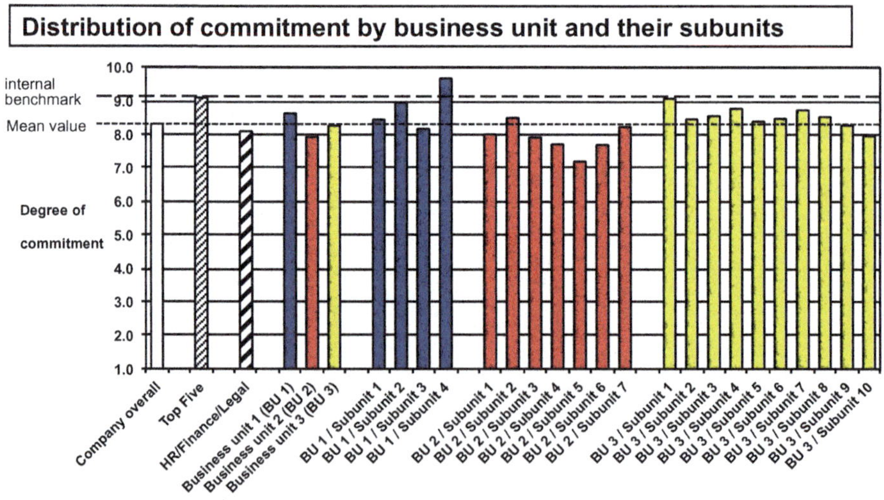

Fig. 5.3 Distribution of commitment in the company (n = 425). *Source* Anker (2012), by courtesy of Erich Schmidt publisher

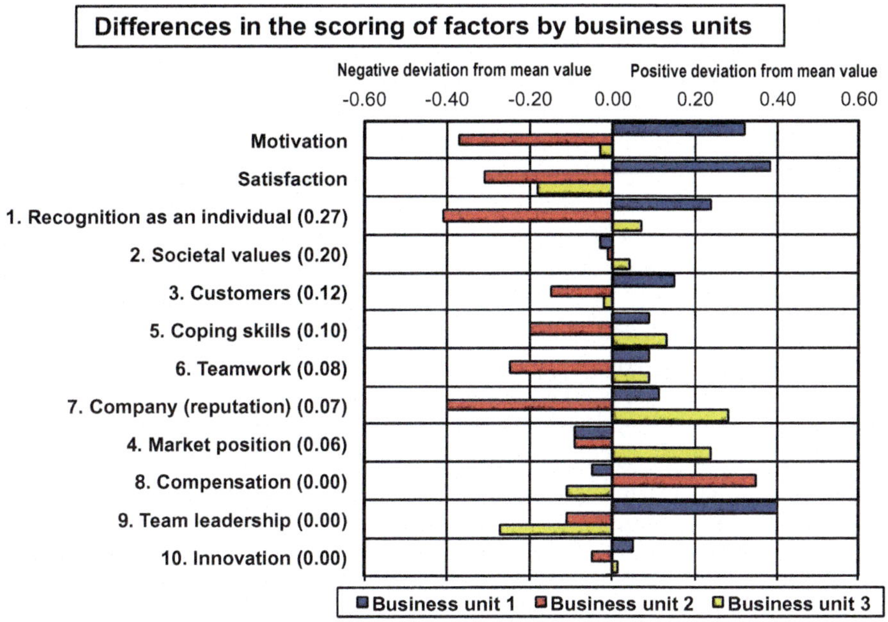

Fig. 5.4 Differences between the business units with regard to the scoring of the individual factors of commitment, expressed in deviation from the mean value of the company (n = 425). Bars to the right show positive deviation from the mean value, bars to the left refer to negative deviation from the mean value of the company. *Source* Anker (2012), by courtesy of Erich Schmidt publisher

Further, it is shown: In the parent company (BU 1) the commitment is above average, in UE 2—the business unit, which was integrated a year before—statistically significantly lower. This also applies to most of the subunits of BU 2. This suggests that the integration of BU 2 staff has not yet been successful. At BU 3, the situation is somewhat different: the parent company—the new employer—has an excellent reputation in the industry, among others due to its leadership culture, and the new employees are looking forward to the change.

In the following diagram (Fig. 5.4), the 10 factors for the three business units are broken down separately. This will show us, among other things, where the problem lies in the integration of BU 2. At the zero point (0.00), the average value of all the factors determined for the entire company is shown. From the zero point (0.00) to the right pointing bars indicate that the corresponding factor in the concerned business unit is above average in comparison to the overall company. For example, in BU 1 (in the parent company), the commitment is significantly higher than the average commitment in the company as a whole. Bars which are offset from the zero point (0.00) to the left indicate that the corresponding business unit has a value with respect to the factor concerned, which is below the company average. For example, the commitment in BU 2 significantly points in the negative direction: it is clearly below that of BU 1.

Why this is so can be seen immediately: parallel to the commitment of BU 2, there are clear deviations to the left for factor 1 "appreciation as people" as well as for factor 7 "company", which means the reputation of the company. Obviously the employees of BU 2 have not yet arrived properly in their "new home"—factor 1 shows clearly the fact that they feel little valued as humans and that they hardly appreciate their new employer or his reputation (factor 7). At the same time, however, factor 8 ("compensation") implies that the integration, which has not been successful so far, is not a question of remuneration. In this respect, the employees assess their new employer even more positively than the employees of BU 1 and BU 3.

An in-depth analysis led to the following: as the employees of BU 2 see it, the poor reputation of the company (factor 7) is a direct consequence of the lack of appreciation according to factor 1. For the same reason, the employees of BU 2 also critically evaluate the customer orientation of their new employer (factor 3 "customers"). The problem was aggravated by a lack of team spirit according to factor 6 (which was not considered important by the former employer) and comparatively weak coping skills according to factor 5 (dealing with uncertainties and failures). A weak team structure obviously makes it difficult to deal constructively with uncertainties and failures. Conversely, this means: "Shared suffering is half the pain." It seems to be easier to deal with uncertainties and failure when one feels supported by a team than when one is a lone fighter. This clearly illustrates the importance of the sociocultural Sense of Coherence (SOC) for the individual SOC (and the damage that can be caused by individual incentive systems).

The deficit of personal appreciation of the staff of BU 2 can be explained with the experience, that the new employer did not consider them for promotion. Another reason was that no one from their ranks was in the upper management of the parent company. They also felt left out in this respect and believed not to have a voice in the company management. Consequently, the company management entered into an intensive dialogue with those concerned, the human resources department revised their training and promotion system, and very soon BU 2 was also involved in management through a committee member.

5.2.4 The Value Balance in Business® Reveals a "Clash of Cultures"

Behind the unsatisfying integration of BU 2 an even deeper and more profound problem was hidden.

The employees of BU 2 came from a company with an extremely shareholder- and short-term profit-oriented culture with rigid structures. They were managed authoritatively; self-initiative and teamwork were not popular. Their scope of action in the sense of manageability was very limited, as was the component of comprehensibility. These circumstances are also of little help to the component of meaningfulness. In the new headquarters, on the other hand, a culture of self-initiative, non-bureaucratic, self-responsible cooperation and team spirit had already been established for a very long time. The motto was "help yourself!" This led to disastrous misunderstandings. As the new staff of BU 2 was accustomed to an authoritative culture, they were waiting for instructions from "above" and from their new team colleagues from the headquarters. However, there nobody understood what the new colleagues were waiting for. The BU 2 employees were increasingly marginalized, and consequently, hardly anybody from their ranks was promoted.

Ultimately, the frustration of the BU 2 staff and their associated lack of commitment have to be understood against the background of the clash between these two opposing cultures. A mentoring and coaching system was set up following these findings. This allowed the employees of BU 2 to freely communicate with colleagues from UE 1 and, if necessary, get advice from them. Thanks to these contacts, the understanding of BU 1 employees for their new colleagues also grew, and the situation relaxed.

This study allows all 10 factors to be analyzed down to the team level (see Fig. 5.5). It turned out that even in BU 2 there were clear differences in team-to-team commitment—not all units of BU 2 were in a real crisis. This allowed the forces to be deployed in the first place where something had to be done urgently, that is to bundle the energies and to use them in a focused manner—and thus also economically.

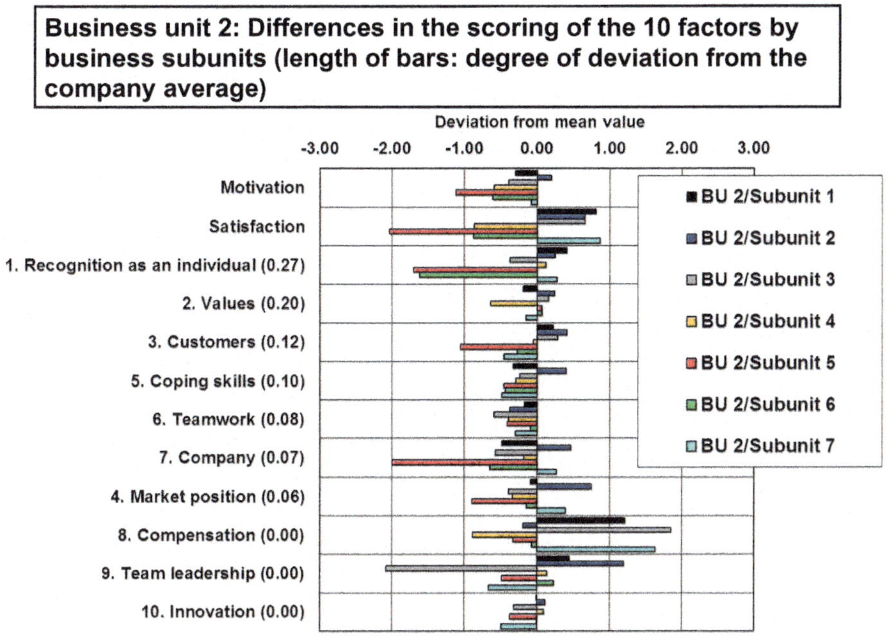

Fig. 5.5 The subunits of BU 2 and their respective degree of commitment (n = 107). *Source* Anker (2012), by courtesy of Erich Schmidt publisher

In this study, for example, the situation of subunit 5 of BU 2 stands out: commitment was the lowest of all business units and subunits. It is immediately apparent: the main problem was the appreciation as people (factor 1). This resulted in the well-known negative attitude to the company (factor 7) and to its benefit for the customers (factor 3). This was a general phenomenon in business unit 2. The special thing about this team, however, was that it took together with its team leader a hedgehog position against the rest of the company. The company management and the HR department were very careful around this team. The team leader ultimately decided to leave the company; the other members slowly built up confidence in the company following the personal attention they had experienced.

Another example: the resolution of the survey down to team level revealed an acute bullying problem in subunit 3: the anonymous survey allowed the team members to express themselves freely, that is, without control by the team leader. The survey resulted in a very rapid intervention and a change of the head of this team.

5.2.5 Facets of a Cluster Analysis Based on Personality Traits of the Employees

The VBB survey also includes questions about the personal attitudes of the employees, their attitude towards work itself, the degree of self-responsibility, their general performance orientation, their team orientation and willingness to cooperate, etc. On the basis of the answers given by employees on such questions, they were put in groups with the same or similar characteristics (clusters).

In this case (Fig. 5.6), five groups were defined. Almost a quarter of all employees have a very close relationship with the company and a much above-average level of commitment. Another eighth of the employees show a similarly high level of commitment, but these employees are worried about the company's future. They are skeptical to pessimistic. They are people who need special attention and appreciation; this is how they feel grounded; if left alone, they are particularly prone to burnout.

Another good quarter of the workforce also consider other things important in life. The company is not their center of life, and therefore, they do not have any career plans, but they are grateful to the company for the freedoms it provides in shaping their lives—they feel themselves to be taken seriously, valued and connected with the company.

An interesting case is the 14% of employees with frustrated career expectations. An above-average amount of employees of this group is characterized by a high level of self-initiative and sense of responsibility—their merely average commitment is a strange contrast. Investigations showed interesting results: many members of this group were once team leaders and thus formed the company's bottom management. In order to reduce costs, this lowest (and widest) hierarchical level

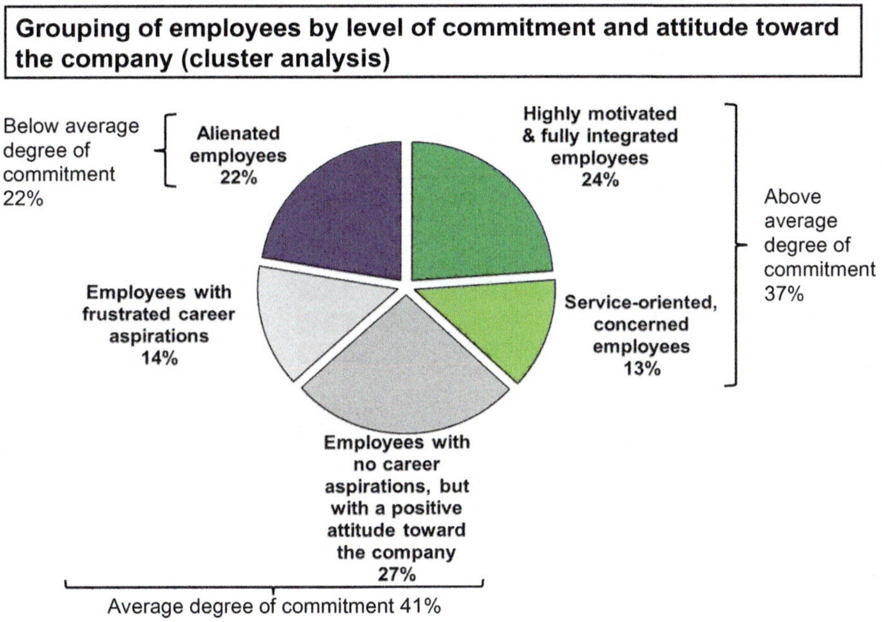

Fig. 5.6 Grouping of employees according to their psychological disposition (n = 425). *Source* Anker (2012), by courtesy of Erich Schmidt publisher

was cancelled two years before the Value Balance in Business® assessment, and the corresponding employees were downgraded. From the point of view of human appreciation, this was a hard blow for those affected. Evidently, many had not yet overcome this after two years—see commitment.

A fifth of all employees are completely alienated from the company: they neither feel appreciated as human beings, nor do they know why they are in this company, that is, what meaning their work has. Here, on the basis of the cluster analysis, we encounter the same phenomenon, which the factor analysis has already shown with regard to the employees of BU 2. This estrangement is accentuated by the fact that a good two-thirds of these employees state that professional work is of great importance in their lives. For them, today's situation is highly stressful from the viewpoint of meaning and appreciation or from the point of view of the SOC components of meaningfulness, comprehensibility and manageability, and, with regard to salutogenesis, their health is therefore particularly threatened.

These five groups of employees can again be represented according to functional areas and business units (Fig. 5.7).

The line "total" contains the grouping already described in Fig. 5.6. If we take a look at the three business units, the picture of the previous analysis is confirmed: the highest proportion of alienated employees (34%) is found in BU 2. Another result: every eighth manager (17%) feels alienated from the company—from the point of view of the multiplier effect of the superiors, this is a fact that cannot be overlooked.

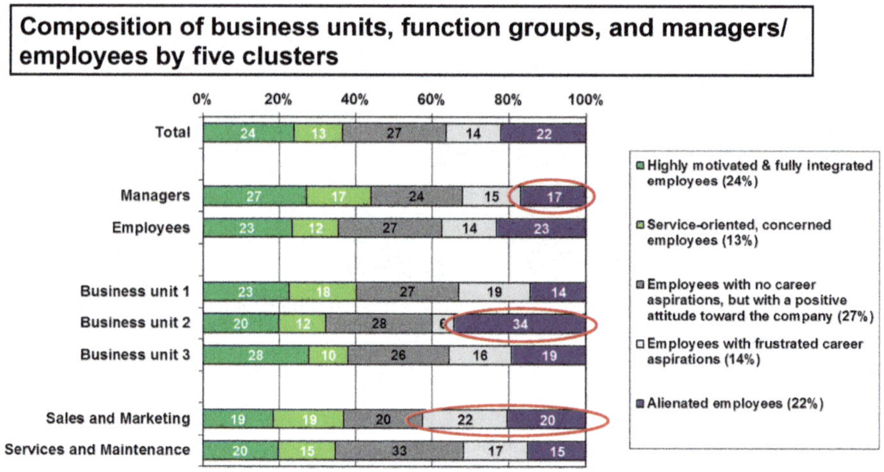

Fig. 5.7 The five groups of employees, divided according to business units and functional groups (n = 425). *Source* Anker (2012), by courtesy of Erich Schmidt publisher

Similarly, the fact that in the marketing and sales units—the company's face to the customers—more than 40% of the employees are critical or very critical of the company: 20% belong to the group of alienated employees, 22% are those who have been degraded from team leaders to non-executive employees.

Above information provides some insight into what the Value Balance in Business® does as an audit and assessment, or diagnostic and development tool. Based on the results of this study, an action plan was developed with the HR managers of the company. In its development and implementation, the company management as well as experts from the areas of HR, management training, company, personnel and organizational development were included. We have pointed out a few measures.

The example of a merger, briefly presented here, shows, among other things, how closely the commitment of the employees and thus the performance capacity of the company are connected with the culture of the company, and how important it is to keep this issue in mind—in the interest of the people and companies, their well-being, health and success.

Good, respectful and responsible entrepreneurship towards customers, employees, shareholders, society and the natural environment is a basic but specific health factor that constitutes a reliable way to long-lasting high profit.

- Success and ethics do not exclude each other; on the contrary, in the long run they are mutually dependent factors. Only healthy people i.e. employees experiencing meaning and personal appreciation make flourishing enterprises.

Reference

Anker H (2012) Ko-Evolution versus Eigennützigkeit. Creating Shared Value mit der Balanced Valuecard®. Erich Schmidt, Berlin

Part II
The Working People and Their Resources

Chapter 6
The Working Human—The Exhausted Human

Ingrid Pirker-Binder

Contents

People do not resist change; they resist being changed (Peter Senge).

The real voyage of discovery consists not in seeking new lands but seeing with new eyes (Marcel Proust).

Nowadays working life and life itself are often seen as two different terms. The term "Work-Life Balance" is considered a keyword suggesting that it is only about the right balance between work and life. However, completely disregarded is the fact that life takes place twenty-four hours every day with a mere change in the distribution of tasks. This means that individual thought patterns and attitudes not only characterize the private everyday life, but also the lifetime spent at work and with work.

In the popular imagination, there is the world of work and on the other hand the private world, the personal life where the "I" can be lived, where people are there for themselves, pursue their hobbies, maintain relationships.

But as attitudes, intrapersonal conflicts, thought and behavior patterns are constant companions of a person, any active preventive measure of a fatigue syndrome

I. Pirker-Binder (✉)
Saileräckergasse 43/26, 1190 Vienna, Austria
e-mail: office@pirker-binder.at

I. Pirker-Binder (ed.), *Mindful Prevention of Burnout in Workplace Health Management*, https://doi.org/10.1007/978-3-319-61337-6_6

at the workplace, and also its therapeutic treatment, has to incorporate the life story of the person concerned, his/her desires and needs, striving for meaning and his/her values.

Work takes place at the workplace in a mutual relationship pattern between board members and executives, executives and employees and between employees. If the workplace is not in the company, but in other places, such as a Home Office space, the interaction pattern is extended to the respective structure of the workplace at the respective location.

Often there are disparities or misunderstandings that lead to problems in work life. Misunderstandings that cause depletion and drain of human resources (physical and mental exhaustion), may be manifold, such as:

- misunderstandings between corporate culture and aspect of meaning or visions of the employees
- disparities in interaction (management styles, organizational processes and structures)
- disparities and misunderstandings in work allocation, work management and in conception of work
- disparities and misunderstandings at the workplace (e.g. as non-compliance with rest periods of shift workers who do not work in the company itself, but at other places; workplaces abroad)
- emotional misunderstanding at the workplace (conflicts, bullying, crises)
- disparities in the design of workplace and location (open-plan offices, noise, lack of separation in the home office, etc.)

The working people, no matter whether they are employees or executives, are involved in the work world with their needs, attitudes and visions, whereby exhaustion may result depending on intrapersonal characteristics, thought patterns, attitudes, personality patterns and disorders, fears, prejudices, etc. An example for this is exaggerated sense of duty or striving for perfection. In this case the prevailing thought would be, "First comes my duty, and only if everything is done and/or perfect, may I take time for myself, is my work finished or can I relax." Unfortunately, the desk never becomes empty, and even the housework is a perpetuum mobile. Anyone who operates a home office is particularly at risk in this respect.

This suggests that fatigue may result both from

- misunderstandings and disparities that are directly related to the company and/or the executives, but also from
- the life history and characteristics of the individuals themselves
- or from both aforementioned areas.

While in Chap. 5 the entrepreneurial aspect was examined in terms of exhaustion and prevention options, the focus is now on the question of what mechanisms act within and on people and can, if they are not changed, lead to a deterioration of psychological, physiological and mental vitality. To capture the individual mechanisms and areas that can lead to exhaustion, it is useful to consider various aspects, which are listed here, as follows:

1. Dimension psyche: the model of Life-Script-Analysis
2. Dimension work: the model of Work-Life-Analysis
3. Dimension physicality (energy, physical performance): the model of Life-Energy-Analysis
4. Spiritual dimension: knowledge and change potential

Ad 1: Dimension Psyche So as to understand one's own life landscape, I have developed the **Life-Script-Analysis** model as an existential analysis of life. In a structured process a close look can be taken at the gateway to understanding causes and effects, the unconscious and subconscious life script, and in a further step the scope for personal reaction and change options can be opened.

Ad 2: Dimension Work In the working environment the psychological connection between life and work has to be scrutinized. As a guide to research this aspect I have created the **Work-Life-Analysis**.

Ad 3: Physicality As a connection and bridge between psyche, body and mind, **Life-Energy-Analysis** is a great tool. It promotes understanding between unconscious and conscious experience. Biofeedback methods are used as development tools in this context.

Ad 4: Spiritual Dimension Existential analysis and logotherapy according to Frankl sees humans as acting beings that, due to their spiritual (noetic) dimension, are able to reflect upon themselves and change attitudes and behavior, if necessary and useful. However, long-term changes can only happen if recognition of the need or opportunity and the will to do so exist.

6.1 Life-Script-Analysis—An Existential Reminiscence on Life

In the model of the Life-Script-Analysis (LSA) anything inherited, acquired, learned, experienced and lived is brought into consciousness, observed and analyzed, and insights are generated. From these findings, experiences and thought patterns, attitudes, desires, visions, needs, positive and negative dispositions of humans can be learned and discussed. It is essential to recognize that all experiences a person gathers in the course of his/her life are stored mentally, physically, emotionally and on a cellular level, and represent a "script" for the present life.

If a human does not live what he/she is, but rather what he/she believes should or has to be done in his/her life script, an inner negative tension is built up. This tension produces constant internal activation, which drains power and energy.

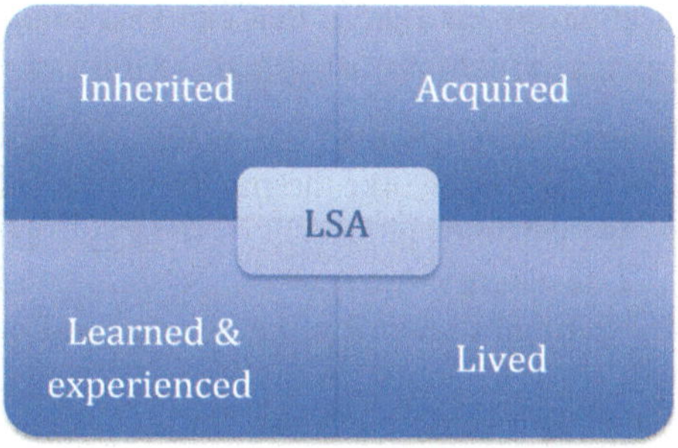

Fig. 6.1 Four formative worlds of experiences (Life-Script-Analysis)

Activation that persists too long, exploits the resources, and results in an exhaustion process.

The life experiences and dispositions are situated in the life script. The individual stages of the disposition can be summarized as IALEL

- Inherited
- Acquired
- Learned and Experienced
- Lived

The Life-Script-Analysis (LSA) helps to uncover content from the four areas and to look out for change options (Fig. 6.1).

Prevention is not only about imparting coping mechanisms, but also primarily about creating an understanding of why nothing is done about psychological stress and strain at an early stage or why humans do not confront smoldering problems sooner.

The explanation is that the affected individual does not even recognize his/her possibilities for action. He/she is more or less caught up and squeezed into his/her life story and unaware of the shaping influence of the world of experiences. Only once the individual life landscape has been unraveled and is clearly visible, is it possible to learn new, adapted action mechanisms. In this case they are formed from the inner understanding of the respective person, otherwise they would merely be imposed.

This suggests that before any preventive measure, clarification and understanding processes have to happen inasmuch as the beliefs, mental obstacles, ways of thinking, emotions, tensions and relationship patterns which influence life, and particularly work life, negatively, have to be made visible, tangible and perceptible.

The story of the frog and hot the water by Charles Hardy, which is retold below, illustrates how calls for action are often not noticed.

The Frog and the Hot Water

It came to pass that an old man was sitting in front of his house on the lakeshore, thinking about life. A frog on the shore drew his attention. He caught it and brought it into his hut. Once there, he threw it into a pot of boiling water. The startled frog leaped out of the pot in a shock and disappeared. After a while the old man was sitting in front of his house again musing about life. Suddenly he remembered the frog that spontaneously saved itself from the hot water in the pot to enjoy life again. Once more a small frog caught the man's attention, and again he took it back into his hut. As he did not have any boiling water on the stove, he put the frog into a pot of cold water and set it on the hotplate. Then he made a fire. The frog did not move to get out of it and kept sitting quietly. The frog did not even make a move to escape this threatening situation when the water was getting hotter. The old man was very pleased and enjoyed his frog soup, while he continued thinking about life.

The story of the frog and the hot water can lead people to the conclusion that it makes sense to sensitize one's individual perception in thinking, feeling and acting to be able to counteract negative influences as soon as possible and to become aware of the free space for an array of choices.

As an example I would like to mention the computer workstation. Stress-related distorted postures are not only connected with non-ergonomic office chairs or tables, but much rather with how the employees use them. A tense posture sooner or later leads to pain with or without an appropriate chair. If the person concerned knows about the relationship (posture and pain) and he/she can get in touch with himself/herself well, he/she is able to notice physical strain early on and respond adequately to it; that is, he/she has a decision space, i.e. "do I keep sitting on my chair this way and accept pain or do I change my position."

The Computer Screen

In many offices, the computer screen is adjusted incorrectly. Mostly it is vertical and the user virtually has to bend unnaturally, especially in the neck, in order to see properly. The problem: nobody notices it even though the solution is quite simple: as soon as pain occurs, one has either been sitting in a cramped and concentrated position in front of the screen for too long and/or the screen is too vertical.

Do a test: bring a book in the same position as your computer screen—would you read like this?

The Life-Script-Analysis, which I have developed from my logotherapeutic work, should lead to an increased awareness, and aims at opening up free space for knowledge and decisions to facilitate development and possibilities for change. It serves as a tool for personal development and as an intervention measure for psychological exhaustion.

6.2 The Process Model of Life-Script-Analysis

An analysis of individual life characteristics, a person's life script, the pattern a person thinks, feels and acts in, permits an understanding of the relationships and enables self-knowledge. Only understanding and feeling how internal tension or a negative belief are formed and what they do, can build a link to freedom and opens the door for possibilities to change (Fig. 6.2).

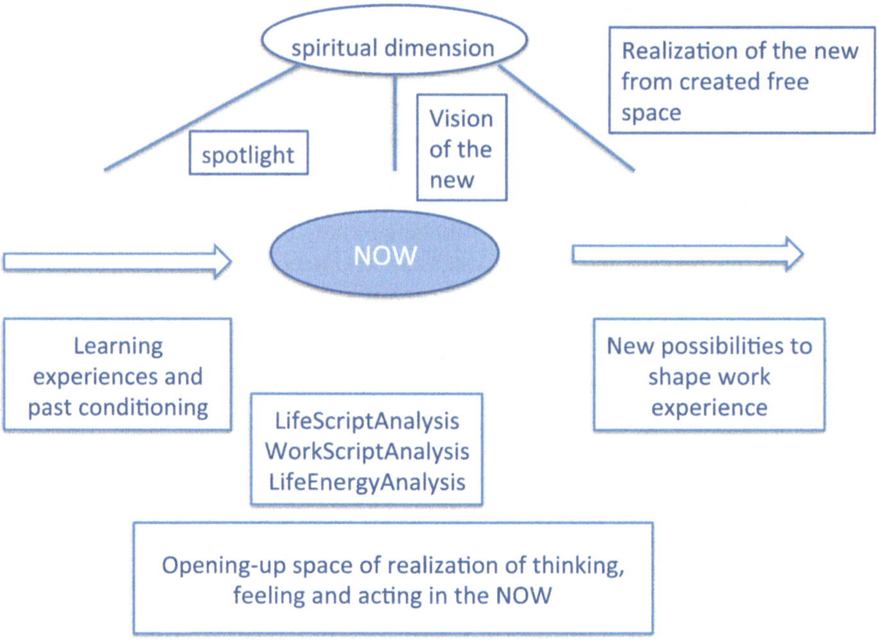

Fig. 6.2 Opening-up of future possibilities to shape life and work (Pirker-Binder)

The spotlight of analysis includes the past and reaches into the present. The four worlds of experience are considered and checked for exhaustion promoting content. Through the freedom in the spiritual dimension (Chap. 3) a vision of the new, the healthy, the things worth living for, grows and can be designed from the present moment and projected into the future. The Life-Script-, Work-Script-, and the Life-Energy-Analysis provide clues and methods for that.

The fundamental principle for this opening of one's free space is looking at the links and mutual influence of psychological experiences and concepts on the physicality. From the dimension of the mind (noetic dimension) the spotlight is directed towards it, which enables knowledge. Out of the neutral, value-free distance can the recognition of one's personal freedom for decisions to strengthen one's desire for change develop (Fig. 6.3).

The process is divided into five steps:

1. question of "what is"
2. contemplation of the process
3. recognizing the individual basic pattern
4. opening-up of personal freedom and recognizing the possibilities for shaping one's life
5. personal development

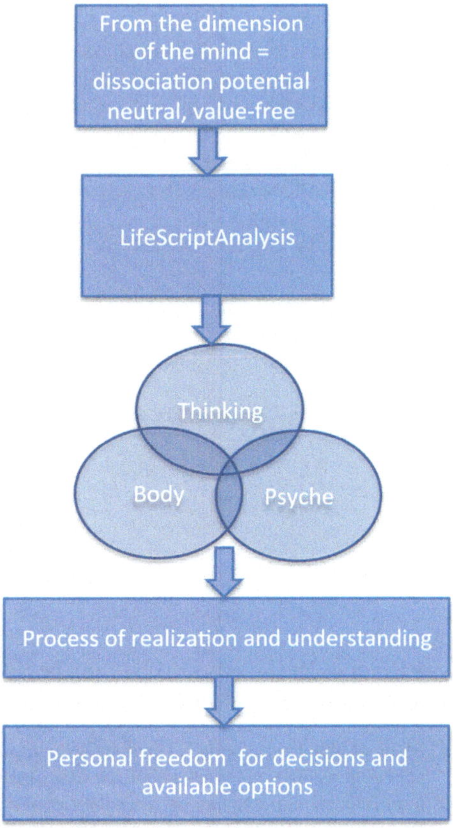

Fig. 6.3 Dissociation potential due to dimension of the mind (Pirker-Binder)

6.2.1 *Step 1: Question of "What Is" and the Desire for Change and Information*

Humans come into my private practice with a desire for change. The first question may be, "Why are you here today?" It is about the "actual state analysis" of the current mental state. The second question will be: "What do you want to achieve, what is **your** aim?"

After analyzing the condition, the client receives information about biological and psychological interrelations of an exhaustion process. They form the starting point of the Life-Script-Analysis with the explanatory model on the three factors of influence on a successful life (body, psyche, spiritual dimension) from the perspective of existential analysis and logotherapy. They provide an explanation for the subsequent reminiscence of life.

In a first step, the correlations and interactions between soma and psyche are explained, as well as the possibility of free decision in the spiritual (noetic) dimension,

Table 6.1 Explanatory model: factors of influence on life and work in flow (Pirker-Binder)

Body	Autonomous nervous system (regulation, regeneration): Cell muscles/physical condition cardiovascular system	I sense: Nervous system Hormonal system Immune system	Energy management
Psyche thinking	Emotions/emotional life	I feel: Affect situation	Emotion management
	Mental processes	I think: Mental concepts	Thought management
Mind	Personal freedom for decisions	I design: My philosophy of life	Attitude management Living and working in flow
My spirituality My mindfulness My connectedness			

which empowers humans to be acting beings. The person must realize what he/she has let others do to himself/herself or what he/she has done to himself/herself.

> Most of what we see is shaped by our impressions, our history, our baggage, our preconceptions. We can't see people as they really are because we're too busy reacting to our own internal experiences of what they evoke in us, so we rarely actually relate to reality. We mostly relate to internal remembrances of our own history, stimulated and evoked by whatever is externally before us (Jaworski 1998)

From the explanatory model the following three aspects can be used for subsequent personality development: knowledge acquisition and opening of creative space takes place under the spotlight of the interactions in these three fields

- attitude management—spiritual dimension
- emotion, thought management—psyche, thinking
- energy management—body

The recovered information opens up a new room for available options (Table 6.1).

6.2.2 *Step 2: Contemplation Process*

Through the steps of the Life-Script-Analysis the unconscious and subconscious interactions between the three aspects are brought into consciousness in the spotlight of the spiritual dimension, the distancing and the freedom of decision. The aim of the contemplation process is to record, recognize, process, let go or fit into the life story obstacles, resistances, traumas or freely accepted loads and sorrows. For illustration, I would like to present the story of the hiker by Nossrat Peseschkian.

The Hiker
In Persian mysticism there is a story of a hiker who was walking painfully along a seemingly endless road. He was hung all over with different loads. Groaning and moaning he was moving forward step by step, complaining about his hard fate and agonizing fatigue. Trudging along he met a farmer in the glowing midday heat, who asked him, "Tired hiker, why do you load yourself with these rocks?"—"Too bad," answered the hiker, "but I have not noticed them yet." At that he threw the chunks of rock away and felt much lighter. After a long distance, another farmer approached him, who inquired, "Say, tired hiker, why are you lugging around a half-rotten pumpkin on your head and are dragging such heavy iron weights on chains?" The hiker replied, "I am glad that you've made me aware of it; I had no idea, what I was doing to myself". He shed the chains and smashed the pumpkin in the ditch. Again he felt lighter. But the farther he went, the more he began to suffer again. A farmer, who was coming from the field, looked at the hiker, amazed, "Good man, you are carrying sand in your backpack, but what you see in the distance, is more sand than you could ever carry. And how big your water container is—as if you wanted to cross the Kawir desert. Beside you a clear river flows, which will accompany your way for a long distance!"—"Thanks to you, dear farmer, now I see what I have been lugging around with me." With these words, the hiker tore open the water container, its brackish water trickling away on the path, and filled a pothole with the sand from the backpack. He looked down at him, saw the heavy millstone on his hand and suddenly realized that it was the stone that still let him walk with a stoop. He untied it and threw it as far as he could down into the river. Free from all his loads he wandered through the cool evening to look for lodging (Peseschkian 2003, p. 56. By courtesy of Herder Publishing House).

6.2.3 Step 3: Recognize the Individual Basic Pattern of Thinking, Feeling and Acting

By recognizing the basic patterns of the past, present actions can be understood better. In the Now, it is possible to create a new future of thinking, feeling and acting (Table 6.2).

Table 6.2 The four Life-Script-Analysis steps (Pirker-Binder)

Inherited	Disposition in DNA	Cell structure	Prenatal, antepartum, peripartum, postpartum	"What I inherited from my ancestors"
Acquired	Conditioning from the environment	Parents	Until about 7 years, role models, sensed life	"What was demonstrated to me"
Learned and experienced	Conditioning through social interactions	Parents, school, peer groups	7 years until now Learning new ways of behavior and thinking	"What my environment taught me"
Lived	Feeling, thinking and acting according to points 1–3	Everyday work and private life	Everyday life	"How I design and live my private and work life"
Intuition (conscience) Meta-life plan and master plan Life in harmony with the individual purpose			"What life means for me"	
			Quality of life	

6.2.4 *Step 4: Opening-Up Personal Freedom and Recognizing the Possibilities for Shaping One's Life*

Through existential reminiscence on life a recognition and understanding of the individual life landscape is created.

Thinking, feeling and acting become visible. The distance of the noetic dimension facilitates grasping the freedom of one's possibilities for shaping life. Thereby stepping towards future transformation and reorganization is facilitated.

All freedom has a "What from" and "What for":
"what" humans can be free "from" is being driven.
The I is free from the It; but "what" humans are free "for", is being responsible.
So, the freedom of the human will is freedom "from" being driven "to" being responsible, to having a conscience (Frankl 2004, p. 39).

6.2.5 *Step 5: Personal Development (ASTI)*

By recognizing the individual freedom strategies and alternatives one's actions can be initiated and directed towards the change objective. This results in two work approaches:

- individual visions and goals: originate in the life script ASTI
- individual goals in terms of the relationship to others, embedded in the work context

Individual goals in terms of the relationship to others refer to the ASTI process (Chap. 3). This does not only involve the individual, but also the respective group, the team, the individual is embedded in. Development steps are:

- **a**wareness and respect towards oneself and others
- **s**ocial thinking: working on the "you"—and "us" feeling
- **t**olerance: dropping (pre-) conceptions and judgment of others
- **i**ntuition: trusting one's feelings, perceiving and noticing somatic markers.

6.3 Suitable Work: Work and Life in Flow

Basic patterns of thinking, feeling and acting accompany humans in their private and professional environment. Based on the experience of work the affected person explores his/her understanding of work, work experience, interactions and emotions at work with the aim of experiencing working time as lifetime, as realization of meaning, away from "being driven". This can best be considered living and working in **flow**.

- understanding that working time means lifetime. Work is part of life, it should not be seen as removed from life, in the sense of "let's work fast so that there is time for life afterwards." One may also live during work!

Ms. Y is a teacher; she loves her job. She comes to my practice because she feels "exhausted", and also in the summer months, the feeling of being under stress seems to persist – it's the stress of having to recover quickly. So far she has lived to the motto: school time is working time and during the summer holidays I recover. Unfortunately, this way of thinking does not work indefinitely, i.e. only until the resources are running in reserve power. Then one can feel that recovery no longer works. Ms. Y did not know what exactly recovery might be for her; she says that for her quietly sitting in a deckchair in the garden does not work, as she is permanently under pressure of having to recover.
Through analyzing her life script and in particular her relationship to her very difficult and demanding mother, she gets to know herself and her inner drives and her needs. She begins to understand and comprehend that during the school year she constantly puts herself under pressure by subordinating her needs to the wishes of others. Both, colleagues and the family exploit her helpfulness. As a result, she learns to distance and re-orientate herself.
The result: at the end of the next school year she is neither exhausted nor frustrated. She has learned, that even during working time she may live; she has learned to distance herself and has thereby gained a new quality of life. She has de-cluttered her judgments and attitudes, has added new perspectives and ways of thinking and learned to listen to and trust her inner voice.

- suitable work: work that corresponds to the skills and competencies of people
- a suitable workplace: design options and control of and at one's workplace

- working in flow presupposes the meaning aspect of work (see below quote: Frankl 2004, p. 84)
- working in flow demands being mindful and present in the **now**: in harmony with oneself and with one's goals and visions = the individual perspective of life
- working in flow in relation to the work context means: being attentive, present with concentrated composure in the **now**: at a suitable work place with adequate conditions and culture, a pleasant environment etc. = the individual perspective of working
- working in flow in terms of social context means: being embedded in the interactions at work, in a collective "Us" = corresponds to the WAVE process (Chap. 3).

> … humans are not interested in any inner states, be it lust, inner balance, but they are oriented towards the world, the outside world, and within the world they seek meaning that they strive to find, or another human whom they could love. And due to a pre-reflective ontological self-image, they also know somehow that they fulfill themselves to the extent in which they forget themselves, and they forget themselves again exactly to the extent that they surrender, surrender to a cause they serve, or a person they love (Frankl 2004, p. 84).

Living and working in flow means meaningful living and working. Frankl coined the concept of self-transcendence (Frankl 1990) as a way of meaningful fulfillment. This means directing one's doing and acting towards something that is not the individual himself/herself; e.g. not regarding work as a means to more money or success, but as a process that creates meaning through action. Success or more money may be the resulting reward, but is not an end in itself.

> Only tasks, one is willing and able to devote oneself to, have the motivational, meaningful character that stabilizes and keeps under self-control an individual's life as well as living together… we, too, need to learn; everyone for himself or herself; learning "to stand above it all" – things and judgments of others, and doing things for their own sake. The decision-making body determining what is correct and "the real thing" for us, what we can justify can only lie within ourselves and not at the discretion of the environment (Böckmann 1981, pp. 62, 58).

In the experience of work it is important what the person does in life, with others, or what he/she experiences. Böckmann regards as life success "the sum of all meaningful situations in life." Accordingly, professional activity leads to professional success through one's inner calling (Böckmann 1981, p. 142, 1984). Böckmann speaks of "performance drive as an expression of mental health, while eagerness to succeed represents an expression of distrust against oneself: its trauma is the fear of failure" (Böckmann 1981, p. 94).

According to Frankl success cannot be forced, it rather has to arise from self-determination and personal responsibility. People should not predicate their success on particular situations, it rather arises from realization of meaning and values. Success stems from meaningful actions, expressed by performance (Böckmann 1981, pp. 85, 114).

If the realization of meaning is the realization of values, what categories can values be divided into in terms of work?

Frankl assigns three areas to values as motivation for living:

- **creative values**: contain active, productive activity and creation
- **experience levels**: the experience of life
- **attitudinal values**: opinion on something, on life, on oneself (Riedel et al. 2002)

The value system of work according to Böckmann (1981, p. 65):

- **creative values**: develop, organize, improve, plan, design, and produce
- **experience values** are divided into
  - socially bound experience values; they refer to the relationship, role, status within a group
  - socially unbound experience values; artistic values
- **attitudinal values**: attitude to life, to work itself, human image, dedication to something.

If realization of meaning exists in the three value areas, they relate to each other. Then, basically, the person experiences himself/herself as being in the right workplace. He/she is at the right place and the work corresponds to his/her abilities and skills, i.e. the conditions for work in flow are given.

If the individual loses himself/herself in ambitious pursuit for more (more money, more power) and all happiness depends on it, he/she loses himself/herself and also his/her life. Tolstoy's story of Pachom, the farmer, should be a warning for us in this respect.

How Much Land Does a Person Need?
Pachom, the farmer, buys a piece of land and becomes a landowner. He is "proud and happy". But his sense of ownership is now awakened. He becomes hostile to his neighbors because of minor damage to crops they cause along the field boundaries. Also, things are stolen from him. He cannot catch the thief; his charge is dismissed. Now Pachom is quarrelling with the judges and the neighbors. The farmers threatened him with the red rooster. So, even though Pachom has enough space on his land, he feels crowded in the community. Eastward, further inland, good land is supposed to be on sale cheaply. After verifying this rumor, he sells his property and settles four hundred versts located east of the Volga. Now Pachom lives ten times better than before. But there are richer farmers than him. In the urge to grow, he also falls out with his neighbors here. Then he hears from a passing

merchant that one could cheaply buy good steppe country from the Bashkirs, even further to the east. With his servant Pachom travels five hundred versts to the steppe dwellers. He is given a friendly welcome in their camp and is allowed to buy as much land as he can circle on foot from sunrise to sunset. However, when assessing his future property, Pachom overestimates his powers. He collapses and dies from exhaustion, after having circled a tremendous piece of land, because towards the end, during sunset, he was running desperately. "The servant took the hoe and dug a grave for Pachom, just as long as the piece of earth, which he covered with his body, from top to toe, - six cubits - and buried him" (Tolstoy, retold on Wikipedia 2015).

Csikszentmihalyi (2000, p. 72 ff.) describes flow as flowing, as recognizing that humans are continuously flowing. The purpose of this flow is to stay flowing and not seek highlights or utopian goals, but to stay in the flow.

The flow contains consistent action requirements, a sense of control and the feeling of selflessness. The flow experience has autotelic character, that is, it needs no goals or rewards that lie outside it. This also explains why financial incentives as a motivation factor only have an effect to a certain degree.

What flow offers is an opportunity to increase the quality of existence (Csikszentmihalyi 2004, p. 87). A flow experience is a condition that arises through self-transcendence, dedication to something, a situation, or people. Tolstoy's description in *Anna Karenina*, of how the rich landowner Levin learns to scythe, gives an impression of what may be a flow experience.

The Wealthy Landowner Lewin

"I'll reach back less with the arm and press more with the whole body," he thought when he compared Tit's uniform, perfectly straight strip with his uneven and messy one next to it … He thought of nothing, wished nothing more than not staying behind the farmers and doing his task as well as possible. He heard nothing but the clatter of scythes, and saw in front of him only Tit's receding shape … Lewin lost any awareness of time and no longer knew whether it was late or early. Now a change happened in his work, which gave him the greatest enjoyment. In the midst of his work he had moments when he forgot what he was doing; he felt lighthearted, and in these moments his strip was just as smooth and beautiful as Tit's. But as soon he focused his mind on what he was doing and wanted to make an effort to do a better job, he immediately felt the difficulty of the work and his strip turned out badly… And more and more often those moments of semi-unconsciousness arose, during which one did not have to think about what one was doing. The scythe was mowing by itself. Those were happy moments (Tolstoy 1959).

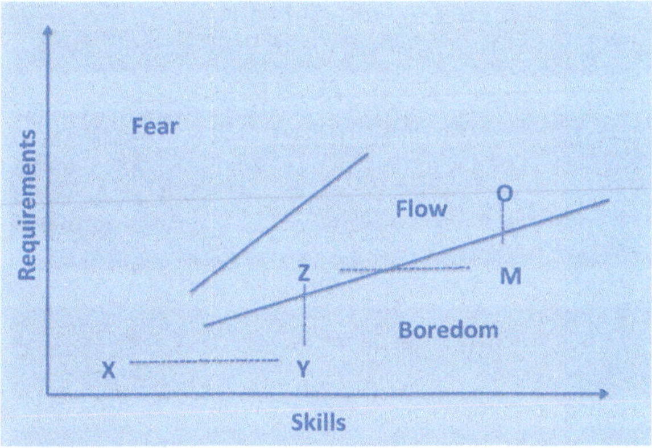

Fig. 6.4 Flow experience (modified according to Csikszentmihalyi 2004). X = start of an activity; the activity is new, challenge and curiosity are present. Y = after some time boredom sets in, the activity becomes routine. Y to Z = new challenges are needed so as not to get lost in boredom (this is where the so-called "Bore-out-Syndrome" arises; an exhaustion syndrome may develop due to insufficient life tasks). Z to M = the process starts anew

Self-transcendence leads to a flow experience. What is needed in professional life is the right mix of skills, competencies and challenge, a happy medium between fear and boredom (Fig. 6.4).

Hence, living and working in flow requires

- bringing one's own life into a state of flow: in inner harmony with oneself, one's needs and visions,
- being embedded in a social and work culture,
- a suitable job: consistent with the individual skills and competences,
- an adequate workplace: design options and control over and at the workplace/ place where work takes place.

In Fig. 6.5 the way to flow or burnout can be traced. Starting from the given conditions, such as individual habits, past conditioning, and given structure and culture in the workplace, like leadership style, work culture, job content, location and its connected cognitions, emotions, physical and mental state, an inner tension arises, which develops either as a positive, motivating and challenging tension or as a negative, stressful, anxious tension.

Through happiness at work, concentrated composure and mindfulness when dealing with oneself, positive, motivating tension leads to flow without burning out. If composure and mindfulness are missing, a fatigue syndrome may develop despite motivating work, because the individual energy reserves are being depleted.

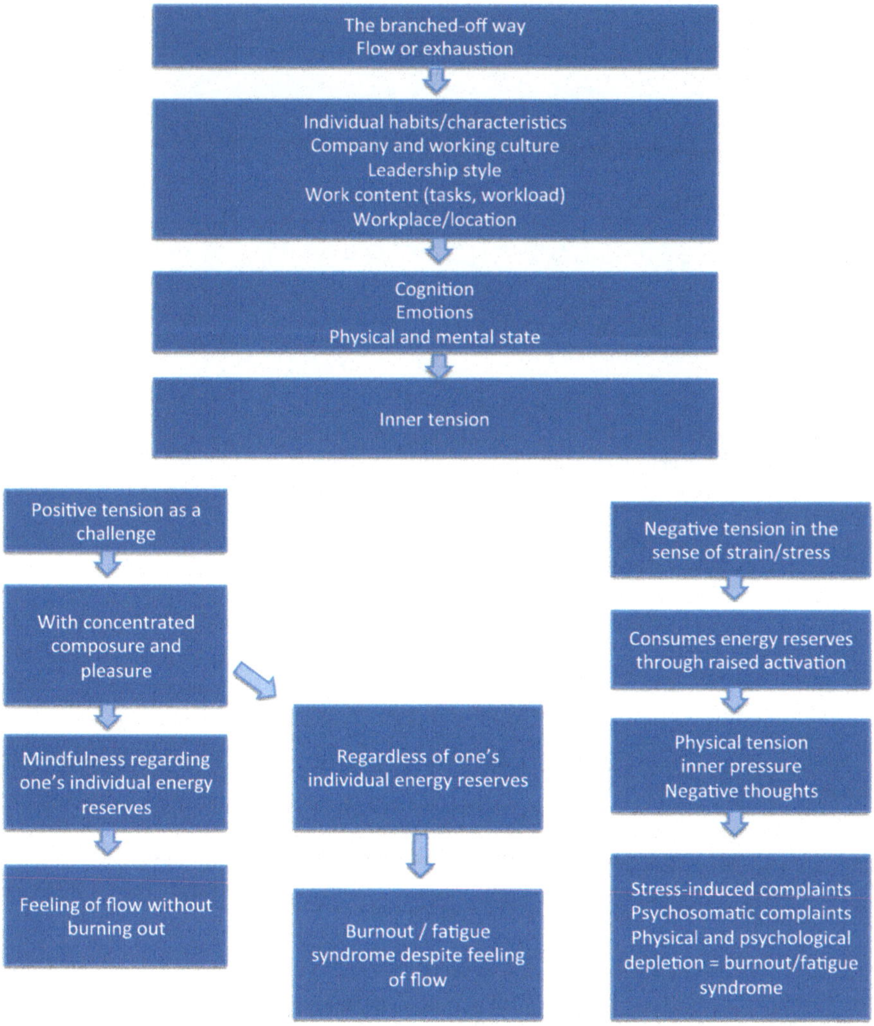

Fig. 6.5 Flow or exhaustion (Pirker-Binder)

Negative tension chronically uses up too much energy to be able to sustain attention and concentration. Nightly rumination and tensed-up working unavoidably lead to psychosomatic and/or stress-induced complaints if not interrupted.

References

Böckmann W (1981) Das Sinn-system. Psychotherapie des Erfolgsstrebens und der Misserfolgsangst. Econ, Düsseldorf Wien
Böckmann W (1984) Wer Leistung fordert, muss Sinn bieten; moderne Menschenführung in Wirtschaft und Gesellschaft. Econ
Csikszentmihalyi M (2000) Das Flow-Erlebnis. 8. Aufl. Klett-Cotta, Stuttgart
Csikszentmihalyi M (2004) Flow im Beruf. Das Geheimnis des Glücks am Arbeitsplatz. Klett Cotta, Stuttgart
Frankl V (1990) Der leidende Mensch. Anthropologische Grundlagen der Psychotherapie. Piper, München
Frankl V (2004) Der unbewusste Gott. Psychotherapie und Religion. 7. Aufl, DTV München
Jaworski J (1998) Synchronicity: the inner path of leadership. Berrett-Koehler, San Francisco
Peseschkian N (2003) Klug ist jeder. Der eine vorher, der andere nachher. Geschichten und Lebensweisheiten. Herder Freiburg im Breisgau
Riedel C, Deckart R, Noyon A (2002) Existenzanalyse und Logotherapie. Ein Handbuch für Studium und Praxis. Primus Darmstadt
Tolstoj L (1959) Anna Karenina. Walter-Verlag, Olten
Wikipedia (2015) Nacherzählung von Leo Tolstoj (1885). Stichwort "Wieviel Erde braucht der Mensch?" URL: https://de.wikipedia.org/wiki/Wieviel_Erde_braucht_der_Mensch%3F. Last access on 10 July 2015

Chapter 7
The Working People and Their Energy

Ingrid Pirker-Binder

Contents

When the heartbeat becomes as regular as the tapping of the woodpecker or the rhythm of the rain droplet on the roof, the patient will die within four days (Wang Shuhe, 3rd century. Chr.).

For a better understanding of what processes lead to people feeling exhausted and/or being exhausted, a glimpse into energy production and control is required. Below a brief overview of the key stakeholders, the mitochondria, the brain and the autonomic nervous system is provided.

7.1 Energy Production—The Mitochondria

Prevention cannot be practiced without including the needs of the body, i.e. particularly its requirement of nutrients. The Nobel Prize laureate Linus Pauling coined the term orthomolecular psychiatry for the first time.

I. Pirker-Binder (✉)
Sailerӓckergasse 43/26, 1190 Vienna, Austria
e-mail: office@pirker-binder.at

I. Pirker-Binder (ed.), *Mindful Prevention of Burnout in Workplace Health Management*, https://doi.org/10.1007/978-3-319-61337-6_7

Orthomolecular Medicine According to Pauling
Pauling defined orthomolecular medicine as "prevention of good health and treatment of illnesses through changes to the concentration of substances in the human body, which are usually present in the body and are necessary for staying healthy" (Pauling 2015).

The Österreichische Akademie der Ärzte (2015) writes in its Preamble to the Diploma Directive Orthomolecular Medicine:

> The method of orthomolecular medicine for the prevention, recovery or cure of diseases comprises selective variations in the molecular concentrations of the substances that are normally present in the body. These biochemical stimuli are processed and answered by the body. This leads to an activation and reactivation of cell metabolism, stabilization of the physiological balance, timely intervention in the energy metabolism, optimization of repair mechanisms, fight of free radicals etc. (Austrian Academy of Physicians 2015)

The production of energy takes place in the mitochondria. They are the power plants of the cells. They produce energy not only from oxygen, but also from glucose (sugar) without oxygen. Besides, they are also responsible for the degradation of fatty acids. The production of energy takes place in two different ways:

- in normal mode
- in economy mode

The energy saving mode normally takes place during the time period when cells divide in order to resume full production afterwards. In the event of unnatural stress caused by free radicals, mitochondria also switch to economy mode as a protective measure against destruction (Kuklinski and Schemionek 2012, p. 72 ff.). During the energy production free radicals, i.e. waste, accrue, which can destroy cells if they appear in too large a quantity. The body's antioxidant systems prevent the cell from that and protect it against free radicals.

Such protection systems are

- essential micronutrients: necessary micronutrients that the body cannot produce itself
- secondary phytochemicals
- glutathione, a protein compound from amino acids

Free radicals also arise from

- chronic physical and psychological strain
- chronic intestinal disorders or inflammation
- nicotine, alcohol, light stress
- environmental toxins

Too high a proportion of free radicals (oxidative stress) in the blood, can overburden the body's own protective mechanisms. The result is the mitochondria switching into economy mode: too little energy.

Counteractive measures and support of the antioxidants are:

- Regeneration
  - micro-breaks during everyday life
  - regeneration during sleep (Chap. 11)
- diet containing sufficient quantities of macro and micronutrients

We receive macronutrients from our diet; these include carbohydrates, proteins and fats. The body requires micronutrients in smaller amounts, but they are essential for metabolism.

A particular form of oxidative stress is an overload by nitro stress (NO gas).

It is an overproduction of nitrogen monoxide gas. A result might be adrenal dysfunction (adrenal fatigue), which affects the production of cortisol, adrenalin and noradrenalin. Its result is a lack of energy production and the feeling of exhaustion (Eichinger and Hoffmann-Nachum 2012, p. 24 ff).

Besides oxidative stress, neuro stress is also a main focus point in the case of exhaustion. It is a dysfunction in the stress axis hypothalamus-pituitary gland-adrenal gland, the so-called neuroendocrine stress axis. Affected are cortisol, DHEA, adrenalin, noradrenalin, serotonin, dopamine, GABA and glutamate (Rau 2015).

A micronutrient deficiency can be recognized by laboratory diagnostics and corrected through orthomolecular medicine. For prevention to be successful not only educating people about macro- and micronutrients is important, but also making canteen staff consider this information. Suspected exhaustion should in any case include laboratory diagnostics to review the impact of oxidative, neuro and nitro stress in addition to a medical check. Laboratory diagnostics is a complementary element of the Life-Energy-Analysis.

7.2 Stress and the Intestine: The Leaky-Gut Syndrome

Science is now putting a stronger focus on the intestine and its significance for a functioning immune system. About 33% of all autoimmune diseases are associated with a leaky intestine, the leaky gut syndrome. Stark (2014, p. 96 ff) provides a first overview of diseases and ailments connected with a leaky gut syndrome.

In addition to many harmful effects on the intestine, the importance of acute and chronic stress is in the foreground in this context. If the intestinal mucosa is damaged and permeable, toxins can get into the blood. Often also chronic fatigue and lack of concentration can be traced back to this, as toxins hinder the immune system and thought processes of the brain.

In her study Van Hemert (2014) points out the influence of a leaky gut on migraine and brain dysfunction. In the case of chronic stress cortisol is produced in the adrenal medulla to protect the organism. It inhibits inflammation and pain, increases in emergency situations and stress and decreases with relaxation and regeneration (Rauland 2001, p. 84 ff).

Consequences of Permanent Stress
If stress lasts too long, cortisol keeps being produced. It cannot maintain its anti-inflammatory effect any longer, which results in a weakened immune system. In the case of chronic stress the level of adrenalin may be up to ten times higher than normal. Not only anxiety and inner pressure lead to an activation of the sympathetic system but also anger and joy.

Mr. Z is busy employee in a large company. Taking breaks is unfamiliar to him; his weekly working time is about 60 h. He starts his holidays right from the office. He rushes to catch his flight; his wife has previously packed his suitcase and is waiting for him at the airport. Once arrived, Mr. Z already feels bad. He gets sick and can only begin to enjoy his vacation in the third week. This symptom is known as "manager disease". Once the stress subsides, the weakened immune system collapses.

Metabolic disorders are also closely related to stress and poor nutrition (Fig. 7.1).

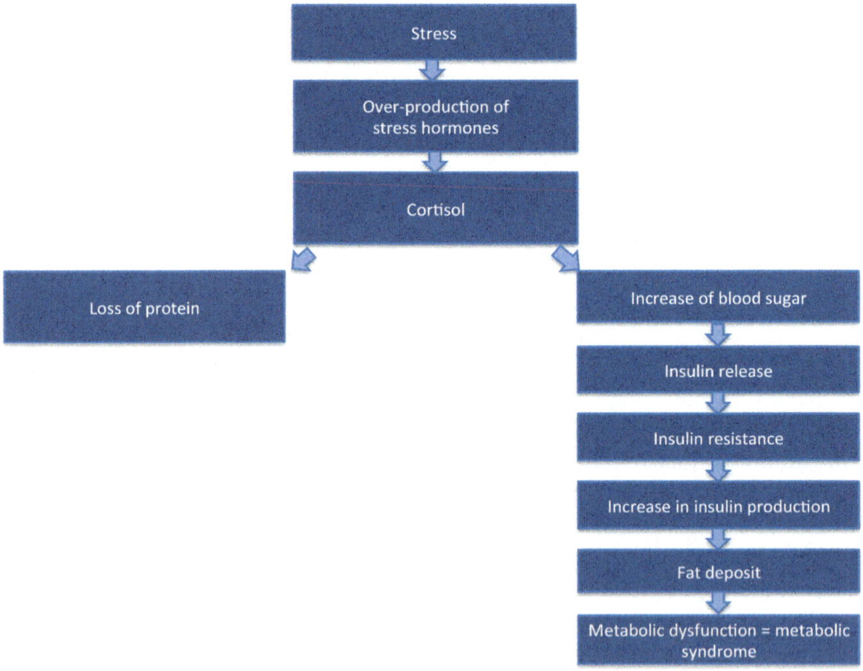

Fig. 7.1 Stress and metabolic syndrome (adapted from Stark 2014)

7.3 Food Intolerance and Allergy

Clinical psycho-neuro-immunology deals with the relationships between the psyche, neurological processes and the immune system, primarily on cellular level. Its focus is the study of new insights into nutrition.

As a new approach in this regard, a kind of diet following the Stone Age people, called "Stone Age" or "paleo-diet", is frequently mentioned. It is a diet made up of fresh, GMO-free biological food, high in protein and healthy fats, and little, and if so, gluten-free cereal. In case of physical ailments or just to treat one's body to a recovery, it makes sense to have oneself tested as to which foods are conducive to one's organism and which are not, or which foods one should leave out for a certain time.

At least once a year detoxifying the body under professional guidance should be considered. Stress makes the body acidic; basic diets combined with a gentle detox cleanse and refresh the whole person.

Rising food intolerances and allergies are a cause for concern. Too much stress promotes allergies, because the body no longer has sufficient strength for compensation. Nonetheless, the scientific question arises why allergies occur in the first place. There are interesting theories in specialist journals, which I would like to refer readers to at this point.

Complaints caused by food intolerances have been rising sharply in recent years. Particularly noteworthy in this respect are wheat and products from cow's milk. While many adults do not tolerate cow's milk any longer and ought to switch to other dairy products, the highly cultivated wheat varieties pose a huge risk for many diseases. In particular the wheat protein gliadin should be pointed out here, an appetizing substance that is added to many foods. In this respect the *Wheat Belly* books by Williams Davis, need to be mentioned, which are devoted to this topic in detail.

Ms. Y had been suffering from bad asthma since childhood. At the age of 45 her general practitioner, who focuses on holistic medicine, tells her that she is suffering from wheat intolerance. In the following months she completely left out any wheat products—with an astonishing result: firstly, her asthma disappeared and secondly she lost eight kilos without ever going hungry.

Ms. M was suffering from incredible fatigue; nobody could find the reason for it. She did know that she had histamine intolerance and was already leaving out foods high in histamine. But only a special food intolerance test and cutting out different foods and the treatment of her leaky gut syndrome could provide help.

A gluten allergy is, if undetected, a long ordeal for those affected. Fatigue, shortness of breath, abdominal pain, intestinal damage, diarrhea and also depression may be associated concomitantly. Gluten is protein that occurs in very many foods. If the gluten allergy is not treated, it can lead to an inflammation of the mucous membrane of the small intestine, which results in deficiency symptoms. Since vitamins cannot be absorbed sufficiently, further complaints might appear. For the purpose of successful prevention and intervention it is useful to provide training and further education for executives and employees about

- the effect of stress hormones in the body
- intestinal health
- the consequences of malnutrition (too many carbohydrates, too little healthy fat)
- new diagnostic methods offered by holistic medicine in the event of complaints of unclear origin or for stress diagnostics

New ideas for a healthy cuisine at work, which meets all requirements, are important for preventive measures. Sports facilities and the daily green apple are not enough.

7.4 The Busy Manager and the Desire to Have Children

More and more often couples that would like to have children come to my practice. Taking a look at the above-mentioned regarding stress and nutrition, the influence of a healthy and mindful lifestyle on the preconditions for a woman to become pregnant and the quality of a man's sperm cannot be denied. Too much stress not only makes the body acidic, but also infertile. An adequate supply of micronutrients has to be taken into account. If medical reasons can be excluded, a program for inner balance and learning how to gain inner peace and regeneration is recommended (Chap. 11).

7.5 Stress, Nutrition and Sleep

Poor sleep, disorders of initiating and maintaining sleep can have various causes. Stress-related causes such as lack of distancing oneself from work, worries and fears can be reasons, but also certain dietary habits (e.g. only eating in the evenings, eating too much and too heavily for dinner) or the sleeping place (Sect. 7.5.1) and sleeping habits. Frequent travel and irregular bedtimes can cause problems as well. Therapeutic interventions, regeneration and relaxation training can help.

A Somewhat Paradoxical Situation

Mr. O comes to see me in my practice because of his state of exhaustion. When asked whether he sleeps well, he says "like a rock". However he does not feel like having recovered at all in the morning. This situation occurs often when the body is already so exhausted, that it falls into a deep rest; therefore we call it coma sleep, during which regeneration cannot take place anymore. This means that the organism cannot recover during sleep. By means of a vegetative functional diagnostics, a 24-h heart rate variability analysis, this state can be proven. Then, a comprehensive therapeutic program to relearn inner peace, relaxation and regenerative ability is strongly advised (Chap. 11).

7.5.1 *Electrosmog and Interference Fields*

Recently electrosmog has been discussed more frequently and heatedly, and justifiably so, as for many sensitive people it has become a scourge of the new technologies. A man without a mobile phone in a trouser or breast pocket is an exception nowadays. Whether being concerned is justified or not, is discussed in different studies on this issue. In any case, sensitive people should remember: strain and interference fields can be verified with the modern heart rate variability measurement.

Interference fields are

- water veins. They produce a weak electric field
- faults, geological fracture
- magnetic lines and intersections of the earth's magnetic field. Hartmann discovered the "Global Grid". The intersection points are disruptive, but not the lines.
- the Curry diagonal grid. It was discovered by Curry and runs along the 45th grade to the Global Grid and may promote nightmares, depression, anxiety states.
- the Benker system, a grid system discovered by Benker, that overlaps every fourth Hartmann-line. It involves high-energy ionizing radiation (Dahlke 2013).

Migraine and Sleeping Place

A mother and her son come to my practice for biofeedback therapy. Both suffer from headaches. Testing for stress induced by interference fields before starting pain therapy is one of my standard procedures. The testing was positive, and I pointed out that she might want to consult a building biologist so as to refurbish the sleeping place or at least to get the head out of this area. The mother confirmed that there were interference issues in the house; she had already had it tested. Her bed was located a floor up, but it was in the same location as her son's. She was aware of the interference but would not make any changes. In this case, biofeedback therapy to reduce the headaches cannot be successful.

Interference Field Sleeping Place and Workplace

Mr. Z, a young, athletic man in his mid-twenties, came to my practice with a suspected diagnosis of severe fatigue/burnout. He was incredibly pale and was so tired that he was trudging along slowly. According to conventional medicine he was completely healthy. A geopathic testing revealed both, a negative charge of his sleeping place and his workplace. Small changes showed a major effect. After a short period of time Mr. Z could train in his soccer club again; his power of concentration and performance capability were re-established.

In case of ailments of unclear cause it is advisable to consult a building biologist for clarification whether interference fields or electrosmog at the sleeping or workplace are contributing factors.

Consequences of Chronic Stress and Anxiety

The human being is a physical, psychological and energetic work of art. Negative emotions, problems and stress can cause blockages in the energy system of the body and vice versa. In particular, blockages in the meridian system and complaints caused by blocked vertebrae (spine) need to be pointed out here. From traditional Chinese medicine it is known that teeth are in connection with meridians and organs, which can influence each other. This shows why a holistic view of humans, whether medically and/or therapeutically, is useful and necessary. Chronic stress and anxiety can lead to blockages!

7.6 Control of Energy Production: Brain and Autonomic Nervous System

The brain communicates over twelve pairs of nerves directly with the organism, each from the right and left hemisphere. The analysis of stimuli and their evaluation are assumed by the limbic system, the amygdala and associated parts. These include:

- **amygdala**: it assigns an emotion to an incoming stimulus, selects a mode of reaction and passes on the respective command for an action to the hypothalamus.
- **thalamus**: it is also called the gateway to consciousness. All incoming stimuli are received here and forwarded to the cerebral cortex for analysis and review. In life-threatening situations stimuli are directly transferred to the amygdala; in that case analysis and review only happen after the situation has eased.
- **hypothalamus**: it controls all vegetative and hormonal processes as well as the release of adrenaline and noradrenaline via the adrenal medulla and the release of cortisol via the adrenal cortex. These effect the activity of the autonomic nervous system, the sympathetic and parasympathetic nerves. The pituitary gland works together with the hypothalamus and is involved in the release of the hormone (ACTH), which in turn supports the release of cortisol.
- **hippocampus**: it works together with the amygdala. It stores the facts, whereas the amygdala adds the emotional evaluation (Rauland 2001; Morschitzky 2004)

The control of energy use is up to the brain in collaboration with the autonomous nervous system. In the brain, the analysis of incoming stimuli happens, which is followed by passing on an impulse to the central nervous system. The central nervous system is divided into the

- peripheral nervous system: for arbitrary reactions
- autonomous nervous system: responsible for the functioning of the organism

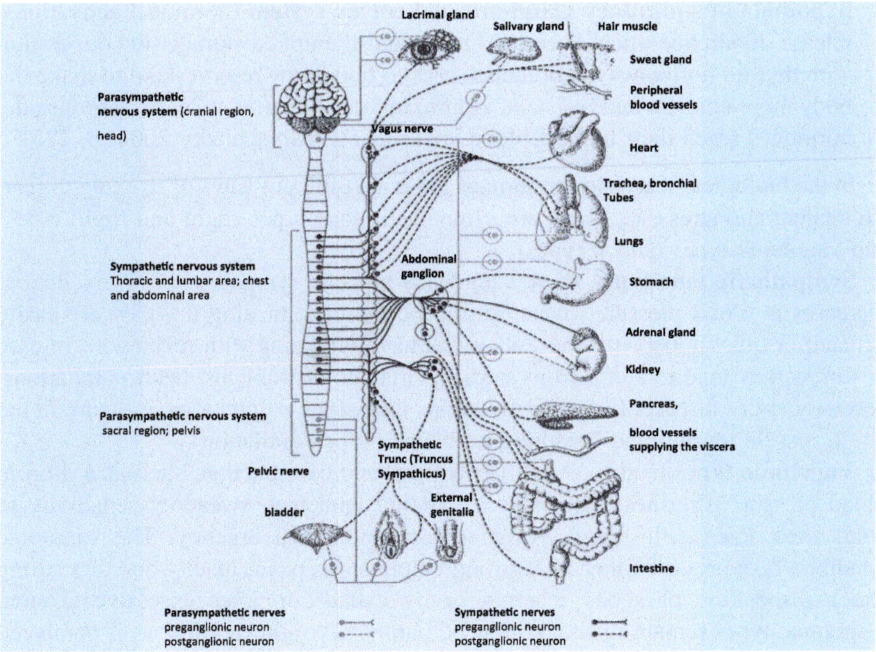

Fig. 7.2 Sympathetic and parasympathetic nerve and their connection to the viscera. Sympathetic nerves organize and mobilize energy resources, parasympathetic nerves help build up energy reserves (modified from Pinel 1997, p. 54)

- enteric nervous system: also called gut brain.

The autonomic nervous system consists of two protagonists that are responsible for activating and deactivating energy production (Fig. 7.2):

- sympathetic nerve: responsible for providing energy required for activity and performance
- parasympathetic nerve: recreation, regeneration, and energy build-up.

- **The most important player in the parasympathetic system is the vagus nerve, the 10th cranial nerve. It also regulates the parasympathetic control of the heart and is responsible for regeneration.**

Its strength or weakness shows in the **respiratory sinus arrhythmia** (Chap. 11). Activation of the sympathetic nerve takes place on two levels (Morschitzky 2004, pp. 224–225):

- **hypothalamus-adrenal medulla system**
  (neural activation): short-term energy mobilization, release of 80% of adrenaline and 20% of noradrenaline and recourse to stored energy reserves.

- **hypothalamus-pituitary gland-adrenal cortex system** (hormonal activation): release of adrenocortical hormones to replenish emptied storage. In cooperation with thyroid hormones the organism tries to build new reserves and to make the body more efficient and resistant. Approximately 4 h after an alarm response the hormones reach their highest blood sugar levels (Morschitzky 2004, p. 225).

In the biological reactivity of humans there are different ways of reacting to fear, excitement and stress, i.e. there are sympathetic tone types (fight and flight types) and vagotonic types (shock types).

Sympathetic tone types show a tendency towards sympathetic over-excitation, increases in blood pressure, overstrain in the muscles, heating up, they are easily irritated or quickly become aggressive and have problems with relaxation. In case of illness they tend to suffer from cardiac, circulatory problems, heart palpitations, coronary artery disease. In fearful situations they show palpitations, pressure in the chest, muscle tension and breathing problems (hyperventilation).

Vagotonic types tend to show parasympathetic overreaction, such as a drop in blood pressure, dizziness, drowsiness, fainting tendency, sweating, sensitivity to cold, weak knees, blushing, crying, urinary and rectal urgency. The vagotonic condition is expressed either by a strong helplessness or incapacity due to a strong shock disposition or shock reaction or by exhaustion after excessive tension. Vagotonic types remain in shock-induced paralysis/"fright rigidity" as if paralyzed and are unable to reach resistance and active engagement with the stressor. The psychological feeling of powerlessness appears physically through constant drowsiness, dizziness and fainting tendency (Morschitzky 2004, p. 229). In case of illness those affected complain about dizziness, nausea, diarrhea and bladder pressure and have the feeling of collapsing or fainting.

- In diagnostics it makes sense to consider various ways of reacting to strain and stress. Even if they are individually predefined they can be changed to a certain degree.

7.7 Polyvagal Theory According to Porges

With his theory Porges moves the brain-heart axis to the center of consideration. The Polyvagal Theory provides a bidirectional brain-body model, which understands the regulation of the peripheral physiology through the brain (neuronal regulation of the cardiovascular and endocrine functions) as a neural platform for developing adaptive social and defensive behavior (Porges 2010, p. 21). The aim of the Poyvagal Theory is to develop methods that strengthen the social vagus. In this context the heart rate variability training offers a very effective solution; however, the training is to be embedded in a therapeutic concept.

Porges builds on the researches of Darwin and James and extends the general understanding of the antagonists sympathetic and parasympathetic nerves to the model of the social, myelinated and the non-myelinated vagus. He attributes to them two different affect-regulation functions in threat situations:

1. **Mobilization**: combat and flight behavior when danger looms, initiated by the sympatho-adrenal activation system (sympathetic nervous system) and the inhibiting influence of the vagus (social vagus). Additionally, facial expression, voice, rhythm and information from the viscera (the inner organs) are determining factors. Information from the internal organs is so important, because early-childhood stress (trauma, attachment disorders, etc.) is "encoded in the body" (stored) (Van der Kolk 1994).
   - **System of social commitment**: the social vagus (originates in the nucleus ambiguus) regulates the assessment of signals (such as threat or security) of other people and from the environment; it facilitates the recognition of positive signals and the proper assessment of and reaction to dangers.
2. **Immobilization**: if the risk is too great, the mobilization system might fail and the non-myelinated vagus (dorsal motor vagus center) with its reaction pattern of freezing and/or fainting occurs. Immobilization goes along with a slowdown of the heart rate and a decrease of blood pressure.

Porges summarizes the function of the social vagus under the term "system of social commitment" (SSC). When working with people under high levels of stress, it is important to bear these two reaction patterns to stress in mind. In coaching processes the increasing importance of somatic markers is becoming more and more evident, for example by advising, "Pay attention to your physical sensation when making decisions; listen to your inner voice".

With reference to Porges' theory, feeling and listening to the messages of the body can work very well (psychosomatic intelligence), but only in people whose system of social commitment is not affected by early trauma.

During the Life-Skript-Analysis (Chap. 2) dysfunctional patterns are collected and registered and discussed in an interactive process. The heart rate variability (HRV) training research provides hope that in combination with psychotherapy changes in the neural network of the affected people can happen. Subsequently, a tailor-made concept for victims of traumatic experiences is necessary.

Trauma researchers such as Van der Kolk point out that the body does not forget, and numerous methods deal with releasing body blockages (Dennison 1990; Levine 2013; Klinghardt 2006; Gallo and Vincenzi 2005, Van der Kolk 2000). Exciting in this context is that in the preface to Porges' book, Van der Kolk mentions his good friend Packer, who works on the soothing effect of hexameters. In his own practice it has been found out in a 24-h HRV measurement that chanting (a particular meditation form with pre-defined singing) can lead to a change of heart rate variability towards the desired optimum of 0.1 Hz in the low frequency range. States of excitement act from the brain to the heart and back again (Chap. 3).

Porges tries to obtain a neurobiological answer to the question of why certain behaviors of people and environmental stimuli evoke a sense of security in some people and a feeling of threat in others. The reason for this lies in neurobiologically congenital or acquired defense mechanisms, whose roots are in the vagus complex, i.e. in a healthy or dysfunctional neuroception.

For the ability to establish positive human relationships, control over the individual neurobiological defense mechanisms is necessary. Adaptive systems for prosocial and defensive behavior are required that are able to assess information from the environment properly (as threatening or safe). Impaired assessment is considered **dysfunctional neuroception**.

The human nervous system allows expressing emotions, communication and influencing physical and behavioral states. Polyvagal Theory combines the development of the ability of neuronal control of heart activity with affective experience, emotional expression, the expressive powers of the face, vocal communication and the part of social behavior that reacts to the behavior of other people.

- **Polyvagal Theory points out that the neuronal control of the heart is neuro-anatomically connected with the neuronal control of the muscles of the face and head**.

7.7.1 Polyvagal Theory and Stress

Based on Gellhorn (1967, in Porges 2010, Gellhorn 1979), who describes the parasympathetic nervous system as a trophotropic system and the sympathetic nervous system as an ergotropic one, Porges regards the parasympathetic nervous system as the homeostasis regulating system. According to his view, homeostasis is an autonomous state, which supports the fulfillment of visceral needs in the absence of external requirements (Porges 2010, p. 101).

In this sense stress could be seen as a disturbance of the homeostasis, which is represented by a decrease in the tone of the parasympathetic nervous system. If so required due to external influences, the sympathetic nervous system becomes involved as well. Homoeostatic processes regulate themselves through feedback loops, which result in a rhythmic pattern. They express a phasic rise and decrease of neuronally efferent signals to the organs (e.g. the heart). The results are: the higher the amplitude of this organized rhythmic, physiological variability, the greater the flexibility of the reaction modulation (Porges 2010, p. 101).

It is also interesting in this context that a rising vagal tone not only results in an increased energy production in the organism but is also important for the digestive organs (also swallowing, esophagus, etc.), the gastric motility (Porges 2010, p. 107) and breathing (bronchial tubes). This facilitates making a potential connection between the complaint of reflux and a weakened vagus.

Physiological Link Between Stress and Muscles

Green and Green (1999) describe a physiological link between stress and unneeded muscles (during stress only those particular muscles are well supplied with blood that are required for fight or flight). As in a dangerous situation no food is taken in, the lower esophageal muscles become somewhat slacker. This can lead to reflux. Stomach and intestinal ailments and vagus are also closely linked.

A long list of complaints caused by a weakened vagus could be cited here. In prevention management an understanding should be promoted of how the parasympathetic system of humans can be trained in a regenerative break, for example through breathing technique.

Porges postulated that the one-sided focus in the definition of stress on the sympathetic nervous system has reached its end. The quantification of the cardiac vagal tone is novel; it can be calculated from the heart rate and thus provides feedback on the power of the parasympathetic system.[1] The vagal tonus is expressed as the power of the respiratory sinus arrhythmia (RSA, Chap. 11). A reduction in the tone of the parasympathetic system before confronting a difficult task may be a reference to physiological vulnerability or susceptibility to stress (Porges 2010, p. 100).

Note: In the Biofeedback section in Chap. 11 various stress response tests are discussed as well as the associated validity of the psychophysiological, measurable changes using biofeedback. In the passive reaction test the respective people are signaled a stimulus without showing stimuli on the computer screen.

The client is completely alone with his/her expectations. This test method could be used in accordance with Porges to measure the vulnerability of the physiological system. Due to the physiological changes of the measured values during the expectation phase a link can be established between psychosomatic or stress-related complaints. For example, a narrowing of the pulse amplitude might indicate sensitivity in the vascular system, etc. For the evaluation of 24-h heart rate variability measurement the change of the RSA before and during stress provides helpful information in the coaching or psychotherapeutic process.

[1]The term "cardiac vagal tone" is a construct that describes the functional relationship between the brain stem and the heart (Porges 2010, p. 109, 1995).

7.8 The Heart: Power Source for Life

The heart is a high performance machine and the center of life. It is developed even before the brain and is an electromagnetic power source of 2.4 W. Its vibrations and signals are measurable down to the smallest cell.

But not only the heart, also every other organ swings in its very own life melody. When all these rhythms (brain, heart, breathing) are in consistency and coherence, we feel the body is healthy, i.e. in flow.

In this state, humans feel creative, dynamic, buoyant and vital. This vitality is dependent on the adaptability of the body to emotional, psychological and physical challenges of life. The organism is in constant interaction with the outside world. It reacts "unconsciously" to incoming stimuli and automatically adapts the required energy demand to the respective situation. This is done through the heart frequency in combination with different other organ systems, such as breathing, nervous system, hormonal system and vascular system (Pirker-Binder 2008, p. 32 ff.). Consequently, the heart rate is not a fixed value but individually adapts to external and internal conditions. This adaptation is achieved by changing the time intervals between the individual heartbeats (heart rate variability, Fig. 7.3).

Heart Rate Variability as a Global Indicator
Mück-Weymann describes heart rate variability as a global indicator of the ability and adaptivity of vibration (resonance) of bio-psycho-social function in exchange between organism and environment. It works like a buffer or

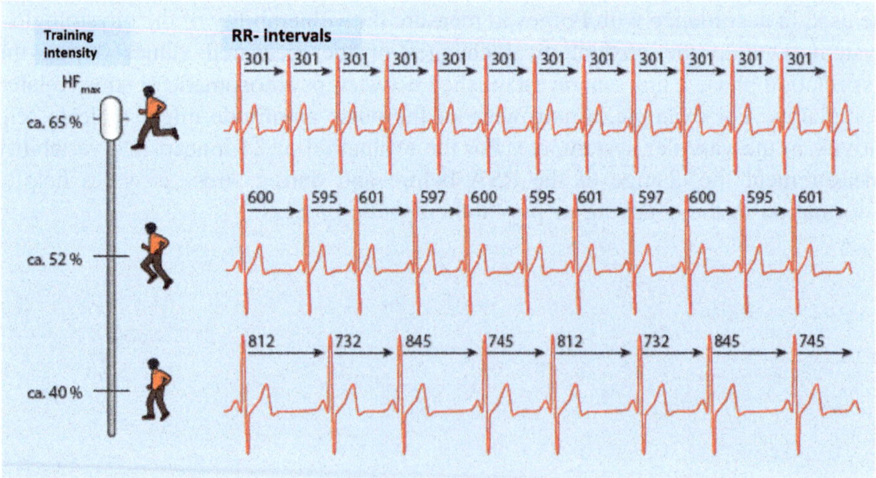

Fig. 7.3 Change of heart rate variability in different stress conditions. Picture used with the courtesy of Hottenrott (2006)

interface that helps the body to communicate with the inner and outer environment (Mück-Weymann 2010).

The better the body can adapt to the daily challenges, strain and stress, the greater the harmony of the vibrations generated in the body. This harmony of rhythms (brain, heart, breathing) is called **coherence**.

As shown in Fig. 7.3, it can be seen that with increasing strain the variability is decreasing and the heart rate is getting more and more regular.

If a spotlight is placed on the physiological processes with respect to successful prevention, it becomes obvious that intervention measures, which do not involve a general understanding of connections and wholeness, cannot bring about any longer lasting change towards increased health. It is necessary to observe energy production and control in the organism as well when exhaustion occurs. Activation that lasts too long can exhaust the energy reserves, but also make energy production impossible and even prevent the release of necessary hormones through weakened associated organs. Here, the question often arises where the cycle begins; perhaps in the thought and experience patterns of each person. The Life-Script- and the Work-Script-Analysis build on this in combination with the Life-Energy-Analysis.

In Chap. 11 the method, measurement and training and, in particular, the heart rate variability of the **biofeedback method** are explained in detail. Biofeedback serves the opening of the consciousness for the above described.

Objectives of a biofeedback measurement and training are:

- gaining insight on unconscious feelings and thought patterns and experience models that have an influence on energy consumption,
- recognizing the interplay between activation, deactivation and regeneration and
- achieving increased functionality of the vagus nerve in heart rate variability training.

An essential aspect for prevention and intervention is generating a basic understanding about how stimuli are processed and how evaluation is anchored in the brain. This explains why changing a thought process or a negative attitude is not so easy to manage. The Life-Script- and the

Work-Script-Analysis are guides for the content in the exchange with people, their assessments, thought patterns and feelings. In a further step, the respective people can take a stance on their thought patterns and feelings if the contexts are understandable. Now they can think about changes, make revaluations and take the first steps.

References

Dahlke R (2013) Störfelder und Kraftplätze, wie man die einen beseitigt und die anderen nutzt. Crotona Verlag, Amerang

Dennison PE (1990) Befreite Bahnen. Angewandte Kinesiologie. VAK, Kirchzarten

Eichinger U, Hoffmann-Nachum K (2012) Der Burnout-Irrtum, ausgebrannt durch Vitalstoffmangel – Burnout fängt in der Körperzelle an; das Präventionsprogramm mit Praxistipps und Fallbeispielen. Systemed, Lünen

Gallo FP, Vincenzi H (2005) Gelöst, befreit, entlastet. Klopfakupressur bei emotionalem Stress. 4. Aufl VAK, Kirchzarten

Gellhorn E (1967) Principles of autonomic-somatic integrations: physiological basis and psychological and clinical implications. NED - New edition ed., University of Minnesota Press, in Porges 2010

Gellhorn E (1979) Principles of autonomic—somatic integrations: physiological basis and psychophysiological and clinical implications. University of Minnesota, Minneapolis

Green E, Green A (1999) Biofeedback, eine neue Möglichkeit zu heilen. 2. Aufl Hermann Bauer, Breisgau

Hottenrott K (2006) Trainingskontrolle mit Herzfrequenz- Messgeräten. Meyer und Meyer, Aachen

Klinghardt D (2006) Lehrbuch der Psychokinesiologie. 7. Aufl. Ink, Stuttgart

Kuklinski B, Schemionek A (2012) Schwachstelle Genick, Ursachen, Auswirkungen und erfolgreiche Therapie. 12. Aufl, Urban und Fischer, München

Levine PA (2013) Vom Trauma befreien. Wie Sie seelische und körperliche Blockaden lösen. 7. Aufl, Kösel München

Morschitzky H (2004) Angststörungen. Diagnostik, Konzepte, Therapie, Selbsthilfe. 3. Aufl, Springer, Wien, NY

Mück Weymann (2010) Was verrät die „Herzratenvariabilität"? http://www.hrv24.de/HRV-Einfuehrung.htm. Last accessed on 21 Dec 2015

Österreichische Akademie der Ärzte (2015) Orthomolekulare Medizin. http://www.arztakademie.at/fileadmin/template/main/OeAeKDiplomePDFs/Diplom-Richtlinien/RL07_Orthomolekulare_Medizin.pdf. Last accessed on 2 Feb 2015

Pauling L (2015) Orthomolekulare Medizin. http://de.wikipedia.org/wiki/Orthomolekulare_Medizin. Last accessed on 2 Feb 2015

Pinel JP (1997) Biopsychologie, eine Einführung. Spektrum, Heidelberg, Berlin

Pirker-Binder I (2008) Biofeedback in der Praxis, Bd. II Erwachsene. Springer, Wien, New York

Porges SW (1995) Cardial vagal tone: a physiological index of stress. Neurosci Biobehav Rev 19:225–233

Porges SW (2010) Die Polyvagal-Theorie. Neurophysiologische Grundlagen der Therapie. Emotion, Bindung, Kommunikation und ihre Entstehung. Junfermann Paderborn

Rau M (2015) Nebennierenschwäche (Adrenal fatigue). Selbsthilfe bei chronischer Erschöpfung. http://www.adrenal-fatigue.de/. Last accessed on 12 Mar 2015

Rauland M (2001) Chemie der Gefühle. Hirzel, Stuttgart

Stark M (2014) Nahrung als Medizin. Wiedenhofer

Van der Kolk (1994) The body keeps the score; memory and evolving psychobiology of posttraumatic stress. Havard Rev Psychiatry January/February 1994:253–265

Van der Kolk BA, McFarlane A, Weisaeth L (2000) Grundlagen und Behandlungsansätze. Theorie, Praxis, Forschung zu posttraumatischem Stress und Traumatherapie. Junfermann, Paderborn

Van Hemert S, Breedveld AC, Rovers JMP et al (2014) Migraine associated with gastrointestinal disorders: review of the literature and clinical implications. Front Neurol. 5:241. doi:10.3389/fneur.2014.00241

Chapter 8
Food Supplements = Supplement to Food

Ingrid Spona

Contents

Chronic high stress can lead to a multitude of complaints ranging from intestinal problems, insulin resistance and silent inflammation to related secondary diseases. Relevant dietary supplements can support the organism in this context; yet, the supply is huge, but what substance is useful and when?

I. Spona (✉)
Vitalogic Dr. Spona VertriebsgmbH, Praterstrasse 45/12, 1020 Vienna, Austria
e-mail: ingrid.spona@vitalogic.com

I. Pirker-Binder (ed.), *Mindful Prevention of Burnout in Workplace Health Management*, https://doi.org/10.1007/978-3-319-61337-6_8

The physical basis for a successful adaptation to changing living conditions will always be a good diet.

Food supplements cannot and are not intended to replace that. However, they can undoubtedly support the organism with regard to adaptation to high and specific requirements.

The physician Dr. Ingrid Spona and the biochemist Prof. Dr. Jürgen Spona have been working intensively in this field for more than 20 years.

This chapter discusses the effects of stress on the organism and briefly examines the relationship between stress, insulin resistance and silent inflammations, together with the corresponding consequences.

In the context of stress, the main focus is on supporting the adrenal glands and the mental power. The gut-brain axis is also addressed.

On the one hand, it is explained which substances are increasingly consumed in this context and thus also required in an increased manner, while they can subsequently also prevent or at least mitigate the harmful effects on the organism. This advice is intended as a suggestion and should under no circumstances replace the instructions of a doctor or therapist.

8.1 Do We Need Food Supplements at All?

The answer is no. The organism can compensate for a great deal, and today it is unlikely that anyone suffers from scurvy or beriberi, the wide-spread deficiency diseases of the past.

The other question, however, is whether one wants to do this to one's organism and whether it does not make sense after all to provide best possible support; particularly in times of high stress. In this case it definitely makes sense to specifically use food supplements.

A solid basis for controlled digestion, for smooth metabolism and thus for optimal energy supply, is provided by good nutrition adapted to the individual requirements. This topic fills entire libraries and has almost assumed the character of ideologies rather than hard scientific facts. Therefore, it cannot be the topic of this short article.

However, one thing is clear: it is about optimally providing the organism with energy in order to cope with the respective requirements.

The "energy currency" of the body is ATP, which is generated in the energy power plants of the body, the mitochondria. Ideally, 38 "units" of ATP are created, whereas in the event of an emergency only 2 ATPs are generated. Without going into specific biochemistry right now, this dimension alone makes it clear that the energy resources also play a big role in how you feel and, of course, how productive you are.

The approach with regard to using dietary supplements in chronic stress situations or chronic stress exposure can only be to take into account the increased need in stress situations. It is obvious and also scientifically proven that the demand for nutrients in stress situations is considerably higher.

It is clear that the main focus must be on mental measures to relieve the organism in the long term. The fact that the basis for a certain level of mental power has to be created first, is also obvious.

This applies, on the one hand, to the consumption of substances that affect the stress response itself and, on the other hand, the substances that are required to a greater degree due to the stress response.

The organ, which is at the forefront of stress responses, is the adrenal gland. There, among other things, the hormones are produced that enable the organism to cope with stress.

8.2 Why Is Long-Term Stress So Harmful?

Because chronic stress activates disastrous chain reactions. Stress causes inflammations, silent inflammations, inflammations lead to insulin resistance, insulin resistance causes inflammations and inflammations cause diabetes, cardiovascular disease, cancer and dementia.

- Chronic stress leads to a series of metabolic disorders, which means that stress leads to diabetes, and diabetes increasingly triggers stress reactions. This is only one of the “vicious circles” that have to be broken.

In addition, stress has a negative effect on the intestinal flora, which can ultimately lead to digestive problems, food intolerances, migraine and depression.

The occurrence of these secondary diseases is certainly partly lifestyle-dependent. This has now been scientifically investigated and proven. In this context, numerous scientific studies provide evidence of the value of a sensible, targeted use of high-quality food supplements.

8.3 As a Reminder: A Brief Clarification of the Terms from a Medical Point of View

8.3.1 Stress—Briefly Summarized with Regard to Food Supplements

Stress mobilizes the so-called HPA axis to cope with a threat. This means that the brain is told that there is a threat, whereupon the pituitary gland instructs the adrenal glands to release stress hormones. These mobilize the reserves of the organism. The threat, however, has an enormously high subjective component. Is it really a saber-tooth tiger, or unfinished files or a difficult situation with (supposedly) difficult fellow human beings? The response is always the same: release of stress hormones. This makes a lot of sense for acute short-time stress, but it is very stressful for the organism if it becomes chronic, for the organism does not stop reacting as long as this situation persists.

In essence, this means that all precautions are taken to make the best possible use of the muscles. Ultimately, it is about fight or flight, i.e. either face a fight or run away from danger. Overall, therefore, it is about the greatest possible mobilization of the physical forces, which has precarious consequences for us nowadays: for finishing undone tasks or getting along with difficult people we do not need any special muscular force. The provision of these resources ultimately results in excess energy that is not needed and ends up in any stores of the body, usually in the fat stores.

8.3.2 Silent Inflammation

Silent inflammation—the stage the immune system already enters the scene. This is not the case in the acute stress reaction. When it comes to fight or flight, the organism is not concerned with the defense of any germs, as, pragmatically seen, the formation of antibodies or the mobilization of special cells for defense against penetrating toxicants would take much too long, and therefore no power and energy are used for that. From the point of view of nature, this topic is not the top priority in an acute stress situation, for it might well be that one does not need defense against germs, because one has already fallen victim to the acute threat.

The situation is quite different when all of this takes longer.

The long-term release of stress hormones has precarious consequences:

The vessels are damaged, the adrenal glands are exhausted and the memory is damaged, because after all, long-term reflection is not of primary importance in acute stress situations. So, no resources are used for this either.

8.3.3 Insulin Resistance

… is also a mechanism that is particularly useful in the defense against acute threats. It enables the organism to provide the cells with as many resources as possible.

Insulin is needed to make energy carriers such as glucose usable for the cell. Insulin is a hormone and hormones can affect the cells only via receptors. If a lot of glucose is available, these receptors become increasingly exhausted. The organism compensates this with an increased release of insulin to ensure the supply. However, the receptors become more and more insensitive. This circulus vitiosus ultimately ends in a complete exhaustion of the receptors and, as a result, in an exhaustion of the insulin-producing organs, namely the pancreas, or more precisely, the part of the pancreas, which is responsible for the production of insulin and for the carbohydrate metabolism. Ultimately, this leads to diabetes with all the known resulting sicknesses such as heart attack, stroke and increased risk of dementia and tumors.

8.4 What Do Food Supplements Definitely Not Stand For?

The use of dietary supplements must clearly be separated from the idea of doping.

This means that they are by no means meant to squeeze out even more performance and resources. They should support the organism gently in accordance with the natural conditions and, in the best case, perhaps even prevent permanent damage by chronic stress.

8.5 Which Substances Are Particularly Important with Regard to High Stress Levels?

Let us now go on a journey through the jungle of infinite selection of substances: which are crucially important, which are "nice to have" and which can provide support in certain situations?

Please note that the following substances represent average empirical values. This also means, of course, that you should clarify and discuss any possible intake of food supplements with your physician or curative practitioner.

8.5.1 Magnesium

Currently it is known that magnesium is involved in more than 300 metabolic pathways and reactions. However, this is probably not the end of the story, as certainly not all metabolic pathways have been explored yet, and new discoveries are constantly being made.

Many metabolic processes are even dependent on magnesium.

Numerous scientific studies have shown that a good supply of magnesium improves insulin resistance as well as inflammations. As stress is also an independent risk factor for insulin resistance, the circle closes here. Magnesium is significantly involved in the efficiency of insulin. This in turn means that all people with insulin resistance have a magnesium deficiency.

An increased sympathetic tone, that is, an imbalance of the vegetative nervous system towards the sympathetic, leads to magnesium deficits. If this is not properly treated, all the doors are thrown wide open to the mentioned resulting sicknesses.

The fact that the increased sympathetic activity hinders a restful sleep, and thus the urgently needed regeneration, starts the vicious circle.

The production of ATP, and hence the energy production of the organism, is also dependent on magnesium.

This means that magnesium is certainly a fixed starter within the context of supplementation at high stress levels.

Especially with minerals and trace elements, it is very important to consider whether the respective substance really arrives where it is needed in the body. They can usually be absorbed more easily than chemical compounds. In principle, therefore, the question is whether a substance is bioavailable.

With regard to magnesium it has been proven that, for example, magnesium citrate or magnesium gluconate can be absorbed better by the organism than the cheaper magnesium carbonate.

A good dose for magnesium citrate is for example 300 mg/day. Magnesium is present both in the cell and outside. By the way, it takes a few weeks for the important intracellular reserves to be filled as well.

8.5.2 Potassium

… is another fixed starter with regard to a high stress level, as its consumption is increased in this situation.

As a citrate potassium is also readily bioavailable; again, a dose of 300 mg makes sense.

8.5.3 Vitamin C

…is the 3rd essential nutrient at high stress levels, since the demand increases in the same way as the release of stress hormones.

Interestingly, all mammals, except for apes, guinea pigs and humans, can produce large amounts of vitamin C themselves. Humans are, therefore, dependent on a supply from outside.

Vitamin C can also inhibit some of the contra-productive effects of the stress response, especially in the immune system.

Very recent scientific studies have shown that vitamin C has positive effects on the heart/circulatory system by protecting the vessel walls.

The recommended dose is 75 mg/day, but orthomolecular physicians recommend at least 500 mg/day.

For specific indications, even several grams/day are administered.

Cats, who belong to the species that make vitamin C themselves, produce between 3 and 10 g daily.

8.5.4 Vitamin A

…is predominantly involved in the formation of new mitochondria, i.e. those responsible for the energy of the cells.

It also plays a major role in the immune system as it stimulates certain cells to produce anti-inflammatory enzymes.

The individual dose differs and should always be agreed with a doctor or an alternative practitioner, since there is a risk of overdosing as with all fat-soluble vitamins.

8.5.5 B—Vitamins

…are essential for the energy production in the mitochondria and many other metabolic functions; they are very often deficient. Particularly in the case of high stress levels and insulin resistance, measurements reveal pronounced deficiency states.

For example, the adrenal glands cannot fulfill their central role in stress processing if there is a deficiency of B5. This state may lead to the collapse of the adrenal glands.

This means that measurements and individual supplementation are recommended in cases of high stress. If this is not possible, a common low-dose combination of B vitamins consisting of the vitamins B1, 2, 3, 5, 6, 12 and folic acid is extremely useful, since this is the basic prerequisite for smooth energy production.

8.5.6 Vitamin D—Calcium—Vitamin K2

A vitamin D deficiency is very common. This may also be due to the fact that the basic demand is increased with a high stress load. Apart from this, the long-standing view that 10 min of daylight exposure is sufficient to ensure the vitamin D production has been disproved. This is at best sufficient to prevent rickets, but not to benefit from all other positive vitamin D effects. While it was previously thought that vitamin D is important only for healthy, strong bones, it is now known that the effects of vitamin D go far beyond this.

In connection with stress load it is especially important to point out that vitamin D is essential for a well-functioning immune system, and that the risk for cardiovascular diseases rises sharply in the case of vitamin D deficiency. Since such risk is already increased under stress, adequate supply is crucial.

Important: vitamin D should always be given together with calcium, as it can only be effective when calcium levels are sufficient.

What is more, vitamin K2 is also essential for the optimal interplay of forces. Its effect on healthy vessels has been demonstrated in large scientific studies.

8.5.7 Omega 3 Fatty Acids

Scientific studies show that omega-3 fatty acids are anti-inflammatory, thus reducing the risk of secondary diseases such as cardiovascular diseases, cancer and dementia. The positive effect with regard to cardiovascular diseases is further enhanced by an improvement in the flow properties of the blood.

In addition, Omega 3 fatty acids improve the cognitive abilities demonstrably.

In this respect, DHA is particularly important, whereas EPA has a positive effect on the cardiovascular system.

The main source of this is traditionally fish oil, with krill and algae oil becoming increasingly significant.

Linseed oil is a good Omega 3 source, however, it has to be metabolized first, since in this case the two components DHA and EPA are not yet accessible.

8.5.8 Q 10

A coenzyme that plays a prominent role in the energy production of cells.

It is also important for good muscle function, especially the heart muscle should be mentioned here.

Q 10 should be taken in any case when cholesterol-lowering medication (statins) is taken, as this medication causes a drastic drop of the Q 10 level.

8.5.9 Plant Nutrients

There is a large number of plant nutrients that have adaptogen properties. These are substances, which facilitate the adaptation of the organism to the external conditions.

Representative of many others are Rhodiola (rose root), Passiflora (passion flower) and Ashwaganda (from Ayurveda medicine).

8.5.10 Amino Acids

Amino acids are the building blocks of proteins. While carbohydrates serve almost completely, and fats for the most part, as energy generators for coping with everyday life, it is the main task of proteins to build up body structures.

This means that bones, skin, mucous membranes, connective tissue, hair, nails, muscles and most organs are made up of amino acids. But also a large proportion of the hormones, transport carriers in the blood, immunoglobulin and neurotransmitters in the brain are continuously formed from amino acids.

The current state of science stipulates that 20 amino acids can build up about 1 million different proteins; these construction and conversion processes happen at incredible speed and intensity. Thus, it is assumed that about 2.5 million new red blood cells are formed every second, that the intestinal mucosa is renewed every 7 days and the skin every 28 days.

To make a projection, it means that we are "renewed" every 7 years.

In emergency times, however, amino acids can also act as energy producers. In this case, they are mainly removed from the muscles, which in the long run is, of course, not a desirable effect.

In the particular context of this book, it is above all the neurotransmitters in the brain that are of primary interest, but also the amino acids, which are important for the immune system or as building blocks for hormones.

Of the 20 amino acids, depending on the author, 8–10 are considered essential, which means that they must be supplied to the organism, while the remaining ones can be formed from these essentials. In particular stress situations even the non-essential ones become essential, because the need is much higher.

Amino Acids and the Brain

It is scientifically proven that the presence of certain amino acids is crucial for a smooth transmission between the nerve cells, the mood, the mental faculties and ultimately for a restful sleep.

Amino acids also activate genes that are responsible for stress resistance. In this respect new knowledge is continually being gained, as new metabolic pathways are constantly being discovered.

8.5.11 Tryptophan

One of the most studied substances in this context is the essential amino acid tryptophan. If tryptophan is kept artificially high or particularly low in the course of experiments, characteristic differences in brain function and behavior are observed.

In case of deficiency, mainly depressive moods and increased aggressive behavior occur. It could also be shown that tryptophan administration leads to better sleep and reduced pain perception. These changes correlate with the serotonin level in the brain. Tryptophan is the precursor for this messenger substance, which is ultimately responsible for our mood.

It was also shown that the decision-ability is impaired at a low tryptophan level.

In the presence of stress hormones, tryptophan is increasingly degraded, so the need is greater in this situation.

Tryptophan is the precursor of *melatonin*, whose importance goes far beyond the regulation of the day/night rhythm according to recent studies. It also plays a major role with regard to mood, immune system, and anti-aging and is now considered one of the most important antioxidants.

8.5.12 Phenylalanine/Tyrosine

Tyrosine is a non-essential amino acid that can be formed from the essential amino acid phenylalanine.

It is the starting point for stress hormones adrenaline and noradrenaline, for dopamine and also for thyroid hormones.

Dopamine, next to serotonin, is another crucial messenger substance in the brain, which is commonly referred to as happiness hormone, because it controls the reward system in the brain and thus stimulates pleasant feelings. It also controls attention, learning ability, motivation, and motor skills.

It has been proven that tyrosine has positive effects on stress resistance.

8.5.13 Glutamic Acid (Glutamate)/GABA/Glutamine

These 3 messenger substances are closely related to each other, because, if required, they can be converted very quickly into one another by relatively simple chemical reactions.

Glutamic Acid
is a non-essential amino acid and is particularly interesting in our context with regard to 2 functions:

On the one hand, glutamic acid (also referred to as glutamate in medical literature) is a stimulating neurotransmitter. It is very important for learning and memory performance and plays a crucial role in the transmission of sensory perceptions.

On the other hand, it is one of the 3 amino acids that form glutathione. Glutathione is enormously important because it is the most important radical catcher of the organism. This means that the so-called free radicals, which occur in the metabolism, are neutralized by glutathione. If these free radicals accumulate, as is often the case in stress situations, oxidative stress can occur which can damage the cells and organs. In such situations, glutathione is inherently important.

GABA
Through a special enzyme, glutamate can be traced back to its direct counterpart, GABA. It is an inhibitory messenger substance that acts as a natural sedative. It works to relieve anxiety and promote a restful sleep in a natural way.

Glycin
Is another inhibiting messenger substance. Scientifically studied and proven is its sleep-inducing effect. Very often, the intake of a small amount of glycine is beneficial right before sleeping.

Lysine
Lysine is essential and it is the amino acid that first leads to visible signs of deficiency if the diet mainly consists of cereals.

It could be shown that anxiety states were significantly more frequent due to stress load with lysine deficiency. These could be improved significantly by lysine administration.

Lysine also has a significant effect concerning herpes, the “cold sores”, which occur more frequently in stressful situations.

If lysine is taken at the first signs, such as itching and burning skin, a full outbreak can often be prevented.

Glutamine
represents the largest proportion of the amino acid pool in the human organism. Nevertheless, it is not essential. The quantity of glutamine is usually sufficient, but in particularly stressful situations an additional intake may be very helpful. This can be inferred from its numerous functions.

An important function is the detoxification of ammonia, which occurs within the protein metabolism. In excess, ammonia impedes the energy production in the cells.

It is particularly involved in the formation of glutathione via glutamic acid, into which it can be converted very easily.

Glutamine plays an important role in the immune system because it is the main energy source of leukocytes. These different white blood cells are the basis of any immune reaction. There are studies that show that glutamine prevents the detrimental effects of high stress due to physical stress with regard to a weakening of the immune system.

Glutamine is a key player with regard to intestinal health, because it facilitates the cohesion of intestinal mucosa cells and thereby prevents the entry of bacteria or toxins into the blood circulation, i.e. it prevents the negative effects of “leaky gut”.

Glutamine deficiency can thus lead to disorders of the important intestinal barrier.

Arginine
Is the precursor of NO, nitrogen monoxide.

For this discovery, the Nobel Prize in Medicine was awarded in 2008.

NO is a gas which acts as a vasodilator, that is, in this way, it can promote blood circulation and act against high blood pressure. This effect has also led to the attribution of the name “natural Viagra”.

In addition, it is the first barrier to penetrating germs, thus playing an important role in the immune system.

It improves wound healing, has anti-inflammatory properties and improves resistance to insulin, which are all effects that are of great importance during high stress loads.

Arginine is also essential for the degradation of ammonia.

However, particularly in the case of arginine, the right quantity determines the positive or negative effect, as too much NO is counterproductive.

Methionine/Cysteine
Is an essential amino acid and supplies the organism with sulfur. It is the original substance of cysteine, which in turn is part of glutathione.

Methionine is also the substance that starts any protein synthesis, that is, any structure buildup. The proteins are formed in such a way that the amino acids are lined up in accordance with the genetic code.

Methionine is always the first amino acid in "threading the bead chain".

Methionine is anti-inflammatory as well.

Histidine
Should be mentioned at this point, since it plays an important role in detoxification, especially of metals. Exposure to mercury (amalgam), aluminum or lead from old water pipes is frequent and poses a major burden for the organism.

8.6 Last But Not Least—The Intestine

This topic is now filling libraries and rightly so, because it is an organ that is very sensitive to stress.

The intestine ultimately has two main tasks:

It is responsible for ensuring that the nutrients are duly processed for the organism and transferred into the blood circulation, where they are available for the countless metabolic processes.

However, it represents a barrier, which does not allow inappropriate agents, such as, for example, penetrating germs.

The intestinal mucosa fulfills this task. It is strongly folded and has innumerable protuberances, the so-called intestinal villi. If the intestinal mucosa were spread, it would cover the unimaginable area of more than 300 m^2. The intestine is the largest immune organ and is populated by more than 400 bacterial strains weighing a total of almost 2 kg.

In stressful times it can happen that bad germs populate the intestine. This leads to severe flatulence, food intolerance, defecation problems or stomach pain. Additionally, an increasing number of inflammatory substances are built, which have a negative effect on the immune system in the long run.

Intestinal Repair

Is therefore extremely important in the context of stress and consists of three components:

1. Probiotics:
   These are intestinal germs that correct the negative effects of miscolonization. Good products usually contain several bacterial strains.
2. Prebiotics:
   are indigestible fibers that serve as a food substrate for the intestinal bacteria. They are fermented in the intestine and in this way the beneficial intestinal bacteria are promoted.
3. Amino acids:
   are useful for the intestinal mucosa—on the one hand as building materials for the mucous membrane and on the other as nutrients for the bacteria.

This small collection of useful substances can, of course, only be incomplete in this limited space and can merely be regarded a suggestion. Especially in demanding times the application of supposedly harmless remedies should be carried out in consultation with the treating physician or therapist, also with regard to the quantity. Not always is a more of good things beneficial.

In principle, it is, of course, best if deficits are detected by measurements so that they can then be supplemented precisely.

Further Reading

Dibaba DT et al (2014) Dietary magnesium intake is inversely associated with serum C-reactive protein levels: meta-analysis and systematic review. Eur J Clin Nutr 68(4):510–516. doi:10.1038/ejcn.2014.7 Epub Feb 12

Harding HP et al (2003) An integrated stress response regulates amino acid metabolism and resistance to oxidative stress. Mol Cell 11(3):619–633

Ishrat T et al (2006) Coenzyme Q10 modulates cognitive impairment against intracerebroventricular injection of streptozotocin in rats. Behav Brain Res 171(1):9–16

Jenkins TA et al (2016) Influence of tryptophan and serotonin on mood and cognition with a possible role of the gut-brain axis. Nutrients 8(1). pii: E56. doi:10.3390/nu8010056

Kelly JR et al (2015) Breaking down the barriers: the gut microbiome, intestinal permeability and stress-related psychiatric disorders. Front Cell Neurosci 9:392

Kuebler U et al (2013) Plasma homocysteine levels increase following stress in older but not younger men. Psychoneuroendocrinology 38(8):1381–1387

Lim SY et al (2016) Nutritional factors affecting mental health. Clin Nutr Res 5(3):143–152

Stough C et al (2014) Reducing occupational stress with a B-vitamin focussed intervention: a randomized clinical trial: study protocol. Nutr J 13:122

Swanson D et al (2012) Omega-3 fatty acids EPA and DHA: health benefits throughout life. Adv Nutr 3:1–7. doi:10.3945/an.111.000893

Walker AF et al (2003) Mg citrate found more bioavailable than other Mg preparations in a randomised, double-blind study. Magnes Res 16(3):183–191

Yan YX et al (2016) Investigation of the relationship between chronic stress and insulin resistance in a Chinese population. J Epidemiol 26(7):355–360

Z Jin et al (2013) GABA is an effective immunomodulatory molecule. Amino Acids 45(1):87–94

Żychowska M et al (2015) Vitamin C, A and E supplementation decreases the expression of HSPA1A and HSPB1 genes in the leukocytes of young polish figure skaters during a 10-day training camp. J Int Soc Sports Nutr 12

Chapter 9
Nutrition for Body, Mind and Soul

Gerhard Moser and Ingrid Pirker-Binder

Contents

> The food you eat can be either the safest and most powerful form of medicine or the slowest form of poison (Ann Wigmore).[1]

"Death is located in the intestine"—traditional Chinese medicine has already attributed crucial importance to the intestine. Its significance is by far higher than generally known: the intestinal surface of the digestive tract of an adult corresponds approximately 500 m^2 (skin surface about 2 m^2), the length of the intestine is about 8 m. The intestine is home to about 80% of the immune system cells, 90% of the "happiness hormone" serotonin, and is therefore primarily responsible for the body's defenses. (Priumboom et al. 2014)

Listlessness, fatigue, skin problems, allergies and asthma—these are but a few, widespread examples of symptoms and syndromes that can be attributed to a lack of intestinal health, even if the cause of health problems is often suspected elsewhere.

[1] http://www.goodreads.com/quotes/563016-the-food-you-eat-can-be-either-the-safest-and, last access on 2.1.2017.

G. Moser · I. Pirker-Binder (✉)
Aigenpeterweg 345/4, 5424 Vigaun, Austria
e-mail: office@pirker-binder.at

G. Moser
e-mail: info@nexyt.com

I. Pirker-Binder (ed.), *Mindful Prevention of Burnout in Workplace Health Management*, https://doi.org/10.1007/978-3-319-61337-6_9

The modern, western diet is characterized by sugar, milk and wheat products, which results in a leaky gut. The key to a healthier life is a specific and health-conscious diet. The new science of cPNI—clinical psycho-neuroimmunology shows us in an understandable way how nutrition can promote health, energy and balance.

With her quote, “The food you eat can be either the safest and most powerful form of medicine or the slowest form of poison”, Ann Wigmore gets to the heart of the matter. The importance of a proper diet does not only apply to our beloved pets, but especially to us humans, if we want to have a healthy, vital, satisfying life and use all the life potential available to us. Eating is more than just food intake—it connects us with Mother Nature, with community experiences and emotions: fun, pleasure, taste. What is more, it has an effect: either positive or negative, depending on the importance given to nutrition as a fuel for the power plant called human being—and it affects everyone; child, adult, the sick, athletes, managers.

Nutrition is equally necessary for our survival, performance capability and health as oxygen is for breathing. In addition to caring for our attitude to life and maintaining the functional capacity of the autonomic nervous system, a suitable diet is another fundamental pillar of prevention.

9.1 cPNI—Food as a Health Factor

cPNI-clinical psycho-neuroimmunology is a young science that has its origins in classical psycho-neuro-immunology (PNI). The father of PNI is the psychologist Robert Ader (Ader and Cohen 1975).[2] He was able to prove for the first time that the immune system works together with the central nervous system and that it is capable of learning. PNI is also considered a field of modern psychosomatic and psychotherapeutic research; it deals with the communication, cooperation and interaction of the psyche, nerves, hormone and immune systems in the human body. cPNI transfers the resulting findings into the therapeutic everyday life. Its tool is a suitable diet, herbs, and/or other active substances to support the body’s regenerative and regulatory measures. It is not about symptom control, but about restoring the healthy functioning of the body or supporting it in its operation.

[2]Ader and Cohen (1975), pp. 333–340.

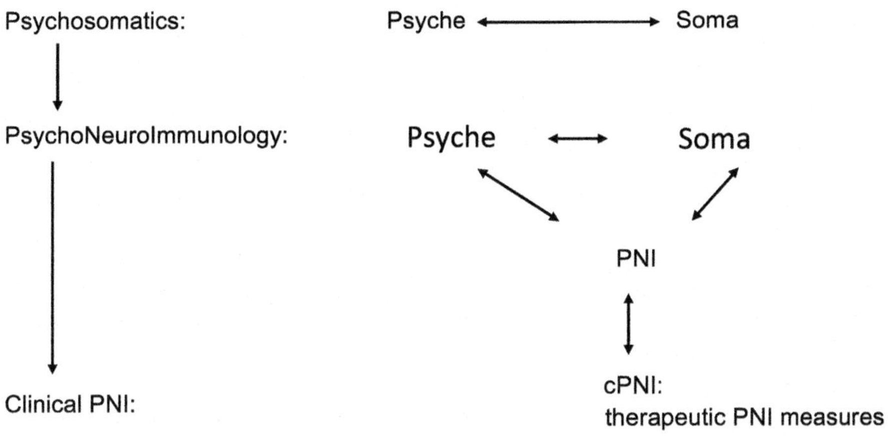

cPNI pioneers were Bram van Dam, Leo Pruimboom (Priumboom et al. 2014) and Kharrazian (2013). In cPNI, the focus of attention is, on the one hand, epigenetics and, on the other hand, on influencing physiological inflammatory processes. In epigenetics it is considered that even though the DNA of humans is created at birth, it is greatly influenced by the environment, attitude towards life (see LifeSkriptAnalysis, Chap. 6) and lifestyle. That is, while an inherited disposition for certain diseases and ailments, such as cardiac diseases, may exist, but the individual does not necessarily have to suffer from it. "However, whether a gene is switched on or switched off is largely dependent on the respective environmental conditions in most genes" (Bauer 2002).[3]

Chronic inflammatory reactions, caused by an unhealthy lifestyle, malnutrition due to a poor diet, lack of movement and stress are the most frequent companions of the 21st century. cPNI states resolemics (from: to resolve) as the most important other task. Inflammatory reactions for the self-healing of the organism are vital processes. However, unhealthy lifestyle, psychological strain and permanent stress, can cause chronic inflammations, which are then the starting point for a variety of diseases and ailments. Resolemics is based on healthy nutrition and an individual diet supported by necessary food supplements.

[3]Bauer (2002), p. 26.

The gene of the immune messenger substance Interleukin 6 can be activated by inflammatory factors as well as by psychological stress. The activation of genes by psychological stress has not only been proven for Interleukin 6 but also for numerous other genes (such as the stress gene CRH) J. Bauer, p. 36.

9.2 cPNI and Frankl's Logotherapy and Existential Analysis

Psychological strain, caused by a transgenerational trauma,[4] birth experience, life and environmental experiences, and/or chronic workloads, lack of exercise and a poor diet, affect the functional capacity of the organism. They disturb the body's balance. The result is a weakened immune system, chronic inflammatory processes, rising infections, allergies, and food intolerances. Both, the soul and the body suffer. This requires careful reflection on life, a re-evaluation of the individual life story. If you know yourself better and understand the signals of your body, a conscious reorientation is easy. In order for this to succeed, a sense of meaning and determination are necessary. This is the task of psychotherapy. In Frankl's logotherapy and existential analysis there is the concept of NOO-psycho-somatics. It means the influence of the mind on the psyche and the soma (body). NOO refers to the word NOUS from ancient Greek philosophy and means *spirit*; translated into the therapeutic language of logotherapy, it is the spiritual dimension from which humans can take a position on themselves and their being (see Chap. 3).

NOO-psycho-somatics

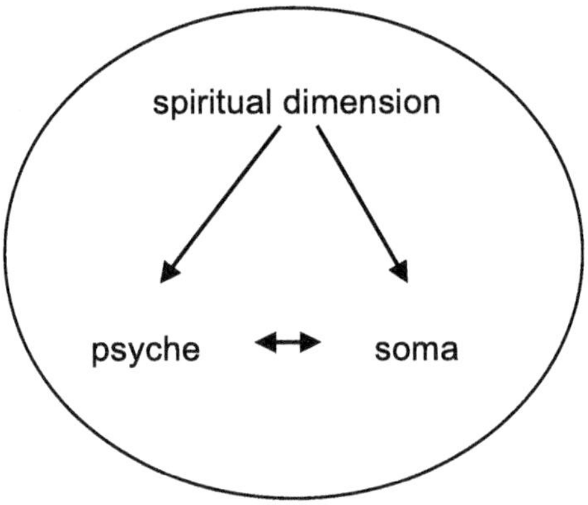

cPNI represents a useful supplement to logotherapeutic interventions in the field of prevention. In particular, it requires the client's active, self-determined collaboration. Psychotherapy, with its tools aiming at a change in attitude, lifestyle change and healing of mental conflicts, has a great influence on the immune system of the organism. Every affect status determines the immune status (Lukas 1998). In contrast, cPNI takes a different scientific approach and supports the immune system with natural food and active ingredients from nature (herbs, etc.).

---

[4]Transgenerational traumas are severe psychological strain (e.g. wartime experiences) whose psychological experience (e.g. inexplicable anxiety, etc.) is passed on to later generations. Traumas can be detected in male semen.

9.3 Gut-Brain Axis: Interactions and Mood Parameter

Physical and mental health are inextricably linked, as are eating and digesting. In traditional Chinese medicine and Ayurveda, the intestine is the center of health. Actually, this is logical, because everything we eat must also be digested and available for the energy production and maintenance of our life energy and health. If the intestine does not get what it needs, the effect on the soul is negative. The saying that people are what they eat is becoming increasingly important. Kirsten Tillisch (ULCA Newsroom 3013) was able to demonstrate the effects of intestinal bacteria on the brain and the emotional condition. In his book "Why isn't my brain working?" Kharrazian describes very convincingly the connections of a non-functional brain with intestinal problems and the related malfunctions and disharmonies in the organism.

The intestine is a highly complex system with its own nervous system, the enteric nervous system. It absorbs information from the inside of the body and food, processes it, and passes it on. For this reason, the digestive system is also called the intestinal brain. How does this connection work? The information carrier is the **vagus nerve**, which emanates from the brain stem and goes through all internal organs. This 10th cranial nerve is decisively involved in the regeneration and regulation capacity of the organism. (More about regeneration and vagus nerve in Chap. 12).

The institute "Initiative Gehirnforschung Steiermark" (Initiative Brain Research Styria) deals with the communication system stomach-intestine-brain (see Fig. 9.1) thereby cooperating with reputable institutions. Together they have been able to locate four information channels between the brain and the gastrointestinal tract:

- Signals of the intestinal microbiome
- Gut hormones
- Messenger substances of the immune system
- Sensory neurons

Through these pathways they exert influence on the psychological condition or susceptibility to stress and the emotions, and with them on the cognitive processes and the amount of food that humans take in.

The latest research is concerned with the influence of the intestinal bacteria on the metabolic processes and thus on the effects on the weight. At the University of Leuven, Belgium, under the supervision of Professor Patrice Cani, examinations have shown that the intestinal flora not only changed due to heavy fat consumption, but also made it permeable, giving toxic molecules unimpeded access to various organs thereby causing inflammatory reactions.

The so-called intestinal flora, or microbiota as it is called today, has an influence on feelings, motivation, immune defense and the early warning system in the case of diseases. They thus influence the behavior more than previously assumed. In order to feel healthy and active, it will be important to avoid or reduce stress stimuli

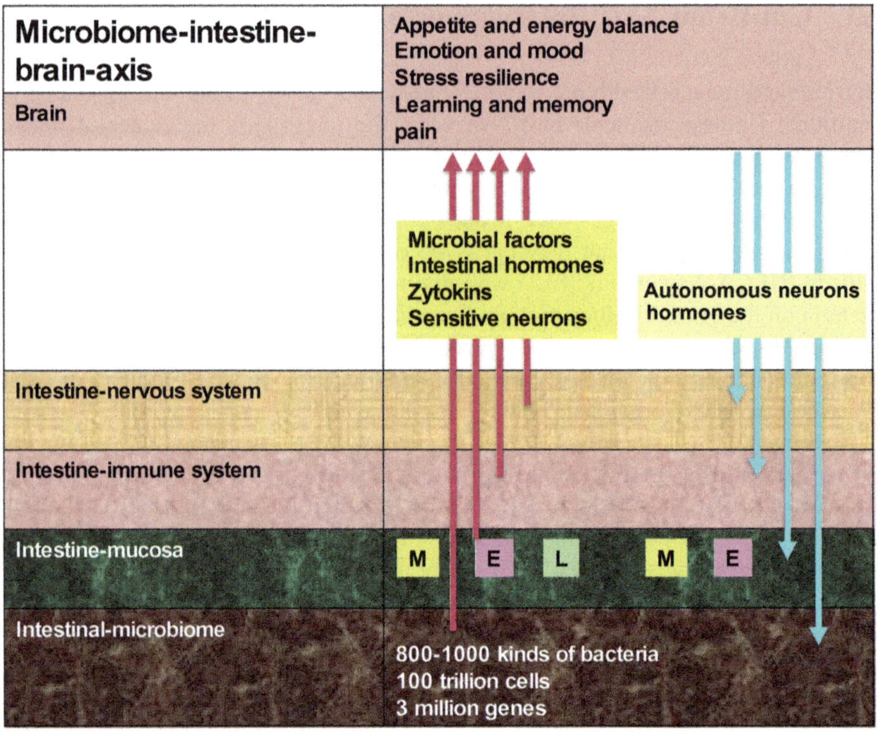

Fig. 9.1 The microbiome-intestine-brain-axis. *Image source* Institute for experimental and clinical pharmacology of the University of Graz; cited according to Prof. Dr. Peter Holzer

and, on the other hand, to take care of the food we give the intestinal bacteria so that they can easily perform their most important task in the human body (Rieser-Lembang 2016, p. 119).

Physical and psychological/mental health are directly linked. The brain plays an essential role in the digestion/metabolism[5]: the "transport" of the food through the body, the release of digestive enzymes, which break down the foodstuffs, as well as the regulation of the blood circulation, which promotes intestinal health and repair, are controlled by the brain.

Through the five sensory organs (eyes, ears, nose, mouth, skin), the brain permanently receives information about the environment. Based on this information, it responds. These responses can be actively controlled to a certain extent; this is the motor system accounting for about 10% of the total brainpower. The majority of the brainpower, namely the remaining 90%, is used for passively controlled processes.

[5]Kharrazian: Why isn't my brain working? p. 164 ff.

In addition to digestion, this includes heartbeat and breathing. Consequently, brain performance is concentrated to a large extent on involuntarily controlled, vital processes!

Decreased brain performance affects the functioning of the intestine. The impairment is noticeable, for example, by reduced memory, articulation or learning difficulties. As a result, digestive disorders (for example, bloating, diarrhea) can occur.

When the brain activity decreased, observations showed that the digestion function was the first to be impaired. If the performance of the brain continues to diminish, further intestinal problems as well as loss of control over the bladder result.

9.4 Leaky Gut Syndrome

Intestinal health has a major influence on the general wellbeing of humans. Unfortunately, the intestine is generally given relatively little attention, although its importance is increasingly emphasized.

Many symptoms emanate from limited intestinal function such as allergies, asthma, celiac disease, Crohn's disease, depression, diabetes mellitus type 1, Hashimoto's disease, migraine, multiple sclerosis, psoriasis, rheumatism, acne, low blood pressure, arthritis and osteoporosis.

Intestinal wall cells are located on the intestinal surfaces. These intestinal wall cells are connected with cell connections "tight junctions" and thus form a barrier for the protection of the intestinal wall. Through the release of stress hormones (noradrenaline and cortisol) or due to a poor diet and malnutrition (lectins, gliadins, saponins[6]), these cell connections are weakened or even destroyed, resulting in an opening in the intestinal wall. Food components (especially gluten), bacteria and viruses enter the intestinal tract, where they are absorbed by macrophages (phagocytes) and identified as intruders. The body's immune system fights these intruders by means of cell-destroying substances and inflammatory reactions. This process also damages other cells. A part of the inflammatory substances enter the organism via the blood channels and lymph and lead to innumerable secondary diseases.

Many people of Western civilization are doubly vulnerable by the release of stress hormones and malnutrition.

Especially long-lasting, so-called permanent stress weakens the organism generally, in particular the intestinal connections and thus the intestinal health.

---

[6]Gliadins occur primarily in cereals and can destroy the connections between the intestinal wall cells; lectins are defenses, which occur mainly in cereals and legumes. They can bind to intestinal wall cells and thereby damage them. Saponins are soap-like substances which can bind to the cholesterol of intestinal wall cells and thus damage them. When potatoes or legumes are boiled, they can be recognized by their foaming property (beer).

The most common dietary habits leave much to be desired. Despite an oversupply and overprovision of food, a serious under-supply of nutrients can be observed. In particular, inflammation-inducing and acid-forming substances in the food lead to permanent defensive reactions of the body. The immune system is permanently active and cannot respond to emergency situations due to a lack of other resources. Diseases occur because of the weakened immune system.

Everybody can actively counteract the destruction of cell compounds and intestinal cells. This is done with simple means, especially a basic diet change focusing on base-producing meals and sufficient liquid intake.

In addition, a multi-phase intestinal rehabilitation, which can easily be integrated in everyday life, is recommended. At the beginning, the intestine is healed, then thoroughly cleansed, and finally, the intestinal flora is restored.

Case Study 1

Ms. C, mid-40, entrepreneur, coach and mother suffers from a lipoedema stage 3. For years, she tried various diets; recently she tried to control her weight and her insulin resistance with an HCG diet (500 kcal, and pregnancy hormones).

Before the weight reduction could be started, the removal of venous weakness was tackled as a first step. By means of adapted nutrient supply, optimal intestinal function was restored. At the same time, the nutrient concept supported and positively influenced the blood flow, fibrosis and low-grade inflammation in the white adipose tissue. The next step was to develop an enhanced nutrient concept for the thyroid function.

After 8 months, the attending physician told Ms. C that the lipoedema had stopped growing. Her condition had improved dramatically, she had normal bowel movement again (she had not had it since she was 14), no inner pain, and the kilos tumbled.

Conclusion: it is always about a restoration of the internal regulatory mechanisms and a change in lifestyle. For this, cPNI provides valuable information.

Case Study 2

Ms. M, 34, owner of a group fitness franchise chain, had gone through a seemingly endless process of unsuccessful therapies.

Her complaints were:

- Allergies (apple, milk, tomato, wool, citrus fruits, grasses, glutamate, aggravated allergy symptoms at night)
- Diabetes II
- Emotional stress, adrenal fatigue,—skin impurities/reactions
- "Toilet paper" allergy
- Concentration weakness
- An emotional collapse
- Massive abdominal pain during the female cycle with suspected endometriosis, chlamydia

The therapy program included:

A change to a nutrient-rich, alkaline-forming and anti-inflammatory diet, free of gluten, lactose and industrial sugar. No food alone is a potent trigger for neurological problems and autoimmunity. It is often the interplay of many minor or major problems, which leads to massive health problems, which inhibit the organism in its functional processes. Routine standard test methods often do not provide the necessary information. Often extensive gluten sensitivity and autoimmunity tests are required.

Special attention should be paid to the intestine to influence the leaky gut positively through special food products. A healthy intestine is a guarantee for the maintenance of life energy and mental health.

Once the nutrient deficiency was cured and the intestine healed, the organism was able to carry out its regeneration and regulation processes, the stress boosts became less and less, the energy increased. After over a year of consistent implementation of all concepts all complaints had disappeared.

- **A poor diet and stress lead to lack of energy and premature aging. Thanks to cPNI numerous ailments can be eased and health can be restored. We have but one health—it absolutely makes sense to preserve it. Health starts with one's individual life style and the fuel we supply for our body.**

References

Ader R, Cohen N (1975) Behaviorally conditioned immunosuppression. Psychosom Med 37(4)

Bauer J (2002) Das Gedächtnis des Körpers; wie Beziehungen und Lebensstile unsere Gene steuern. Eichborn AG, Frankfurt am Main

Kharrazian D (2013) Why isn't my brain working? Elephant Press LP, CA, USA

Lukas E (1998) Lehrbuch der Logotherapie. Profil Verlag München, Wien

Priumboom L, Reheis D, Rinderer M (2014) Wirk-Kochbuch, 2nd edn. Hohenems-Wien,Vaduz

Rieser-Lembang B (2016) Der Darm und seine Gefühle. In: Prävention von Erschöpfung in der Arbeitswelt, German edn. Springer, Berlin-Heidelberg

Wigmore A http://www.goodreads.com/quotes/563016-the-food-you-eat-can-be-either-the-safest-and. Last access on 2 Jan 2017

Chapter 10
People and Their Workplace

Ingrid Pirker-Binder

Contents

Not only the work content and requirements have changed considerably in recent years, but also the workplace, workplace design and working hours. Currently there is a trend away from the individual office towards flexible workplaces, working units, open-plan offices and home office. Despite all the dynamics people and their needs must not be forgotten. The workplace should be conducive to the people's needs. Not all new models are suitable for all people. There must be a development and research, which place the people at the center and do not fit people into the models in retrospect.

Flexibility of workplaces, working hours and work content mean more responsibility and self-management for individuals. Frequently the people lag behind these conditions. Learning steps and responsibility management are necessary. In times of technological progress and permanent availability work-life balance is giving way to a new concept of work-life integration and interaction. It is about the integration of work and leisure in the daily life.

For prevention as well as intervention measures in the case of exhaustion at the workplace, it is necessary to analyze the work area to identify stress fields. While Life-Script-Analysis records the individual or business meaning and experience

I. Pirker-Binder (✉)
Sailerückergasse 43/26, 1190 Vienna, Austria
e-mail: office@pirker-binder.at

I. Pirker-Binder (ed.), *Mindful Prevention of Burnout in Workplace Health Management*, https://doi.org/10.1007/978-3-319-61337-6_10

framework, Work-Script-Analysis refers to the meaning and experience framework of work, the working environment, the physical and psychological effect and experience of work.

10.1 Office Environment

10.1.1 Rising Popularity of Open-Plan Offices

In Austria the space and air requirements per employee are regulated in the Workplace Ordinance (Arbeiterkammer Wien 2015a, b). Amongst others it deals with the control of the room height (3 m, at a size of 100–500 m^2 also 2.8 m, up to 100 m^2—without physical strain—also 2.5 m), the floor area which is allocated to each worker (minimum 8 m^2, for each additional employee 5 m^2) and the air (with low physical stress at least 12 m^3). The objective of the Workplace Ordinance is to adapt the workplace to the needs of the people working in it and not vice versa.

Looking for greater flexibility in the work organization, workflows and means of saving costs, new models of workplace design were developed, such as the open-plan office. This is a large open area, which is divided into smaller working units without walls and doors.

The initial ideas for this model were formed by the following considerations (Oommen 2008, p. 37 ff.):

- lower construction costs due to less space requirement: compared to individual offices, more people can be accommodated on the same area.
- lower maintenance costs (heating, ventilation, air conditioning etc.).
- every employee has the same available space.
- easier communication between employees; this is supposed to increase productivity and creativity.
- greater work flexibility due to the possibility to work in different areas without regard for time and space.
- everything is centrally available.
- technical resources can be used more efficiently (e.g. copiers, printers, etc.).

What was disregarded in the planning of such offices is the uniqueness of every person and the relationship between the physical environment, the need for quiet and performance capability of each individual employee during work. The workplace should be helpful and stimulating to the user; it should not be an obstacle or restrict the employee in his/her capacity to work. Hence, it must support the working people in their needs. Specifically, this can have an impact on the following factors:

- right to privacy: design possibility (pictures, plants, etc.).
- possibility to control one's work environment: one's own workplace that does not have to be shared.
- feeling of security: many people feel observed when others are present.

- right to quiet: conversations, people walking to and fro, subliminal noise caused by conversation and phone calls can impede the attention and focus on difficult tasks.
- right to undisturbed working: in open-plan offices there is no barrier in the form of a closed door.
- status and identity. Work in an open-plan office may entail status loss and/or identity loss within the organization. In the open-plan office the individual is one amongst many others.

If the workplace is used by different people through job rotation (several employees share a workplace), not only the feeling of control is lost, but also privacy (everyone has his/her filing habits, or would like to find the workplace in the same condition as he/she left it).

10.1.2 The Closed Door or the Right to Undisturbed Work

Many employees complain about continuous interruptions through telephone calls or disturbance through colleagues. Many have problems closing their office door or not answering a phone call or e-mail immediately. "My door is always open for everybody," I hear very often. It is a matter of organization to create quiet periods for undisturbed work for oneself, be it closing office doors for certain times or not responding to enquiries immediately. It has also been proven useful to put time for concentrated working into the calendar system just like appointments.

If employees share a room with colleagues, mutual consideration is necessary. It has paid off to work with headphones at times of special concentration.

A young man whose job it is to develop game software, tells me that in his company it works perfectly with headphones, "When I develop something, I put on my headphones not only to be able to fully concentrate but also to enjoy the support of quiet music. It is agreed with the colleagues that no one is to be disturbed as long as the headphones are up."

There is no door in open-plan offices that can be closed to signal the desire for privacy. It is necessary to implement a regulation for undisturbed working. Even if "quiet working islands" are provided, it is not always possible to use them, be it because they are occupied, or documents cannot always be carried around.

Depending on the personality and the area of responsibility some employees are also advocates of open-plan offices. However, in terms of efficiency it is beneficial not to go over people's heads when deciding on their workplaces. The increased noise level in open-plan offices may lead to a stimulus overflow and hyperstimulation among individual employees. Not everyone is the same, particularly when it comes to scheduling, compliance with deadlines, concentration or a high level of responsibility and decision-making for the tasks at hand.

Recent developments make it possible to reduce noise by means of structural measures. Adequate office equipment and resources for the employees (e.g. headsets that reduce the noise of telephone calls or head-phones that provide quiet and concentration for the working people) are conducive to a working atmosphere.

If a company is planning to move from conventional offices into an open-plan office, not only good and thoughtful planning is required but also preparing the employees, who will be working in it, for the new way of working. Open-plan offices demand a different kind of living together. In open-plan offices a new culture of consideration is necessary.

Mr. M, an aspiring employee of a large company, reports on the open-plan office. It has existed for a long time and does not meet the current state-of-the-art anymore. Mr. M is suffering from the constant disturbances, on the one hand by impromptu meetings close to his workspace or, on the other hand, by the smell of a doner kebab, a colleague likes to eat during work. The smell then spreads in the whole office. Mr. M also attributes the source of the disturbances to weak management.

- Sensitive and highly sensitive people particularly suffer in an open-plan office.

Oommen (2008, p. 42) compares the following positive and negative aspects of open-plan offices:

Positive aspects:

- lower construction costs
- lower costs for heating, ventilation, air-conditioning
- more people per area
- equal workspace for all employees
- greater communication possibilities
- improved cooperation
- greater flexibility to work in different areas

Negative aspects:

- high noise level
- loss of concentration
- lower productivity
- reduced privacy
- status problems
- feeling of insecurity
- dissatisfaction with work
- more conflicts at the workplace
- more stress, risk of infection, physical and psychological exhaustion, muscle aches, tiredness and elevated blood pressure
- higher fluctuation

The Stress Research Institute and the Institute for Psychology at the University of Stockholm have pursued the question whether office design has an influence on sickness rates (Bodin Danielsson et al. 2014, p. 139 ff.). Thereby seven different kinds of offices were compared (Table 10.1).

Table 10.1 Different kinds of offices, classification according to Bodin Danielsson et al. (2014)

Cell office	Traditional single room, high level of concentration, all necessary office equipment available in the room		
Shared room office	2–3 people		
Traditional open-plan office	4–9 people/room: "small open-plan office"	10–24 people/room: "medium-sized open-plan office"	More than 24 people/room: "large open-plan office"
Flex office	There are no individual workplaces but workstations, i.e. rooms for concentrated work, for making telephone calls, meeting rooms. Workplaces can be chosen freely		
Combi office	More than 20% does not take place at the individual workplace; there is teamwork. The focus is on rooms for group activities		

1852 people participated in the Swedish study, which could establish a significant link between sickness rates and office design. Traditional open-plan offices showed an increased rate of short sickness rates.

A higher risk of longer sickness absences was documented for women in open-plan offices, for men in flex offices.

1230 people participated in the SBiB study (Amstutz 2010), a Swiss survey on the evaluation of the working conditions. It is notable that the type of office was not rated as decisive in the first place, but rather whether the workplace meets the needs for working qualitatively. Below essential characteristics of a workplace were named:

- possibility of 2–3 hours undisturbed work
- quiet in order to concentrate
- possibility to make phone calls undisturbed

The requirements were met best in the one-person office and were decreasingly met the bigger the office size was.

10.1.3 Home Office

Due to new technologies and multi media applications the paperless office is not a distant reality anymore. Flexible work hours and flexible ways of working contribute to a change of the work world. In the future work will become less and less connected to a workplace. The home office will become prevalent.

"New World of Work means more than merely flexible work. New World of Work in companies appears more like a holistic concept of work innovation in the dimensions people, place and technology (Bartz and Schmutzer 2015).

Within the currently predominant dynamics people and their needs must not be forgotten. The workplace should serve the people. Not all new models fit all people. There must be a development and research that puts the human beings at the center and does not place them into the new system afterwards.

Taking the example of the home office, it can be shown that establishing distance to work is often more difficult than in the office. Statements by people working in their home office like "I don't even dare to have a break because if I'm not online and available anytime, the colleagues in the company think I do not work! "Or" When I work at home, I constantly have a bad conscience about not doing enough; you might think I work too slowly or too little", are very common in therapeutic practice. Distancing oneself from work is difficult. A high level of commitment and strive for perfection, missing tolerance for failure or mistakes directly lead to exhaustion.

However, the home office also offers a great scope of work design and more flexibility in time management. For all those who are able to organize themselves very well, this model will be expanded in the future; new technologies facilitate this. The disadvantage is that one is almost constantly in communication with the company. Constant accessibility or the belief that they must be constantly available, may put a strain on life quality and life energy.

Work-Life-Balance is changing into Work-Life-Integration and Interaction. The working people have to learn that work is an integrated part of life and vice versa. The thoughts, "Business before pleasure", or "I am going to relax when I have finished all the tasks" are outdated, as they do not work anymore nowadays. The new media have made work omnipresent.

10.2 The Workplace at Distant Places: Risks and Possibilities

Global economics makes traveling a necessity. On Monday morning the planes are fully booked by people flying to work, sometimes returning daily or at the end of the week. Without active stress and regeneration management these people run the risk of being exhausted. Whether and what risks the traveler takes when his/her workplace is in a distant place, depends on the following:

- time, frequency, duration of air travel
- shift work locally or abroad

- intensity of work and working time
- ability to eat healthy and regularly

Many travelers take the early morning flight on Monday to get to their workplace abroad. This usually means that they are already dealing with topics on Sunday that are due on Monday, to be well prepared. The suitcase must be packed and the night's sleep is significantly shortened for a timely arrival at the airport. The work then mostly starts on the plane and continues all day, often until late into the night. Everything should be done quickly. Consequently, the daily working time is very long, sometimes interrupted with breaks, but often they are ignored due to time pressure. The return in the middle or at the end of the week is then filled with follow-up work or preparations for next week, informing and delegating.

Case history frequent flyer a manager, who has spent his working hours in Germany from Monday to Wednesday evening, complains that there is no time left for him. Apart from the short night on Sunday, the evening after his return is busy with working on accumulated tasks, so as not to forget anything and to get important issues out of the head. He finds it useful to pack all the information in emails, so that his employees are informed on the next day. With astonishment he notes several times that he receives replies to his emails in the middle of the night. But as soon as he gets an answer, he somehow feels compelled to write back again. So it often happens that the time to sleep is much too short. Due to his frequent travels, he also feels never to have time for himself; somehow he is either arriving or departing. Especially the time missing on Sunday evening has become noticeable. Vegetative functional diagnostics (24-h heart rate variability measurement) clearly points out the strain.

Time pressure, completion dates and deadlines are energy killers. In particular, however, striving for perfection and the inability to relax, but also an exaggerated sense of responsibility towards work, lead to health risks at the workplace.

- Anyone who travels a lot should learn to integrate micro-breaks and regeneration times.

There are chances for a longer or shorter break now and then, e.g. during a meeting, when you are not actively involved, waiting times or just the necessary times you spend on the toilet. In principle, recovery is quite simple, it requires

- letting go of the thoughts for a couple of minutes,
- relaxing the muscles (there are many tense, concentrated faces),
- the right breathing and
- mindfulness to the needs of the body.

– Those who forget about themselves and the needs of their body, fall by the wayside sooner or later. Life goes by without having been lived. However, work does not have to be fatal. It can be integrated into life because working time is also lifetime.

Case history heart attack

Mr. X is 40 years old and loves his profession. He is working on an important project. He has problems with his health, his internist advises him to slow down. Mr. X's attitude, "I know, that I am running out of strength, but I need to finish this task, then I will recover." He made this statement in January. In March, he suffered a heart attack. Those who do not stop the inner pressure and are in tension too long, should not be surprised if the body reacts accordingly.

The assumption of great responsibility without distancing from work combined with anxious expectation or foresight is bad. Foresight is good; expecting something negative may severely impede one's health if it is a life and/or work pattern. Those who have distancing problems or problems shutting off at the workplace, or who constantly worry, should not hesitate to work through these issues with a trained therapist.

Case history health

Mr. O, an executive on a drilling rig, comes into my practice. He is going through a health check, because it has to be clarified whether Mr. O is capable to work again after his last bypass operation (he has already had several). Mr. O is in a very poor health condition. His cardiovascular system is severely damaged, which is visible in both the biofeedback as well as in the 24-hour-heart rate analysis. From a therapeutic perspective Mr. O is no longer able to work - he is psychologically and physically running on empty. His story is shocking. He tells me that he always has four weeks off and then spends a fortnight on the drilling rig. As soon as he is picked up by the helicopter after his vacation and flown to his workplace, he is in a state of emergency. He is constantly worried, "What if fire breaks out?" He constantly goes through the rescue measures in his head. Since he is a senior engineer, a large part of the responsibility is on his shoulders. He has not learnt to switch off, to build up a certain trust or to tense up in case of an emergency only and not constantly. He has been working in this job for over twenty years; nothing has ever happened—but his health, in particular his heart, has been seriously damaged by the chronic tension, worrying and anxiety.

Fear and constant distress facilitate chronic tension and lead to narrowing of the vessels. Being in a constant state of alert about a potential danger deprives the body of sufficient rest and recovery during sleep. This results in the regeneration mechanisms not functioning any more, i.e. the downward spiral begins.

Through therapeutic measures, learning how to achieve inner silence and regeneration, Mr. O would have been able to preserve his health and joy of life. An executive has the function of a role model. It is not without reason to say, "If the executive is well, so are the employees!" A manager is responsible for the human resources. Executives who constantly call their employees after work hours are not an example.

Case history leadership and role model Mr. P is a controller in a company. He puts himself under a lot of pressure, suffering from ruminating and not being able to switch off. He feels burned out. He tells of his boss, who is a role model. She works until late at night every day, because of work she decided not to have children or a husband; work is her sole purpose in life. Therefore Mr. P feels obliged to work equally hard or has a guilty conscience when he goes home early.

- Managers, who cannot distance themselves, disregard their resources and dedicate their lives to work, are no role models.

Shift work, diet at the workplace

People working in exposed positions at home or abroad carry a high responsibility for their health and energy. Often, diet is a special issue, as there are either no shopping opportunities or different eating habits at remote workplaces. It is on the one hand the company's task to prepare its employees for this, but also to encourage them to take up responsibility for their wellbeing. This also applies to sleeping and recreation times in the case of shift work.

Case history shift work Mr. M is a shift worker and works about 800 km from his company location. After his shift he does not switch off his mobile phone, he is virtually on "Standby" while he should actually observe rest periods. He complains that his colleagues in the head office would not show consideration for this. "They must know that now, in the morning, I am ending my shift," he says. It does not occur to him that the colleagues at the head office might not even have considered this. He has not realized yet that he alone is responsible for his rest periods - and that his mobile phone and computer should be switched off during these times. For a successful communication with the parent company fixed times should be arranged.

Flexibility of workplaces, working hours and work content means more responsibility and self-management for the individual. Very often people lag behind with regard to these requirements. Learning steps and responsibility management are necessary. In times of technological progress and permanent availability work-life balance is superseded by a new term: work-life integration. It's about the integration of work and leisure into the daily life. Mindful treatment of oneself is one of the learning objectives of integrating work and leisure into the daily life.

10.3 Process Model: Work-Script Analysis

For preventive measures and for intervention in the case of exhaustion at the workplace it is necessary to analyze the work area to identify stress fields. While the Life-Script Analysis records the individual meaning and experience framework, the Work-Script Analysis focuses on the meaning and experience framework of work. The Work-Script Analysis refers both to the work environment, as well as the physical and psychological influence and experience, which might lead to a rough classification into "hard facts" and "soft facts".

The "**hard facts**" include:

- working contexts and work contracts, such as all-in contracts, work content, areas of responsibility
- working hours: fixed or variable office hours, home office, workshop, shift work, external office hours (in branch offices abroad, in the client's office)
- working place: stable, changing, flexible

The "**soft facts**" include:

- corporate culture: mission, vision, values, meaning
- leadership: leadership culture, personality of the manager
- team: interaction, roles, work distribution, responsibility, conflicts, bullying
- break culture: regenerative break, nutrition (company kitchen), humor
- health awareness: information, workshops, healthy diet
- complaints: physical/psychological; stress-related, workplace-specific (open-plan office, computer, assembly line, construction, travel activity)

Conflicts in the workplace or discomfort due to an inappropriate working environment result in physical and psychological stress. According to the SBiB study (Amstutz 2010) the need to be able to do concentrated work stands at 90%. If the necessary peace and quiet is not given, the person concerned has to invest more energy into keeping up the level of concentration. That means more effort accompanied by an internal negative feeling (e.g. anger, impatience) of being refused the necessary environment for work. Hence, the working time as well as the quality of work suffers. The increased effort consumes more energy; fatigue and the physical and psychological tension rise with the desire to complete the respective task in the specified time.

The equipment of the workplace has a significant impact on the experience of work. However, the best office chair does not help if the user sitting on it is tense. Ergonomically designed and equipped workplaces are a prerequisite, yet training the individual body perception regarding tension and unhealthy working postures should be an integral part of all preventive measures. Perception exercises supported by biofeedback (Chap. 11) can reduce work-related physical tensions.

The Work-Script Analysis aims to receive an overview of necessary prevention and intervention measures in the different work areas. These can be addressed to the whole company, the leadership culture, one or more teams, but also only to

Table 10.2 Work-script analysis

Area	Content	Perception	Questions/solutions
Hard facts			
Work context/ work contract	All-in contract expenditure area	Balanced work content workload	Responsibility?
Working hours	Fixed office hours Variable office hours Home office Shift work External office hours	Physical perception of the strain? Time for regeneration? Air travel?	Are there resulting stress fields?
Workplace	Stable changing flexible	Physical/ psychological stress?	Determining psychological/ physical stress
Office type	Single office, open-plan office	Fields of disruption?	Determining fields of disruption
Soft facts			
Leadership	Mission/vision		Corresponding values and quest for meaning?
Team	Interaction, roles, role patterns	Work distribution, responsibility	Appreciation, respect, interaction? SuMeCo
Information culture	Email, telephone, open office door etc.	Disruption Constant availability	Distancing oneself Rules for communication
Break culture	Regenerative break	Physical	Short regeneration
Health awareness	Company kitchen Health promotion measures	Nutrition = energy Wellbeing	Information Responsibility
Complaints	Stress-related Workplace specific (computer workplace, air travel, shift work etc.)	Physical complaints	Determining stress, sickness rates

individual employees. The Life-Script Analysis and the Work-Script Analysis form the basis for prevention and intervention measures against exhaustion at the workplace (see Table 10.2).

References

Amstutz S (2010) SBiB Studie: Schweizerische Befragung in Büros. URL www.seco.admin.ch oder www.hslu.ch/cctp. www.news.admin.ch/NSBSubscriber/message/attachments/18922.pdf. Last access on 23 March 2015

Arbeiterkammer Wien (2015a) ArbeitnehmerInnenschutz. URL: http://media.Arbeiterkammer.at/wien/PDF/Publikationen/ArbeitnehmerInnenschutz/Arbeitsttaetten.pdf

Arbeiterkammer Wien (2015b) Arbeitsstätten; Gestaltung und Ausstattung von Arbeitsstätten. URL: http://media.Arbeiterkammer.at/wien/PDF/Publikationen/ArbeitnehmerInnenschutz/Arbeitsttaetten.pdf. Last access on 2 Aug 2015

Bartz M, Schmutzer T (2015) New world of work transformation - Herausforderungen auf dem Weg zum Unternehmen der nächsten Generation. In Vorbereitung

Bodin-Danielsson C, Chungkham HS, Wulff C, Westerlund H (2014) Office design's impact on sick leave rates. Ergonomics 57:139–147

Oommen VG et al (2008) Should health service managers embrace open plan work environments? A review. ASIA Pac J Health Manag 3:37 ff

Chapter 11
Mental Profile: Stress and Energy—A Diagnostic Method: The CA Method and Its Use in Practice

Bohdana Fialová, Jiří Šimonek, Marie Šťastná and Ingrid Pirker-Binder

Contents

The article describes the CA method (Color association method) and its possible applications in practice. The CA method is a combined projective technique using calibrated sets of words and Lűscher Color Test. It measures the dynamics of functional processes of consciousness, attitudes, i.e. comprehensive units within the consciousness. The test is carried out via a computer program; the whole administration process takes 20–40 min with regard to personal pace and the extent of the calibrated set of words. The results are computer processed and are available immediately upon completion of the test. In current practice, the CA method is used in HR, sport, education, market surveys and health.

B. Fialová · J. Šimonek · M. Šťastná
DAP Services a.S, Smetanovo Náměstí 328/1, 702 00 Ostrava, Czech Republic
e-mail: fialova@dap-services.cz

I. Pirker-Binder (✉)
Saileräckergasse 43/26, 1190 Vienna, Austria
e-mail: office@pirker-binder.at

I. Pirker-Binder (ed.), *Mindful Prevention of Burnout in Workplace Health Management*, https://doi.org/10.1007/978-3-319-61337-6_11

Furthermore, the utilization in prevention of burnout is described here, where the diagnostic tool **Mental stress and energy profile** is used. This tool focuses on the level of experienced and managed stress. With the help of value word schemes it attempts to identify its sources. Another measured item is body-mind balance, which makes it possible to see whether these parts are in balance and whether they support and complement each other or whether one or the other part is more or less accentuated. With the assistance of constructive types of behavior we are able to observe how we can approach and work with a client and what solutions will be functional and effective.

An advantage of the CA method is its speed, the non-demanding nature of the test and a quick access to results.

11.1 The CA Method

The CA method (Color association method) is a combined projective technique using calibrated sets of words ("verbal modules"—48–130 words) and a test of eight colors by Lűscher (1971). Lűscher's diagnostics is based on evaluating the importance of preference and rejection of certain colors. The basic hypothesis is the reasoning that color preference is in a way dependent on certain personality variables, situational states in the organism as well as objectively active agents (Svoboda 1999). The theory of the test is based on the relationship between physiological mechanisms and color structures, i.e. a specific color relates to specific forms and stereotypes of behaviors or individual experience. There are 8 different colors, which are different in their measurable wavelengths range and form the basis of "Little Lüscher's color test" (LCT). The numerical designation of each color (according to LCT) is maintained, which allows easier recording of specific responses (answers) of analyzed people to the stimulative word. The recording is implemented with the use of a computer. Apart from assessing the two preferential selections and one statistical preferential choice, the client also matches each stimulative word with 3 colors. It is a forced choice with regard to its order (it is not possible to select the same color more than once with one word). 56 possible variations are thus formed (color triads) of reactions to one specific word. The generated tool might then be used to determine the responses of people. Its basis is the documented existence of "cortical association areas". Innovation in the form of putting together Lűscher's color test with color-word associations allows us to focus on various areas of human behavior and perception. The CA method combines advantages of both these methods.

The CA method measures the social-psychological spectrum of attitudes, including their implementation potency—not only what people think but also what they prefer (hierarchy of values) and if they would in fact implement their attitudes in their behavior, if so, how successfully and in what time frame. It measures the dynamics of functional processes of consciousness, attitudes, i.e. comprehensive units within the consciousness (of individuals or groups). Data scanning is carried out using a computer program called Sensor (Šimonek 2007–2009).

In current practice, the CA method is used in HR, sport, education, market surveys and health.

11.1.1 Sensor and Data Collection Method

In practice, we use Internet sensor (Fig. 11.1). The perception field during submitting and choosing combined color word associations has been adapted so that the form of testing

- eliminates perceptual defenses as much as possible
- if possible, does not evoke spatially-perceptual stereotypes

Practical application has been standardized. It has 3 phases and the client follows the given procedure. Instructions are included in the diagnosis and are described at the start of the test in the on-line form. This procedure may be explained by the administrator as well.

(1) initial color selection

- look at the colors and let them work on you for a while
- then select all the eight colors in the order from most pleasant to the least enjoyable one
- once you have entered the complete selection, continue with selecting colors for individual words

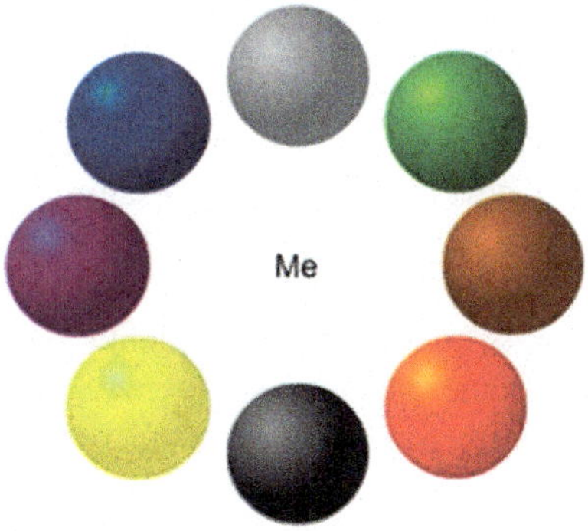

Fig. 11.1 Internet sensor and perception field; color selection

(2) select three colors to match the individual verbal stimulants

- look at the colors and let them work on you for a while
- read the word out loud and then repeat it again in your mind
- take a look at the colors, and select three of them as quickly as possible
- as soon as you have entered all three colors, immediately go to the next word

(3) final color selection

- look at the colors and let them work on you for a while
- then select all the eight colors in the order of how they work on you at the moment (it is not a hidden memory test, the selection may be quite different, similar or the same)
- as soon as you are finished, end the program.

Data scanning can be implemented individually or in a group. The whole application process takes 20–40 min with regard to personal pace and the extent of the calibrated set of words. The results are computer processed and are available immediately upon completion of the test.

11.2 Sample Results of Diagnostics for Mental Stress and Energy Profile

11.2.1 Verbal Schematic

The diagram of consciousness shows the structural map of consciousness composed of verbal objects (words), which have been used for testing.

Objects are divided into 5-value groups—Ideals (idols, i.e. existentially anchoring, long-term positive effects), Satisfactors and Motivators (strong, positively experienced energy resources and rewarding tools of regeneration), Operators (predominantly effective and situationally used tools), Stressors (mostly inefficient situational tools, accompanied by pressure), Destructors (existentially threatening and developmentally devastating long-term influences)—depending on how they are usually preferred in the relevant age category (Fialová and Šimonek 2009).

This creates the typical significance structure of values in consciousness, which has its quantitative and qualitative fulfillment. For each value (verbal object) there are some characteristic general functional and dysfunctional implementation patterns (methods and forms of behavior typical in a certain developmental stage and environment).

The verbal diagram (Fig. 11.2) provides an insight into the current state of the hierarchy of values of the person and it can be used as a guide showing how to work with the person. Working with the verbal diagram allows identifying how to

Company words

Ideals	Satisfactors and Motivators	Operators	Stressors	Destructors
Commissions, Director, Employer, Holiday, I perform physical work, My profession	Employee benefits, I lead the subordinates, I train myself, I work on the computer, My boss, My career, My salary, Rewards, The unions	Business trips, Co-workers, Customer offers, Evaluating interview, Meetings, My job, Suppliers, Work time	Customer claims, I telephone, I work overtime	Administration, Company management, Customers, I go on sick leave, I work shifts, Independent tasks, Meal tickets, Work guidelines

Work words

Ideals	Satisfactors and Motivators	Operators	Stressors	Destructors
Experiencing, I am allowed to, Change, I lead, I organize, I see	Success, I can, I do sports, I feel, I speak, I want, Money, My will, Speed, Advisor, I create, I think, Information, Medicine, People, Reality, Responsibility, Risk	Computers, Cooperation, Independent, My work, Competition, I decide, I hear, My intuition, Property, Self-regulation, Time, I don't want	Control, I am ashamed, My defense, My mistakes, Strain, I am aggressive	I am punished, Obligations, I am not able to, I am not allowed to, My fear, My illness, Slowness, My fault

Fig. 11.2 Verbal schematic—structure of values in consciousness. Company words and work words

motivate the individuals or reward them. You will also find out which tasks and activities they perform **routinely, flexibly** and without any problems and recognize what is a potential **source of tension** or a possible **destructive factor**.

11.2.2 Constructive Types of Behavior

Everyday life and work bring a large and diverse palette of situations and problems, which need to be addressed and, if possible, sorted out successfully. There are a lot of response and behavior types. However, only some enable and facilitate real solutions. By virtue of the CA method, **six basic types** (Šimonek 2007–2009) are defined and measured which include a constructive approach, i.e. support for reaching solutions.

Individual constructive types—individual abilities and strengths are involved in reaching the solution. They include **vitality, ambition and logic. Group**

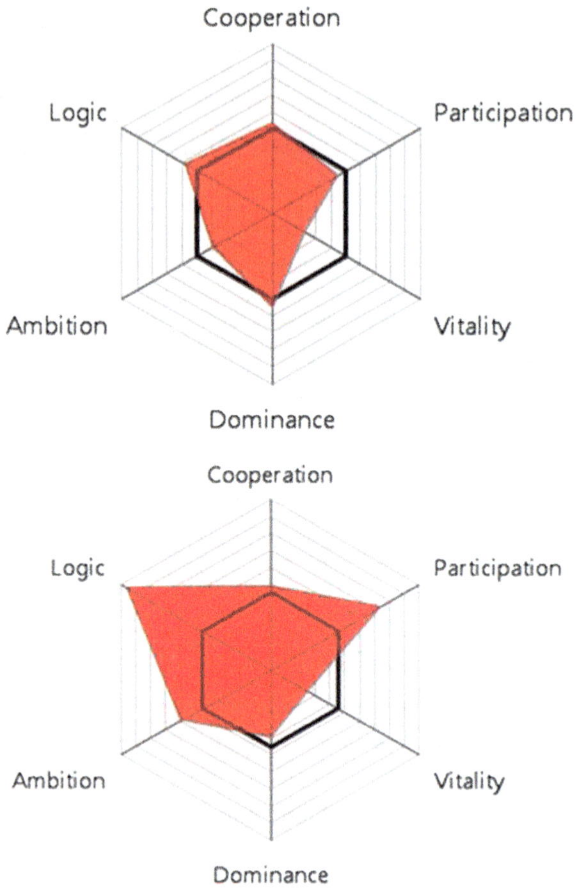

Fig. 11.3 Two different results of constructive type of behaviors

constructive types—group skills and strengths play a role in obtaining a solution. They include **cooperation** and **participation. Mixed constructive types**—individual strengths and skills with functioning and effect in the group are required for reaching the solution. This includes **dominance**.

From this chart (Fig. 11.3) you can see what type of behavior the measured person uses most frequently, what the relationship between the types of behavior is, whether an individual or group type of solution prevails or which way of addressing problems is the least preferred and used. This information can then be used when hiring the best possible candidates or when new work teams are formed.

The images show how different the measured results may be with individuals.

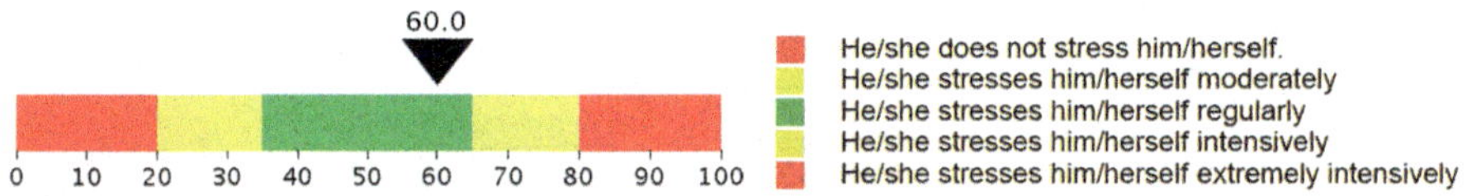

Fig. 11.4 Internally experienced stress; 0 = no stress; 100 = intensive stress

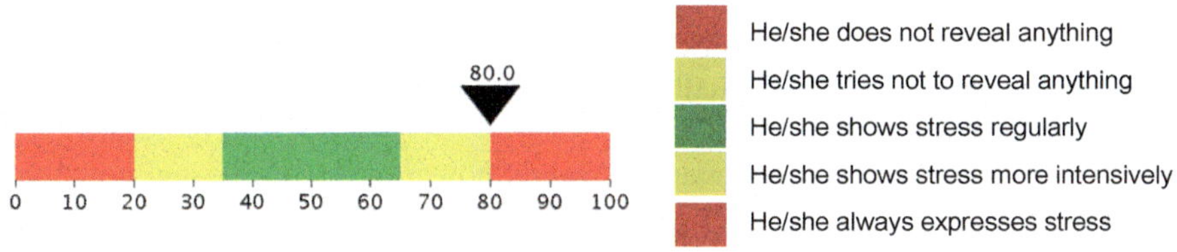

Fig. 11.5 Stress management; 0 = doesn´t reveal anything, 100 always expresses stress

Fig. 11.6 Stress in the company; 0 = no stress, 100 = intensive stress

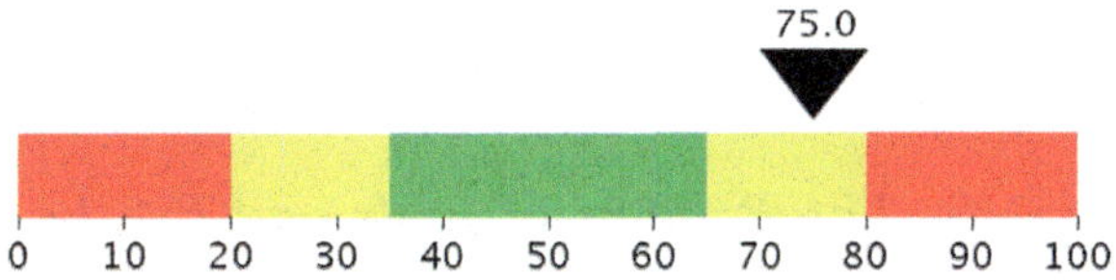

Fig. 11.7 Amount of mental power; 0 = no power; 100 = high power

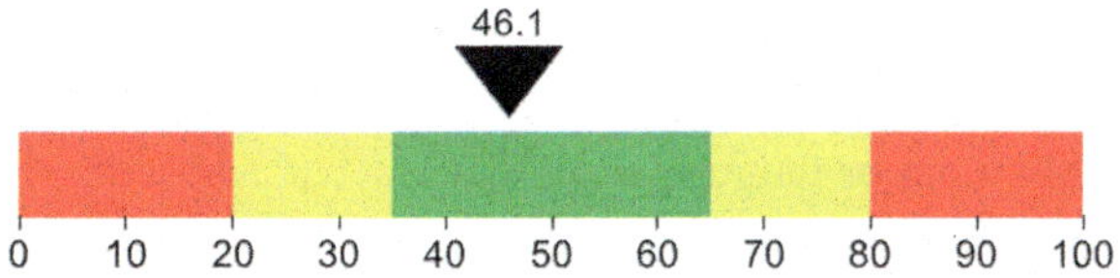

11.2.3 Degree of Stress

It is commonly assumed that it is not possible to avoid stress. It is a normal and integral part of personal and work life.

Stress reaction takes place automatically and it includes both positive (energizing, activation, etc.) and negative factors (excessive load).

Using the CA method, the level of **internally experienced stress** can be measured as well as **stress management** in relation to the outside environment.

Degree of stress (Fig. 11.4).

Degree of stress (Fig. 11.5).

Due to the fact that the CA method works with words, it is possible to measure the degree of stress in different environments, e.g. **stress in the company.**

Degree of stress (Fig. 11.6).

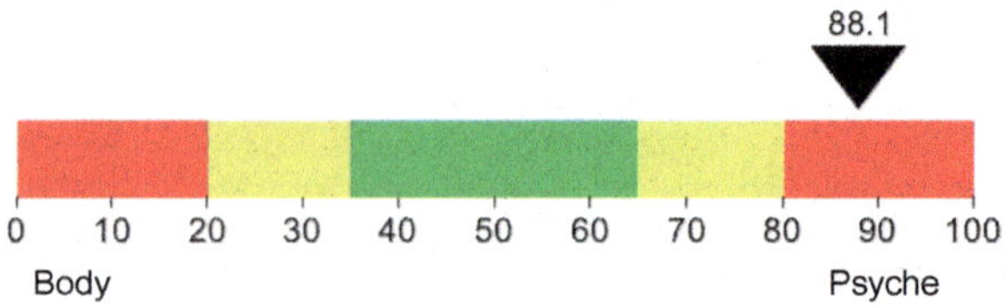

Fig. 11.8 The balance of body and psyche

Stressors can be highly individual, but using verbal diagrams (Sect. 11.2) the stress activator for the individually analyzed person within the company can specifically be identified.

This item can measure the amount of mental power of the clients and how they handle it.

Mental energy (Fig. 11.7).

At the moment, the client has a normal amount of stamina, which he uses in a sensible and balanced way. The resulting scale of energy gained and lost is well balanced.

11.2.4 The Balance of Body and Psyche

The item shows whether the client's body controls their psyche or vice versa (Fig. 11.8).

Such a high measured value means that the client overcomes sensations in the body (pain or fatigue) using their psyche and will. The balance is severely affected. Physical congestion is excessive and the respective client is unaware of the possible consequences. In other words, the psyche and/or will are controlling the body. This state indicates that it might not take long until serious health problems emerge.

11.3 Advantages of Use in Practice

Compared to conventional questionnaires, the CA method diagnostics has several advantages. The progress of the diagnosis feels more like a "game" than testing; thus it is a great advantage that clients' defenses are largely removed. Administration usually takes no longer than 20 min, it is simple, quick and understandable and the results are available in a few minutes from the end of testing owing to computer software. The principles of the CA method and subsequent evaluation allow us to see inner attitudes and experiences, which are not rationally controlled and influenced. Considering this aspect, we obtain results that far more accurately describe the real state of the client's consciousness. This enables us to select the intervention or prevention methods much faster and in a more targeted way. What is more, we cannot only measure both experiential and attitudinal parts of the consciousness, but also their implementation potency in a vast majority of items.

References

Fialová B, Šimonek J (2009) Profil jednotlivce, VOA a VOŠ Masarykova 10, Valašské Meziřící
Lüscher M (1971) Der Lűscher Test. Rowohlt Verlag GmbH, Persönlichkeitsbeurteilung durch Farbwahl. Reinbek bei Hamburg
Šimonek J (2007–2009) Soubor studijních materiálů pro výcvik Profil jednotlivce, DAP Services, Ostrava
Svoboda M (1999) Psychologická diagnostika dospělých. Prague, Portál

Part III
Biofeedback in the Work and Economic World

Chapter 12
Biofeedback: Measurement and Training Methods

Ingrid Pirker-Binder

Contents

The biofeedback measurement and training technology opens up promising opportunities in the combat of fatigue. The process triggered thereby is simple and leads to an understanding of inner psychological and physiological interactions in our body during work. This knowledge provides a new basis for individual personal development, self-management and self-control of one's body's energy efficiency, for the processing of emotions and a new basic understanding of regeneration and prevention.

I. Pirker-Binder (✉)
Saileräckergasse 43/26, 1190 Vienna, Austria
e-mail: office@pirker-binder.at

I. Pirker-Binder (ed.), *Mindful Prevention of Burnout in Workplace Health Management*, https://doi.org/10.1007/978-3-319-61337-6_12

In ergonomics, the use of biofeedback is indispensable for the facilitation of awareness of posture, unconscious tension and tenseness, unrhythmical breathing and related (psycho) somatic, stress and workplace-related complaints. New diagnostic and training methods such as the heart rate variability analysis make it possible to measure activation and stress during work and regeneration capacities during breaks and sleep. With this method, those interested are provided with direct feedback (Life Energy Analysis). Biofeedback training sensitizes the individual for the way to enhanced perception of the needs of the body and to more mindfulness in working life, more relaxed, mindful concentration and flow without unnecessary tension or tenseness.

The biofeedback measurement and training methods provide a solid framework for successful prevention and preservation of human resources in the world of work, for personal development, "high performance" and for the diagnostics of exhaustion. In high-risk professions accompanying strain measurement is a useful tool for the safety of those working in this profession, for the prevention of stress-related accidents or the processing of traumas after distressing events.

- **The company management should provide measures for personal development and an understanding of health care. What is more, the participation in such measures should be appreciated, i.e. with a reward system.**
- **Everyone is responsible for the health of his/her body and its energy.**

12.1 Why Biofeedback in the Work and Economic World?

Biofeedback is one of the most important achievements for the area of personal development, self and resource management. It is a tool that brings about a better understanding of the body and how it functions. By measuring changes in breathing, pulse rate, pulse amplitude or ECG, heart rate variability, skin conductance, muscle tension and finger temperature, the connection between psyche (thought patterns, emotions) and soma (body processes) become visible on the computer screen, understandable, controllable and thereby changeable.

The changes are measured during activation, stress, strain, in breaks and recovery times and during the regeneration phase of sleep. The knowledge about the interactions in one's own body should be the basis of any regeneration management.

- **Everyone knows what stress is and how it feels. But only a few know what regeneration is, how it feels and what you have to do for it.**

The human organism is a miracle of nature. It provides us with energy every day and is endowed with a high self-healing and regeneration potential—provided that it is not disturbed in its inner harmony. Here lies the root of the scourge of our modern age: the exhaustion of human resources due to carelessness regarding the needs of the body and the psyche.

The internal pressure (perfection pressure, pressure to perform, success pressure, etc.) of the working people, which seems to push them forward using a whip making them behave as if they were on the run, and the external pressure (e.g. time pressure), which is voluntarily accepted, are the protagonists in this scenario. It has not been about work-life balance for a long time. Work has generally crept into life and due to the modern media it can take place almost anywhere, regardless of time and place. The main advantage is a high flexibility as to when and where work is done. Still, why do people become exhausted?

The main reason is that we have not learned to regard life energy as a temporary gift. The importance of the preservation or the regenerative capacity of the organism on the one hand and a proper diet (sufficient macro- and micronutrients) only becomes evident, when the body and the psyche no longer cooperate and people become sick. Once the regenerative capacity starts decreasing, the energy production is disturbed. The organism reduces its performance capability to a low flame and if nothing changes, the system collapses at some point. The processes, which lead the working people to stay in chronic activation, are manifold; they are described in the first part of the book.

- **Biofeedback expands awareness, sensitizes perception and supports change processes. Heart rate variability measurement and training protect against burnout and are indispensable for high-risk professions.**

The application areas of biofeedback in modern enterprises are diverse and efficient. Examples include:

- **Personal development**:
  - emotions management (e.g. anger management)
  - attitude management
  - self-control, stress management, "high performance"
  - change processes
  - charisma

- **Regeneration management**:
- letting go (mental processes, quieting the mind through neurofeedback)
- relaxation (physical process of releasing muscular tension)
- regeneration (mindfulness, inner silence, active regeneration, coherence between breathing and heart beat)
- **Opening room** for creativity, inspiration, "becoming aware from the heart" (Scharmer 2009, p. 189 ff.)
- **Feedback on stress** at the workplace and the ability to recover during breaks and sleep.
  - Heart rate variability measurement (HRV)
  - Long-term measurement (24 h or longer) as protection from excessive strain and burnout: especially important in high-risk professions, for "high potentials", shift workers and travelers

- **Heart rate variability training** as a learning method for preserving human resources
  - as a training method for restoring recovery ability (coherence training between breathing and heart activity)
  - to increase perceptual capacity and mindfulness
  - A **must** in case of exhaustion to strengthen the parasympathetic system (braking and recovery system of the body)
- **Pain reduction/stress reduction**

Muscular tension due to non-resource-oriented working and inappropriate physical strain (e.g. shoulder or neck discomfort, headache, back pain, carpal tunnel syndrome etc.)

The gateway to efficient energy management is opened by the following three factors:

- thought processes
- perception and change of tension and inner pressure
- breathing as a time base and corrective

Biofeedback technology is a tool that is very often wrongly degraded to relaxation training or simple breathing training. But it is much more. Biofeedback serves people as a gateway to insight and, under expert guidance, it supports change processes leading to more self-awareness, self-control, self-management and responsibility for health.

Biofeedback technology is always embedded in an individual development concept and/or a training program such as in the processes of the Life Script Analysis, Work Script Analysis and Life Energy Analysis. It is a useful prevention tool in companies.

12.2 Biofeedback—Awareness Bridge to Freedom

The American Association for Psychophysiology and Biofeedback (aapb) places biofeedback in the fields of learning and improving individual health, performance capability and quality of life. Biofeedback is a scientifically recognized method that uses computers and sensors to make visible, and thus experienceable, recognizable and changeable, unconscious psychophysiological processes. Biofeedback provides the trainees with information, which enables them to learn (Pirker-Binder 2015).

> Biofeedback is a process that enables an individual to learn how to change physiological activity for the purposes of improving health and performance. Precise instruments measure physiological activity such as brainwaves, heart function, breathing, muscle activity, and

> skin temperature. These instruments rapidly and accurately "feed back" information to the user. The presentation of this information – often in conjunction with changes in thinking, emotions, and behavior – supports desired physiological changes. Over time, these changes can endure without continued use of an instrument ... Biofeedback has evolved from a fascination in the 1960s and 70s to a mainstream methodology today for treating certain medical conditions and improving human performance. This evolution has been driven by years of scientific research demonstrating that the mind and body are connected, and that people can be taught to harness the power of this connection to change physical activity and improve health and function. (Aapb 2011)

Elmar and Alyce Green write the following about the significance of biofeedback for awareness training:

> ... learning how to move the homeostatic balance points arbitrarily into a certain direction, physically, emotionally and mentally. One can imagine the spreading waves, which will finally influence our society, just like inner law and order spreads from the individual to the family and society. (Green 1999, p. 201)

They refer to the option of choosing one's thoughts, feelings and actions. And it is exactly what is possible in existential analysis and logotherapy by recognizing one's freedom: the freedom of deciding **for** or **against** something, for **this** path or a **different** one.

Biofeedback meets Frankl's requirements (Chap. 1) of the existential act. The people concerned receive information, which they can adopt a position on. They have the choice to recognize this information as an enrichment of their consciousness, to take a position and consider expanding the ways they deal with themselves, or not. During a biofeedback supported measurement or training procedure the responsibility always remains in the hands of the client. The therapist is a companion, explainer and supporter. Biofeedback is a method, which should always be embedded in a process and may never stand as a method on its own. Biofeedback supports the learners in their change process and thereby provides the necessary information for their learning progress.

Biofeedback is a measurement and training method for awareness raising and activating self-regulation and self-healing mechanisms.

> It has been shown that a certain degree of willful control over psychophysiological processes, which are normally not noticed, is possible once they are made conscious. One can also say that with the help of biofeedback training awareness can be expanded to normally unconscious processes in the body. (Green 1999, p. 66)

Green and Green are convinced that biofeedback technology can clarify a physiological principle.

> Any change in the physiological state is combined with a corresponding, consciously or unconsciously initiated change of the mental-emotional state, and reversely, any consciously or unconsciously created change of the mental-emotional state is followed by a corresponding change of the physiological state. In other words: mind and body build a uniform system. (Simonton 2005, p. 44)

> If nowadays medical experts in research can train the heart - or the feelings of the heart – to reverse a pathological condition, then also the practicing physicians need to learn that interrelationship between body and mind is more powerful than has been assumed so far.

> The explanatory models of psychosomatics, which refer to the mental-spiritual origin of pathological phenomena, have long been accepted; the biofeedback research provides the first medically verifiable evidence that mental forces are able to do both, heal diseases and cause them. (Barbara Brown in Simonton 2005, p. 44)

In their psychophysiological diagram (Fig. 12.1) Green and Green establish a relationship between the psychological areas of the conscious and unconscious and the different sectors of the arbitrary and involuntary physiological areas.

The peripheral nervous system is divided into the arbitrary and the autonomous, involuntary nervous system. The protagonists of the autonomous nervous system are the sympathetic and parasympathetic nerves; they control all the vital systems. Whereas the activity of the sympathetic nerve increases the activity or the tension in the body, the parasympathetic nerve reduces tension and initiates regeneration. The impulse of the sympathetic nerve is in the brain, i.e. in the hypothalamus. To reduce excessive energy or a high activation level in the body, the activity of the sympathetic nerve has to be reduced and the parasympathetic nerve, in particular the nervus vagus (10th cranial nerve) has to be strengthened. In biofeedback training, the smallest physiological changes are made accessible to conscious perception and thereby they are under self-control. Green and Green (1999) put the steps of learning self-control into a schematic diagram, which is shown in Fig. 12.2.

Green and Green differentiate in their model between conscious (whether perception takes place is at the will of the person concerned) and unconscious perception and between external influences (OUTS influences/events) and internal influences (INS influences/events). The two fields (emotional and mental reaction) are exactly on this line as they may occur both consciously and unconsciously. The

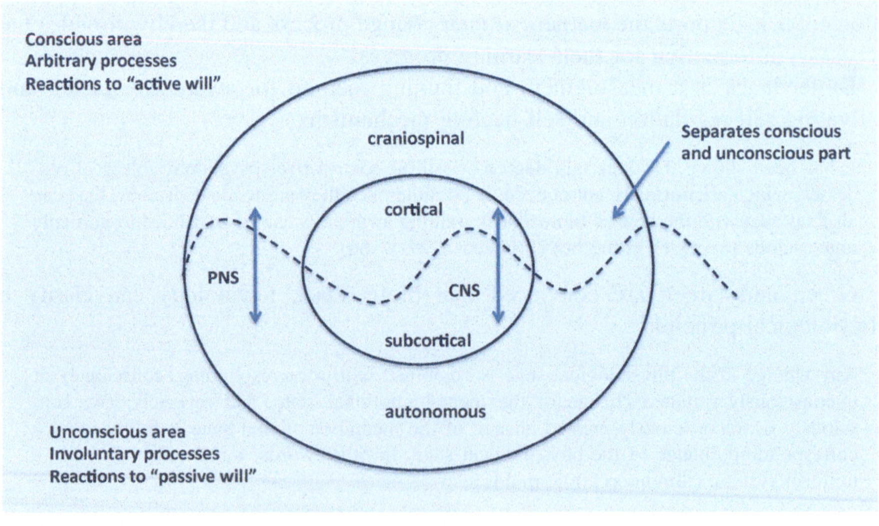

Fig. 12.1 Psychophysiological diagram. PNS: peripheral nervous system, CNS: central nervous system. Modified according to Green and Green (1999, p. 70)

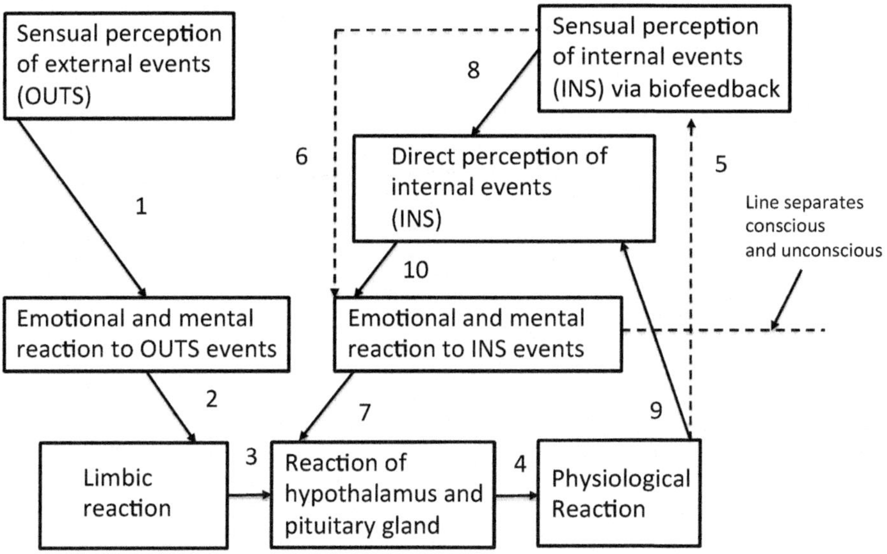

Fig. 12.2 learning of self-control (modified according to Green and Green 1999, p. 71)

limbic system is situated in the unconscious part. It is considered the behavioral assessment system of the brain and is also involved in affective and emotional behavioral control (Roth 1996, p. 197 and 2009, p. 15 ff.).

> The unconscious understood in terms of Freud's conceptions includes those psychological basic structures from a neurobiological and psychological view, which determine our character and personality, i.e. the way we react towards ourselves and our natural, and particularly, social environment, how we make commitments, learn impulse control and develop self-confidence and confidence in others. This is mainly related to the limbic system. (Roth 1996, p. 154)

The assessment system is inseparably linked with the memory system of humans, for memory is not possible without assessment, and any assessment necessitates memory. Earlier experiences and evaluations are saved in the memory and serve as a template for assessment of and behavior in new situations (Roth 1996, p. 198).

The hypothalamus is a part of the limbic system. It is responsible for the reward system and controls the production of endorphins. In another part of the limbic system, the Amygdala, vegetative and affective responses are controlled in combination with the reticular formation and the hypothalamus: an important function for the response to stress and stress management. Figure 12.2 shows the function using arrows.

Arrow 1: External stimuli are involved with both, more conscious as well as unconscious emotional and mental responses.

Arrow 2: The incoming stimuli are processed in the limbic system and lead to a reaction in the hypothalamus and pituitary gland (arrow 3). A physiological reaction (arrow 4) results.
Arrow 5: If the physiological reaction is reported to the respective person through biofeedback, there is a possibility (arrows 6 and 7) to learn new limbic responses. These change the reaction paths 3 and 4 and also the original physiological reaction.

This leads to a learning process that places the homoeostatic balance under willful control. In the process of learning the feedback via biofeedback devices is no longer necessary, as the respective person acquires the ability to practice self-regulation independently through increased sensitization for the incoming "IN-events".

> The new emotional reaction is connected with a new limbic response (arrow 7). It modifies the original limbic response (arrow 2). This new limbic response in turn affects the hypothalamus and pituitary gland secretion, which results in a new physiological state. This creates a closed cybernetic circle, which seems to close the normal gap between conscious and unconscious, arbitrary and involuntary processes. (Green and Green 1999, p. 75)

Biofeedback trains the sensitivity to internal conditions (arrow 8). Learning with biofeedback makes it possible to dispense with the paths 5, 6 and 8. The circle closes between arrows 9–10–7–3–4–9. In their model Green and Green also place a link to the **will**. Unconscious parts of the nervous system respond to the active will, while the normally unconscious parts respond to the passive will (Green and Green 1999, p. 77). The passive will can be developed by biofeedback. The authors distinguish between autogenic training which uses passive concentration as a means of change, and biofeedback training, which activates the passive will, that is, a change is facilitated, and the body works by itself.

According to Green and Green psychosomatic self-regulation follows this principle:

> Our will enables self-regulation in our body. The principle states that the body affects the mind and the mind influences the body and thereupon the new physical state in turn influences the mind, and so on. If the psychophysiological operations are connected to the will, psychosomatic self-regulation happens. (Green and Green 1999, p. 82)

In terms of existential analysis and logotherapy the biofeedback method works like a bridge. It makes connections between psyche and body visible and brings the unconscious and subconscious into consciousness. Knowledge gained thereby expands the freedom to decide between various options (Fig. 12.3).

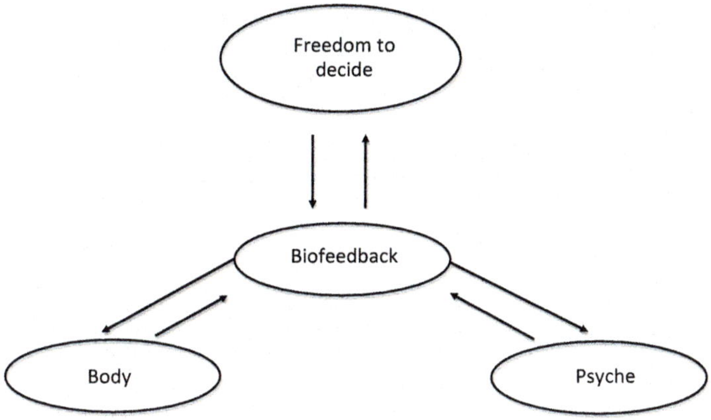

Fig. 12.3 Biofeedback and freedom to decide (Pirker-Binder)

12.3 Biofeedback—On the Way to Inner Resources

12.3.1 Biofeedback as a Measuring Instrument

The measuring possibilities of psychophysiological parameters are diverse. A first classification can be made according to the location of its usage. Everything measured on the head is covered by the term "neurofeedback", while everything measured on the body can be summarized with the term "multimodal biofeedback" (Figs. 12.4 and 12.5).

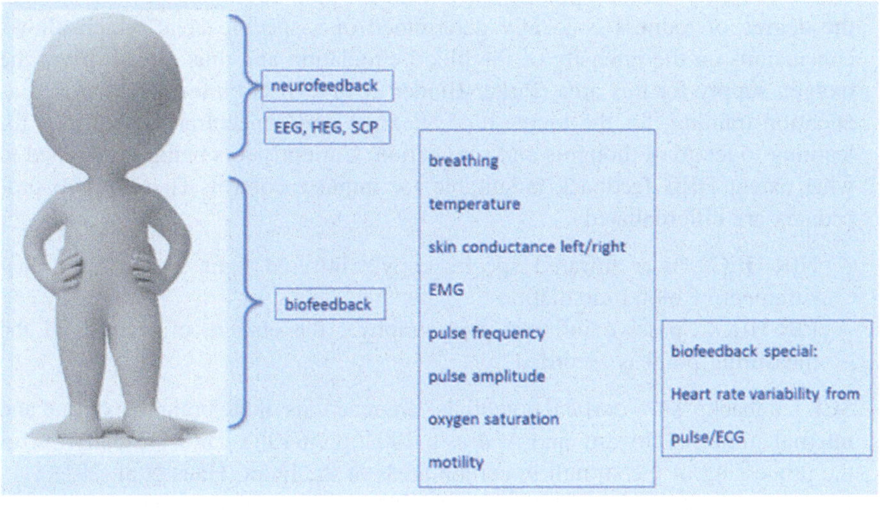

Fig. 12.4 Classification according to neurofeedback and biofeedback (Pirker-Binder)

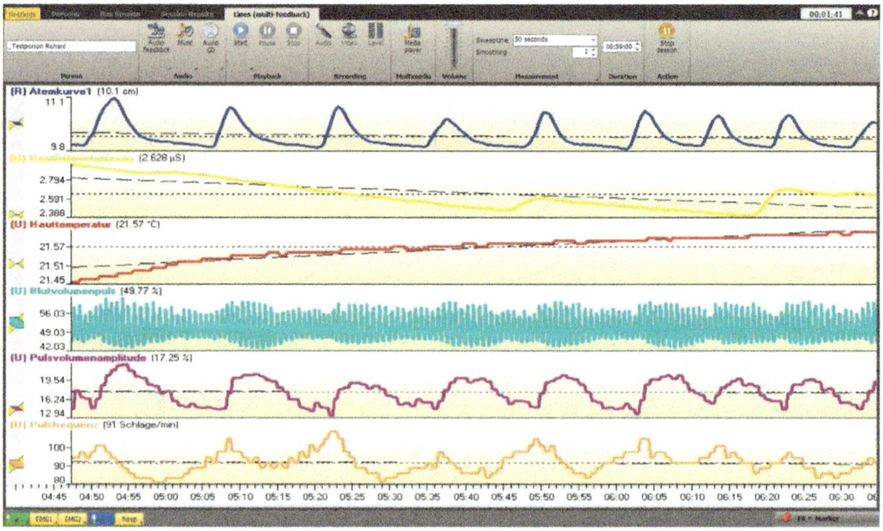

Fig. 12.5 Representation of biofeedback parameters on a computer screen. From top to bottom: breathing, skin conductance, skin temperature, blood volume pulse, blood volume pulse amplitude, pulse frequency. Source of image: Schuhfried GmbH. www.schuhfried.at

Neurofeedback includes:

- EEG feedback = neurofeedback: measurement of brainwaves, which are split up according to frequency components and fed back to the computer screen. The individual frequency components are allocated to different states of attention or consciousness, measured and submitted to training.
- HEG Feedback: hemoecephalography: with the help of red and/or infrared light the degree of redness is locally determined in a specific area, which allows conclusions on the intensity of the blood circulation and thus also displays the oxygen supply for this area (Pirker-Binder 2014). HEG biofeedback is used as attention training, for the increase of attention and concentration, but also for learning to let go of thoughts and rumination. Currently it is being researched to what extent HEG feedback is suitable for impulse control. Thereby two procedures are differentiated
  - NIR-HEG: "near infrared spectroscopy": infrared light is used for measurement of blood circulation
  - PIR-HEG: "passive infrared photography": the change of warmth at the measuring point is recorded
- SCP feedback: "slow cortical potentials" are reactions of the brain to external and internal stimuli (Schwartz and Andrasik 2003, p. 464 ff.). They basically mirror the processing of the stimuli in certain areas of the brain (Haus et al. 2013).

Multimodal biofeedback includes the following parameters:

- pulse frequency and pulse amplitude (ECG)
- breathing rate and breathing depth
- muscle tension
- skin conductance
- temperature
- oxygen saturation
- motility: the movement of the test person is recorded during the measurement

Heart rate variability biofeedback includes the following parameters:

- pulse
- ECG
- breathing

The time intervals between two heartbeats are measured as a peak-to-peak interval (RR interval) or an interbeat-to-interbeat (IBI) from the pulse. Subsequently the RR intervals are converted into frequency spectra using statistical processes and allocated to various areas.

In colloquial use, the visual representation of the heart rate variability measurement data (Fig. 12.7) is also called AutoChrone image (www.heart-balance.org).

Time-related representations, such as a histogram or Poincaré plot as non-linear methods (represents RR intervals in a coordinate system) and minimum and maximum heartbeat difference are a useful and necessary supplement for diagnostic analysis (Fig. 12.6a–d).

The individual frequencies can be read in Table 12.1.

The respective power of the frequency ranges is decisive for measurement and training.

"**High frequency**" (HF) refers to the activity of the paramagnetic nerve and expresses the adjustment of the heart rate to the respiratory rhythm. It is an expression of tonic vagal activity.

"**Low frequency**" (LF) corresponds to the so-called Mayer waves (represent the blood pressure regulating system), and they are associated with the activity of the sympathetic as well as the parasympathetic nervous system. In healthy people (at rest) the parasympathetic nervous system dominates the heart activity through the vagus nerve, i.e. 10th cerebral nerve.

> Mental stress loads are mostly controlled … by withdrawal of the vagus. Reductions of the HRV are an indicator for mental stress. In the case of acute stress, in situations of particular tension, the sympathetic nerve dominates. Everyday life is controlled by variations of the vagus. Accordingly, chronic stress leads to a chronic reduction of vagal activity without sympathetic activity increases. (Sroka 2002, p. 38)

Everyday strain in the lower and medium performance ranges (up to about a heart rate of 100/min) is primarily regulated by taking back the strong rest vagal tone. Only in the upper performance range (approximately in the upper third) is the

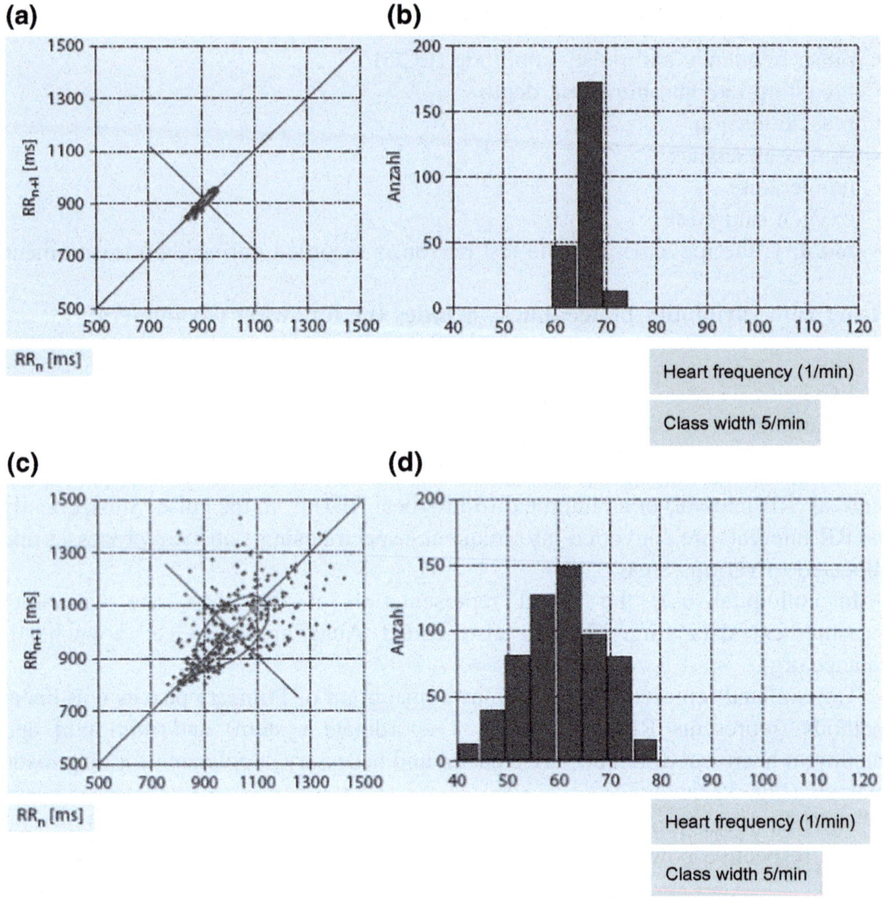

Fig. 12.6 a–d Histogram and Poincaré-diagram (Yang 2006) provide information on the heart rate variability. **a** Histogram showing the measurement of a bad HRV. **b** Poincaré-diagram showing the measurement of a bad HRV. **c** Histogram showing the measurement of a good HRV. **d** Poincaré-diagram showing the measurement of a good HRV. *Source of image* Company Biosign, by courtesy of Dr. Reinhard Beise

Table 12.1 Frequency ranges

ULF	Ultra low frequency	<0.003 Hz
VLF	Very low frequency	0.003–0.04 Hz
LF	Low frequency	0.04–0.15 Hz
HF	High frequency	0.15–0.40 Hz

sympathetic activity connected as well. In acute stress, in situations of particular tension, the sympathetic nerve dominates. Everyday life is controlled by variations of the vagal tone. Accordingly, it can be assumed that chronic stress leads to a chronic reduction of vagal activity without sympathetic activity increases (Sroka 2002, p. 133; Pirker-Binder 2008, p. 33).

The "**very low frequency**" (VLF) is associated with the vascular tone, temperature regulation and also inner psychic activities. A correspondence to the skin conductance value has also been established. (Pirker-Binder 2008, p. 33 ff)

The "**ultra low frequency**" (ULF) reflects the rhythm of the heart activity throughout the day. It is influenced by different factors such as light, food, hormones, etc.) The "ultra low frequency" can only be used in long-term measurement.

Circadian impulse generators control the daytime rhythms of the heart rate and other physiological values. The central circadian impulse generator is the suprachiasmatic nucleus of the ventral hypothalamus. A control element is the light-dark change, which is regulated by the eyes and/or by the melatonin released by the pineal gland (Weippert 2009, p. 8).

12.3.2 Biofeedback as a Prevention Variable

For an effective prevention process, it is necessary to correlate the information from the Life Script Analysis and the Work Script Analysis to the individual energy consumption or activation pattern. As shown in Chap. 2, the organism strives to always supply the energy needed for our thinking, feeling and acting. Prevention means in this context realizing and becoming aware

- of how much energy is consumed for what, whether the use is resource-oriented, or not,
- about the stress, which is individually put on the organism,
- of an opening to a more sensitive perception about the needs of the body,
- of how regeneration works,
- of strengths and weaknesses of the organism.

Everyone has a predisposition, a higher sensitivity, in one or the other functional system,

- for example, if heart function disorders occur frequently in a family, there might be an increased responsiveness in this organ system compared to other organ systems. Specifically, this means that in the case of system overuse this system sends a first alarm signal, such as increased blood pressure, extra systoles (beats). Additionally, tensions, migraine, irritable bowel syndrome, hypersensitivity in the vascular system, etc. can occur.

Biofeedback can, through observation or appropriate test procedures, provide information on how the body responds to stimuli and/or which system of the body is the fastest or the slowest to recover. This realization is integrated into awareness training. Thoughts, attitudes, assessments and expectations control the life energy use. Biofeedback uncovers these relationships, makes them visible on the computer screen and thus controllable.

Controllable impulse generators for energy input are

- cognitive processes,
- muscle tension,
- breathing.

From this follows that with the consideration of inner psychic patterns and mechanisms of regeneration a change process with regard to a resource-oriented use starts (that is, producing only as much energy as is really needed for the corresponding situation and practicing active regeneration), in which unconscious is brought into awareness.

- **Regeneration is more than relaxation; it virtually follows from the processes of letting go and relaxation.**

The learning process results from the understanding that life and daily routine follow a particular rhythm: a change between activation, deactivation and regeneration. If activation is kept up too long, depletion will occur. The inner resources are used up and eventually the human being falls ill. Thereby depletion can surface in different areas:

- problems with thinking, concentration and memory
- exhaustion of the energy production of the cell
- excessive activity of the sympathetic nerve, loss of the activity of the parasympathetic nerve
- physical discomfort and disease

A learning or cognitive process using biofeedback can be initiated in different ways:

- by observation,
- by suitable test methods,
- through a 24-h heart rate variability measurement.

12.3.3 Learning by Observation

During learning by observation, realization and understanding are facilitated by watching the change of the measured parameters. Therefore, the selection of the appropriate sensors is crucial. "Appropriate" means that the biofeedback therapist chooses the correct sensors for creating awareness of the desired situation. If anything is unclear, it has been proven most successful to choose as comprehensively as possible (i.e. using more than one sensor).

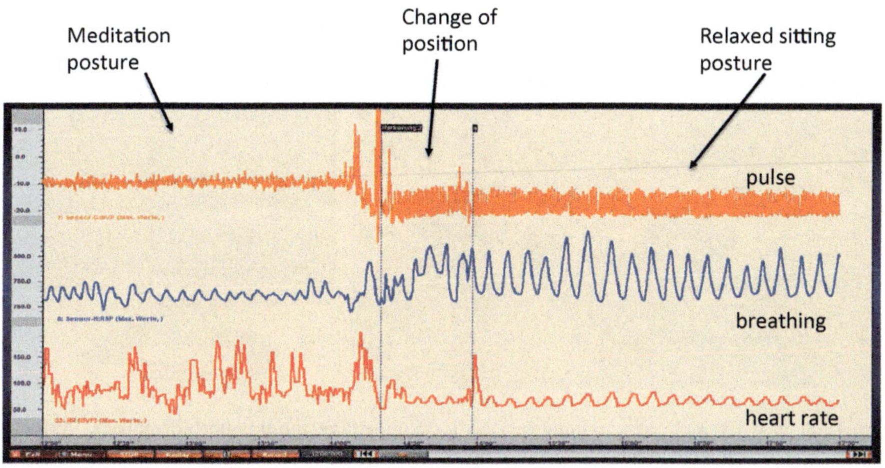

Fig. 12.7 Observation of breathing, pulse and heart rate during meditation posture and in relaxed sitting posture. Screenshot Nexus 10. Left: Meditation posture, middle: change of position, right: relaxed sitting posture (Pirker-Binder)

Figure 12.7 shows the measurement of a client who would like to ease his migraine by means of relaxation meditation. He is asked to practice his way of meditation while his breathing, pulse and heart rate are measured. In the screenshot (copy of the screen) it can clearly be recognized that there is no coherence between breathing and heart rate, a so-called RSA vibration (respiratory sinus arrhythmia, Chap. 5). Once the client starts to relax, focusing on letting go and breathing, the image changes; it indicates that the measured values oscillate with each other and that letting go, a coherence of breathing and heart rate, occurs in the body.

Through observation the client learns to understand the different reactions of his body and the meaning of letting go for a specific topic.

In sports, the strain of various functional systems of the body in different positions is measured and reported back so as to set a basis for "high performance" in the competition. Biofeedback is known in sports as a contribution to high-performance training but it could also be called ergonomics in sports.

- **The aim is to achieve best possible performance with the lowest possible energy input and correct muscle activity and corresponding mental effort.**

The same applies to people working on the PC, driving, working on the assembly line, during and after the shift work, during lectures, meetings, in trainings as a teacher, during leisure time sports, gardening, etc.—the list could be continued as desired. With Biofeedback it is the same as with competitive sports, i.e. it is always about the right energy input, perception, performance and regeneration (Fig. 12.8a, b).

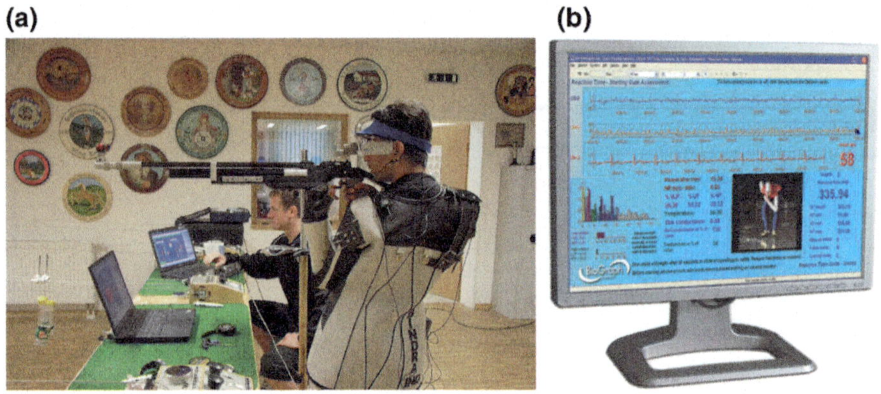

Fig. 12.8 **a**, **b** Example of a training session for competitive sports with biofeedback. Abhinav Bindra, the first Indian winner of the Olympic gold medal for single competition in air gun shooting is training with the sports psychologist Timothy Harkness. b screen with bio and neurofeedback for optimal competition preparation during the training of speed skaters. *Source of image* Courtesy of Thought Technology Ltd. (www.thoughttechnology.com)

12.4 Learning Through Appropriate Test Methods

For the acquisition of knowledge and the development of training steps biofeedback reaction tests can make a valuable contribution when used as an initial test. Various methods are used:

- passive tests
- performance-dependent tests
- combined tests
- 24-h heart rate variability measurement
- short-term measurement of heart rate variability

Depending on the initial situation and information interest a choice between different test procedures is available. In practical work it has proven useful to apply a test method which allows focusing on the individual expectation and the inner experience. This includes passive tests and a 24-h long-term measurement of heart rate variability.

12.4.1 Passive Test Methods

In the passive test method as few inputs as possible are directed towards the person to be tested, i.e. except for a little animation on the screen or few external verbal instructions. The goal is to recognize the change of the measured parameters through internal processing. Passive test methods are particularly suitable for detecting activation through anticipation (lat. "anticipo": to pre-empt), so-called expectation. An example is when the person concerned already gets nervous on Sunday afternoon when he thinks about the upcoming work on Monday.

In such a case a learning goal could be making a difference between creative thinking and visualization and putting oneself into alertness by activation. In this respect learning steps are learning to distance oneself and dealing with the topics of responsibility and inner peace.

The test situation procedure is divided into several steps. The person to be tested is asked to sit down as comfortably as possible into an easy chair. The sensors are chosen by the biofeedback therapist/trainer. The test sequence can be standardized, so that no intervention of the therapist is necessary during the test phase. The procedure is divided into five sections:

1. Relaxation phase. Screen displays the request, "Please relax, keep your eyes open and keep quiet as much as possible" (Movements influence the meaningfulness of the measured values).
2. Announcement phase. Information appears on the screen that the stress is coming soon. Afterwards, the screen returns to the image of the input phase. The client does not know when what kind of stimulus will come to him/her. At this moment the attitude of expectation of the test person begins.

An analysis of the data including the baseline can also show that the client already starts building up expectation before the actual start of the test (Pirker-Binder 2008)

3. Expectation phase.
4. Stimulus. An acoustic and visual stimulus is set as an orientation reaction that lasts a few seconds.
5. Recovery phase. A text field on the screen informs that the stress situation is over and advises to recover again.

In the evaluation it can be seen that after the announcement phase the skin conductance value (also considered an indicator of mental activity, ruminating) recovers very quickly and returns to the starting position, even after the stimulus. In the cardiovascular system an increase (heart rate increase, pulse and blood volume pulse constriction) like anticipation of a future stimulus can be seen during the expectation phase. In the following recovery phase the values return to the original level.

Different biofeedback suppliers offer different stress response tests in their program. If test methods are used, there should always be a clear definition of the goal, what knowledge should be acquired and what motion artifacts will be inherent (Fig. 12.9).

If the test person talks or moves, the validity changes. Having somebody do calculations or solve tasks, tests the performance or the knowledge or concentration of the relevant person. The inner experience is difficult to capture.

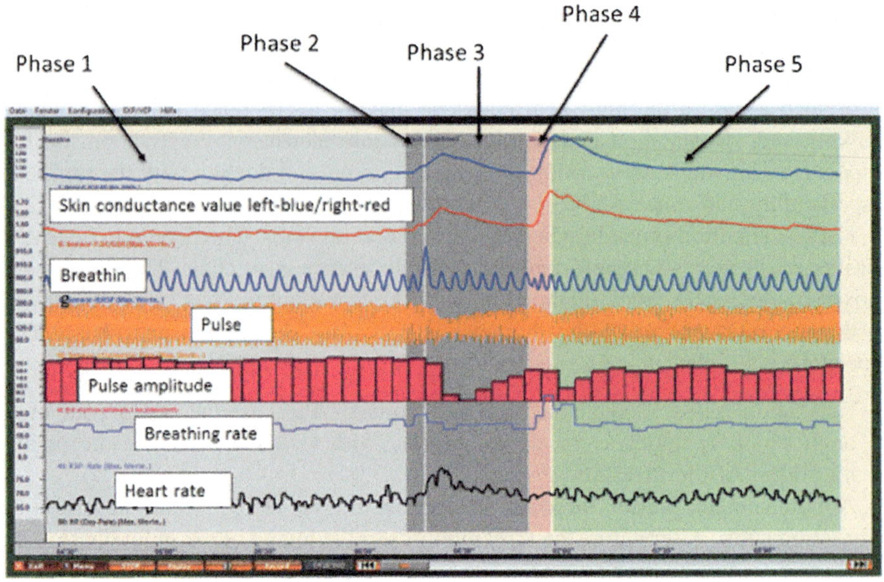

Fig. 12.9 Passive stress reaction test. Screenshot of Nexus 10 (Pirker-Binder)

- **It is very important to select carefully, what test in what form should provide what statement. The therapist should have a clear target definition.**

In training courses and supervision I have repeatedly experienced that participants conduct biofeedback test procedures without knowing or previously defining what statements should be made in the evaluation. For example, if the picture on the screen is changed in the expectation phase or even a second counter is displayed (counting until the appearance of the stimulus), the attention of the test person changes. He/she leaves the inner attention, to turn towards what is happening on the screen. In this case, no longer the innerpsychic processing is measured, but the processing of the information of the image or the processing of a particular task or concentrated attention to something specific in the picture.

- **For the orientation stimulus, objects or sounds that might cause negative or frightening associations should not be selected, such as spiders or sounds of war.**

12.4.2 Performance-Dependent Test Methods

With regard to performance-dependent procedures, a certain performance is demanded, such as calculating, solving brain challenges thinking about a negative event or a conflict, doing a preset test, giving a talk and many more. When such a procedure is used, the target of information acquisition has to be very clear. It is important to remember that the test persons move when solving the various tasks or prefer doing certain tasks to others. I would like to say, on a rather critical note, that the interpretation is difficult because it is the activation during solving a task that is queried, and not inner processes and motion artifacts, which additionally influence the result. It is often easy to confuse activation with stress. Different tasks demand a different level of energy.

This situation is quite different when a trained performance or self-control shall be examined. In such a case the task could be applying something learned previously, e.g. remaining calm when lecturing, not panicking with aircraft noise, not getting annoyed in a traffic jam and use it as a recovery pause instead etc. For impulse control in the case of addictive behavior biofeedback training and control are essential factors. Here pictures of beverages or, with regard to gambling addiction, videos of games, machines and casinos are displayed on the screen with the respective person being supposed to learn to control his/her addictive behavior.

In sports, biofeedback measurements are examined for performance check during visualizations as well. For example, a swimmer gets the task to imagine his/her 100 m distance. He/she keeps the eyes closed and imagines swimming the distance. On the computer screen it can accurately be identified when the athlete makes the turn in the pool.

Performance-related tests make sense to check the application of training content, or to clarify certain questions.

- **It could be said that performance-related tests answer the question how a person deals with a specific situation, whereas passive tests focus on evaluating the innerpsychic processes of a person during the test phases**.

Every test situation has to be considered with its overall connection to the question, and is only a part of information and knowledge acquisition. Activation must not be equated with stress.

In ergonomics performance-related tests can say a lot about stress at the workplace. In this case, it makes sense to measure and make visible the muscle tension during work. A reduction of stress can often be made clear by slight behavioral changes.

In the discussion, findings from the change of the parameters can be related to findings from the Life Script Analysis and Work Script Analysis.

12.4.3 Combined Test Methods

For information acquisition and training supervision combined test methods seem to be useful. Depending on which information is needed to bring unconscious processes to consciousness, different test variations can be combined or applied alternately. A central condition is, however, that the biofeedback therapist has adequate knowledge of psychosomatic relationships, biofeedback application, design of training units and interpretation of the data obtained and a clear idea of which information should be acquired from the evaluation of the measured results.

12.4.4 Heart Rate Variability Measurement: 24-h Long-Term Measurement

In recent years multimodal biofeedback has been at the forefront as a learning method for controlling psychophysical activity. The goal has always been the change of a certain level; e.g. the reduction of muscle tension or the increase of finger temperature.

Heart rate variability measurement and training pursue a different goal. The focus of research, training and therapy are the measurement and positive manipulation of the resonance variability of the heart rate. The aim is to strengthen the endogenous physiological control mechanisms (Lehrer et al. 2007, p. 228 ff.).

A major advance in heart rate variability-biofeedback was initiated by the space industry. Vaschillo et al. (1983, pp. 257–265) conducted the first studies in the Soviet Union when the heart rate variability of cosmonauts was used as a measure of the functional capacity of the autonomous system. Influenced by Vaschillo, Lehrer and his colleagues began to research this method in America (Lehrer et al. 2000, p. 171, 2003, pp. 796–805; Gevirtz and Teacher 2003, pp. 212–244).

> When a biological variable rises, a regulatory reflex is triggered that makes it fall again; and, as it falls, a complementary reflex makes it rise. This sequence causes a pattern of continuing oscillation and also gives us a window to the body's processes for self-regulation and homeostasis. Any one physiological function is usually controlled by multiple reflexes. One could think of them as multiple backup systems for homeostatic control; hence the complexity of the oscillatory patterns, as well as the amplitude, reflects healthy adaptiveness … When the body is well regulated, these oscillations have a complex pattern and are of relatively high amplitude. Reductions in either amplitude or complexity are a sign of vulnerability, indicating that the body's self-regulatory mechanisms are damaged or inefficient and unable to withstand the vicissitudes of stress, disease, in jury, and so forth. (Lehrer 2007, S. 227)

While in America the heart rate variability biofeedback training has been paramount, the research development in Austria focuses more on recording the heart rate variability over 24 h. A great effort is being made to implement this measurement procedure in the prevention and evaluation of therapeutic advances. To my knowledge biofeedback research and training and heart rate variability research and training are regarded as two separate areas, with an increasing tendency towards measurement.

Unfortunately, heart rate variability training has not been integrated into the various therapeutic training directions of psychotherapy or psychosomatic psychotherapy (currently, this term is still not generally used) in Austria. Also, the 24-h long-term measurement is primarily used by business consultants, coaches and psychologists in order to obtain information on the strain on employees. It has to be critically noted that there are no compulsory trainings on the applicability and evaluation of biofeedback measurement data and biofeedback training (heart rate variability measurement and training is a part of biofeedback) for the application and interpretation of heart rate variability measurements. In Austria only certain professions such as psychotherapists, doctors, health psychologists and a limited group of body therapists are entitled to apply these methods in the therapeutic process.

The development of biofeedback measuring devices for the detection of heart rate variability has experienced a huge boom in recent years. The fact that the evaluation and interpretation of the obtained data is not easy, poses a problem. Another weak point is that there are no generally valid statements on the parameters collected, as there is no data pool, which can be resorted to. Each device/software producer more or less draws on their own data. The "Task Force of the European Society of Cardiology and the North American Society of Pacing and Electrophysiology" already set standards for statistical data collection (European Heart Journal 1996) in 1996.

- **Heart rate variability measurement, especially over 24 h, is an excellent tool to gain insight into the performance capacity of the autonomic nervous system, the psychological strain on the body and into sleep quality as an important regeneration factor: as vegetative functional diagnostics or as chronobiological regulation diagnostics, depending on which side one starts.**

Heart rate variability measurements, which more and more companies are offering to their employees, allow statements about the regulation of activation, deactivation and quality of sleep. However, it must be stated that a human being cannot be reduced to a key figure. There is currently a tendency in economic circles to recognize this measuring method for health benchmarking. This could mean that the health of the employees is reduced to a reference number. Here, ethical issues come to the foreground, i.e. how to deal with data obtained with this technology. On the one hand, it is a matter of protection, and on the other hand the psychophysiological data should be interpreted. It must not be forgotten that behind the measured data and the reference numbers there is a human being. This technology provides information that only becomes valuable, meaningful and important through individual anamnesis discussions with experienced therapists. In business consultancy it makes sense to use heart rate variability measurements in prevention, personality formation, ergonomics and in the detection of fatigue symptoms.

Nevertheless, I would like to note here that exhaustion might also occur even though the heart rate variability measurement showed excellent values. Such a phenomenon can be explained in so far as exhaustion of resources can take place at different levels, which more or less intensively also affect the vegetative nervous system, for example disbalance of the energy supply of the cells etc.

It is also worth noting that the health of humans cannot be reduced to a reference number. On a critical note, it should be considered that there are different causes of excessive activation of the sympathetic nerve or disturbed sleep. For example, old traumas or other psychological strain latent in the subconscious, play a role as well (Fig. 12.10).

- **Measurement and interpretation must be treated carefully and fully appreciate the measured person. Premature conclusions must be avoided.**

Depending on the biofeedback measuring device and the stored software, different data are collected and evaluated. The pictorial representation gives a first impression. The example analysis shows the measurement of a 42-year-old man (Fig. 12.10), father of a family, with a fatigue syndrome. The evaluation is carried out according to statistical specifications in frequency domains and, depending on the software provider, also in time domains. For representation all measured heartbeats are submitted to a frequency analysis and subsequently evaluated and proportionally allocated to sympathetic and parasympathetic activity:

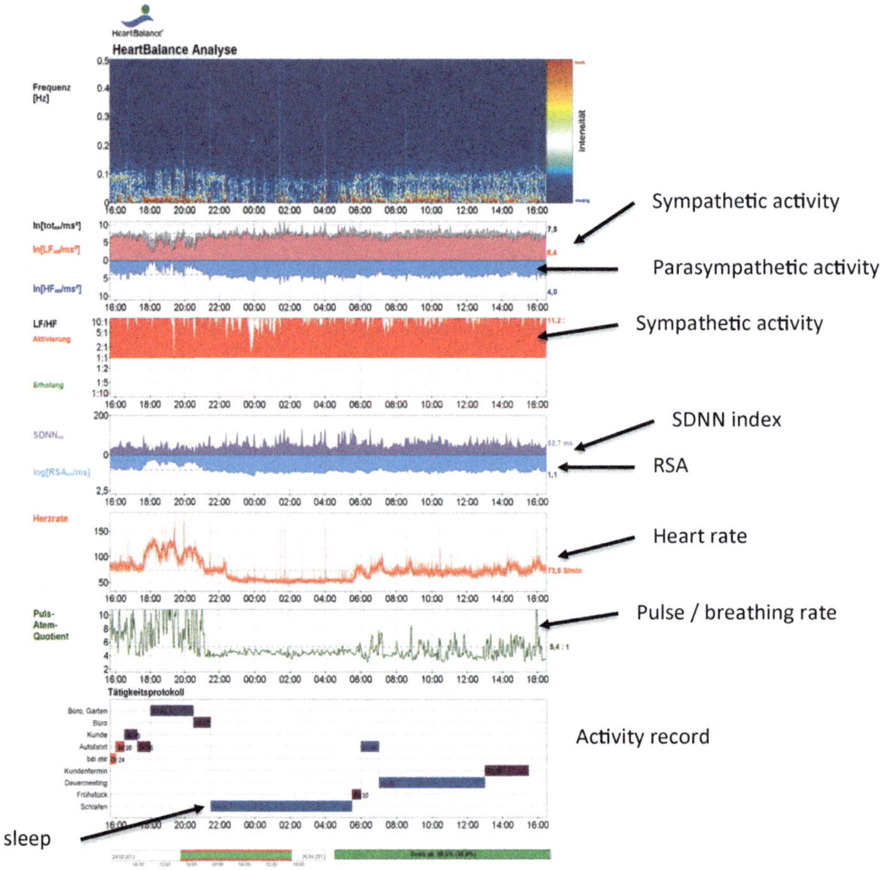

Fig. 12.10 Example of a 24-h heart rate variability measurement by Pirker-Binder with HeartMan (by company HeartBalance Innovations GmbH)

- In (tot_{RR}/m^2): total power divided into In (LF_{RR}/m^2) and In (HF_{RR}/m^2)
- LF/HF: shows the relationship between sympathetic and parasympathetic nervous system. In the American literature it is somewhat controversial to use this value as a core statement:

> … use the LF:HF ratio as a measure of autonomic balance, there is some doubt about validity of this use, particularly in the supine position … because there is evidence that sympathetic system contributes only minimally to supine HRV (Myers et al. 2001, S. 62–75).

- Not all providers offer the evaluation of a further subdivision, a separate evaluation of the VLF, "very low frequency" and the LF, "low frequency"; however, in terms of information this would be very important, since this area is predominantly allocated to the sympathetic nerve, while in the LF range sympathetic and parasympathetic are represented.
- SDNN index: SDNN index is the mean value of the standard deviation of all RR intervals for all 5-min sections of a 24-h measurement (Eller-Berndl 2010, p. 104)
- Heart rate: is calculated from the R-R intervals
- log RSA_{RR}/m^2: statistical calculation of RSA
- QPA: pulse-breath ratio represents the ratio (coherence) between heart rate and breathing; a ratio of 4:1 in sleep is desired
- Vegetative quotient: relationship sympathetic to parasympathetic

All the collected key figures are compared with a database, allocated according to age and gender and evaluated. A weak point of the evaluation is that there are different databases that are partly not created along uniform criteria. This means that evaluations of different providers cannot and should not be compared with each other. However, if several measurements are made with the same person at different times, a trend can be realized, i.e. the current status can be assessed much better.

With the newly launched HeartSensor by HeartBalance it is possible to record a medical ECG, but also a separate evaluation of the individual frequencies. Another advantage is the simplicity of the measurement.

Electrodes to not have to be attached any more; also movement, position, temperature and air pressure can be measured.

A good overview is obtained if in addition to the HRV evaluation also time-related parameters (in the form of a histogram, etc.) are displayed.

For the planning of preventive measures and/or intervention measures, it is necessary to take further diagnostic measures in addition to vegetative functional diagnostics by means of heart rate variability measurement over 24 h:

- the therapeutic conversation,
- questionnaires on work experience and life satisfaction, etc.,
- information from the Work Script Analysis,
- information from the Life Script Analysis,
- medical clarification.

12.5 Biofeedback as a Training Method for Prevention of Exhaustion

In the prevention of exhaustion biofeedback training has an important and heart rate-biofeedback training a special position. It can be divided into three different training areas:

- preservation or restoration of the balance of the autonomous nervous system by internal coherence of the individual oscillation pattern in the organism. This includes the respiratory sinus arrhythmia (RSA) and heart rate variability biofeedback training (HRV-BF).
- perception or awareness training: multimodal biofeedback or perception and control of the energy consumption, the inner peace as well as learning regeneration.
- biofeedback in ergonomics: here, the focus is especially on the perception of muscle tension and learning a situation-adjusted posture and muscle tension. Also, the issue of dysponesis (tension as a protection mechanism) can be mentioned here.

In a training program, these three different training contents are properly integrated into each other, so as to achieve an overall effect.

- **Inner peace and control over the autonomous nervous system can only be achieved when the whole organism is in resonance**.

The idea behind the 24-h heart rate variability measurement is the attempt to detect strain of the vegetative functional capacity early on and to inform the affected people, or to initiate training programs. It is always about measuring the oscillation capacity of the autonomous nervous system, which is an essential part of the regulatory reflexes of the organism.

> These oscillations represent the body‘s self regulatory reflexes. When the body is well regulated, these oscillations have a complex pattern, and are of relatively high amplitude (Lehrer 2007, p. 227).

Another important rhythm is the 90–120-min rhythm, which appears very clearly in the structure of the night sleep. A rhythm of parasympathetic (green) and sympathetic (red) system expresses deep sleep and REM phases. This rhythm is influenced chronobiologically and controlled via the autonomic nervous system.

It is called BRAC (Basic Rest and Activity Cycle), i.e. a basic relaxation and activation rhythm. This important rhythm represents the balance between activation and recreation in people and provides for the long-term health and sustainable performance capability of the organism.

This rhythm, i.e. the ability of people for activation and performance, deactivation, regeneration and relaxation, depends on the regulatory capacity of the autonomic nervous system.

- The regulatory capacity of the autonomic nervous system becomes one of the most important parameters for the assessment of longer-term stable health.

Figure 12.11 shows a comparison between good and poor regulation capability. Poor regulatory ability can be caused by chronic activation, stress, over-training of athletes or traumatic experiences, allergies or physical disorders.

The process of reducing the vital potential can lead to psychological and physical deficits and disorders. Figure 12.12 shows in an ideal-type manner the course of good vitality (stage 1) up to burnout (stage 12). The reduction in the course of each stadium becomes clearly visible.

- **The goal of a training program with heart rate biofeedback in prevention can be defined as the preservation and/or restoration of the regulatory capacity of the autonomic nervous system, the reduction of stress-induced and psychosomatic complaints and an increased perception of health.**

Due to the results of the research on heart rate variability two training steps have been established in biofeedback training:

- Respiratory Sinus Arrhythmia (RSA)—biofeedback training
- Heart rate variability biofeedback training

Fig. 12.11 *Image source* Courtesy of HeartBalance Innovations GmbH (www.heartbalance.org)

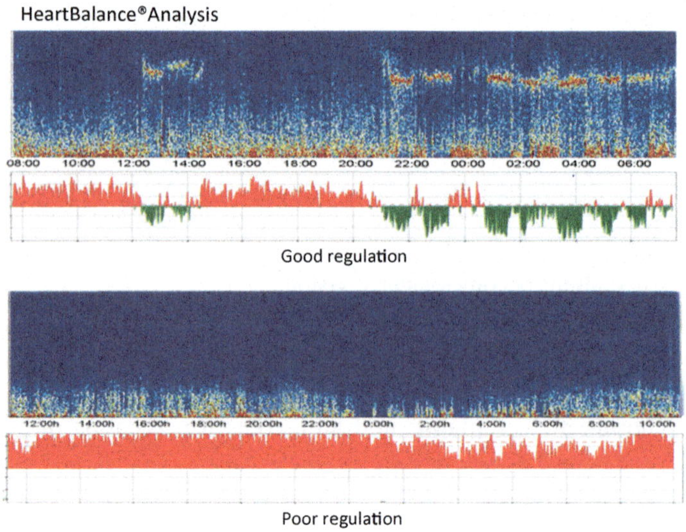

Fig. 12.12 Good and poor regulatory capacity compared. *Image source* By courtesy of HeartBalance Innovations GmbH, www.heartbalance.org

12.5.1 Respiratory Sinus Arrhythmia (RSA)

Respiratory sinus arrhythmia means the change of the heart rate by the breathing; that is, the heart rate increases during the inhalation phase and decreases during the exhalation phase (Porges 1995, pp. 225–233, 2010). The RSA, which is influenced by the breathing, appears at a breathing rate from 6 to 24 breaths per minute in healthy people, which corresponds to the range of "high frequency" (HF) 0.15–0.4 Hz on the frequency band.

The power of the RSA is considered the strength of the parasympathetic system ("vagal tone"). The RSA is influenced by the vagus nerve (10th cranial nerve), which, in the exhalation phase, is responsible for the release of acetylcholine, the transmitter substance of the parasympathetic nervous system (Fig. 12.13).

However, merely determining the strength of the vagal tone through RSA is not always easy:

> It is important to consider respiration rate while evaluating HRV as a measure of autonomic function. If increases in RSA occur independently of respiration rate and are coupled with decreases in HR, then one can confidently interpret these effects as reflecting increased vagal tone. (Lehrer 2007, S. 229)

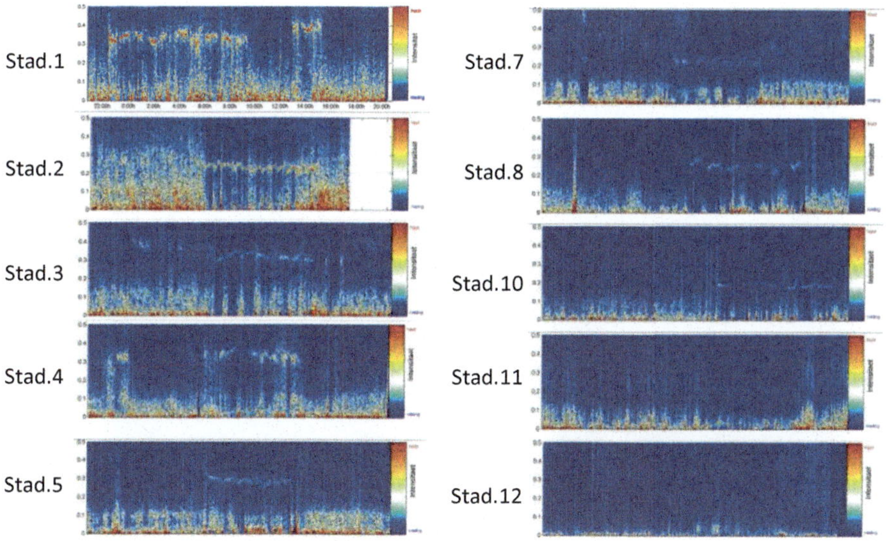

Fig. 12.13 Simulation of burnout. *Image source* By courtesy of HeartBalance Innovations GmbH, www.heartbalance.org

12.5.2 Heart Rate Variability-Biofeedback Training

In addition to respiratory sinus arrhythmia, the heart rate variability is affected by the baroreceptors. They control the blood pressure and are located in the aortic arch (influenced by the vagus nerve) and in the carotid sinus (influenced by the glossopharyngeal nerve).

The baroreflex can be represented in the "low frequency" area 0.04–0.15 Hz, with a peak at 0.1 Hz. The power of the baroreflex is an indicator for the adaptability of the cardiovascular system to life's challenges. The peak at 0.1 Hz means that at this frequency coherent oscillation occurs between heart rate and blood pressure (Vaschillo et al. 2002, pp. 1–27 and 2004, pp. 1385–1386).

> We have found that the phase relationship between HR and blood pressure oscillations at the resonant frequency (and only at this frequency) is exactly 180°, that the phase relationship between HR oscillations and respiration is exactly 0° with inhalation coinciding with HR accelerations, and that the highest amplitudes of Biofeedback-produced HRV are achievable when people breathe at this frequency. Thus is associated with increases in HR (presumably driven by respiration-RSA) and decreases in blood pressure. The decrease in blood pressure then stimulates the BRs (Baroreflexes- added by author), so that they also produce increases in HR at this time, thus enhancing the respiratory-induced increases in HR. (Lehrer 2007, S. 231).

Such coherence, also known as cardiac coherence, happens at a breathing rate of around 6 breaths per minute. This breathing rate, or "**resonant frequency**", is

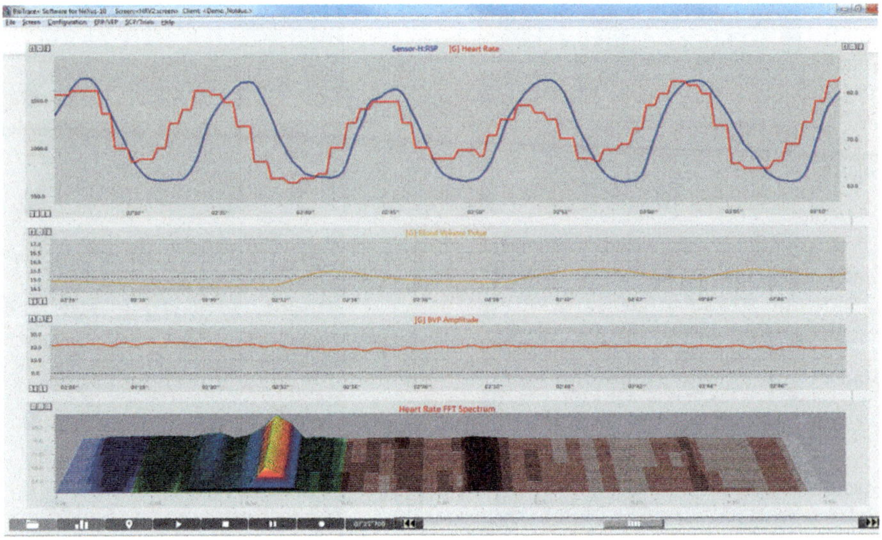

Fig. 12.14 RSA training and power spectra/frequency analysis, screenshot. *Image source* By courtesy of Mind Media www.mindmedia.nl

individual and differs between 4.5 and 7 breaths per minute (Johnson and Piscataway 2000; Harvard Business Review 2015; Fig. 12.14).

Heart rate variability training in the area of "resonant frequency", i.e. the breathing rate, which enables the highest amplitude in the RSA, leads to

- strengthening of the vagus nerve,
- high amplitudes in the heart rate,
- higher heart rate variability,
- strengthening of the pulmonary function,
- strengthening the baroreflex,
- a "mindful mental state" (Gevirtz, Lehrer in Schwartz and Andrasik 2003),
- an increase in health,
- a reduction of stress-induced and psychosomatic complaints,
- and blood pressure regulation.

New research approaches by Vaschillo (2002 in Schwartz and Andrasik 2003, p. 248) deal with influences of the baroreflex system and blood pressure oscillations of around 0.05 Hz. The research results might prove that special heart rate variability training in this frequency range also greatly affects the strength of the baroreflex and the control of the autonomic nervous system.

- **It is to be noted that for efficient training not only well-equipped biofeedback devices are necessary, but therapists who can operate them and are able to design useful training concepts.**

Efficient heart rate variability biofeedback training requires consciousness and perception training. Without proper breathing, mental, psychological and physical letting go, the desired success is very difficult to achieve. The goal should be life and wellbeing without the support of devices. Inner mindfulness and concentrated serenity should be our daily companions without having to practice continuously. This requires professional support during change processes with biofeedback. Learning and discovering with biofeedback should be an integrated component of prevention programs. Advisors and coaches should undergo self-awareness training before practical application of measuring or training methods.

Patient Report September 2015

In November 2004 I suffered a hypertension crisis and was admitted to hospital. After my condition had stabilized, the treating physicians prescribed blood pressure medicines. These should keep my blood pressure stable during the next few years. With continuously rising stress at work the dose kept being increased over the years until it reached a level in the spring of 2015 that I no longer wanted to increase. A further increase of the dose had only resulted in short-term improvement. The use of psychotherapeutic drugs did indeed have a positive effect, but seemed to me no viable alternative.

At the advice of my general practitioner, I decided to try biofeedback. The training should, on the one hand, provide me with an instrument for extreme stress situations and, on the other hand, it should help to freeze the drug dose, which had been increasing in recent years, or, ideally, even reduce it.

After an initial talk with Ms. Mag. Dr. Pirker-Binder, we decided on a training series of ten sessions. These were divided into an analysis of the causes of stress and corresponding respiratory training (heart rate variability biofeedback training, therapist's note). Both parts were necessary for me to recognize where my problems were in the daily workflow or in stress management. The sessions took place at intervals of two to three weeks.

The training quickly showed that I could positively influence my body's regeneration system. I started with daily breathing exercises before and during work, measured my blood pressure and my finger temperature (part of the hand warm-up training) at the same time every day and followed the instructions during the daily endurance training. The records rapidly showed significant improvements in blood pressure, so that I started the next step, which was measuring my blood pressure at different times of the day and indicating particularly stressful days in my notes.

Spiritual anchors like "The anger over the mistakes of others makes sure my mood is indirectly controlled by these people", or "Keep working slowly; not everything has to be finished immediately" helped me with upcoming anger or stress, or avoided such a crisis situation all together. Scheduled breaks and a relaxed sitting posture at the PC have become important for me to facilitate mental letting-go and relaxation in between.

The analysis of the blood pressure values after a recording phase of three months showed that my values had not only normalized, but also sunk. My physical wellbeing has risen significantly. The training has helped me to better manage my stressful everyday life and to use my energy more efficiently and purposefully. In consultation with the general practitioner we therefore began to reduce the medication on individual days and on weekends. The lower dose has so far had no effect on the blood pressure values.

Development of blood pressure values:

Apr.15: 150/100 (before the training)
Jul.15: 128/81 (after 5 weeks of training)
Dec.15: 119/71 (after 5 months of training)

Different biofeedback units are available for individual heart rate variability training at home. These small appliances (www.vital-monitor.com or www.heartmath.org) are used for the reduction of stress-induced and psychosomatic complaints (according to a predefined plan of the treating therapist) and/or for health control and sports training control. These small appliances are easy to use via mobile phone or tablet. Based on the progressive graphs the daily stress and regeneration factor can be read. It is particularly exciting to see the course of the biological age ("bioage"), which results from daily measurement and analysis of the statistical evaluation of peers. Stress after an intensive working day or too intensive sports activities can be recognized quickly, but also the efficiency of active regeneration units (Fig. 12.15a, b).

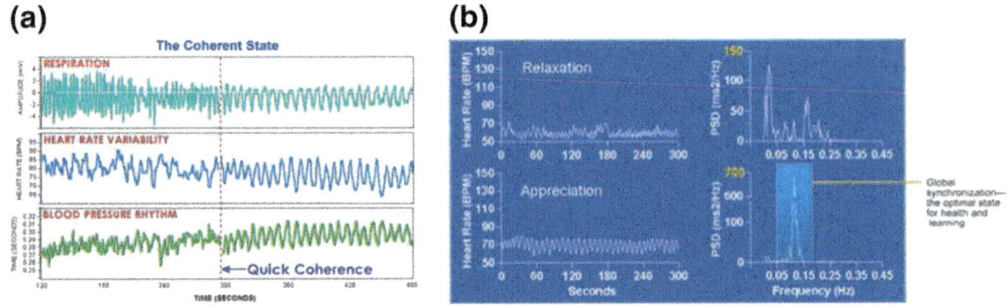

Fig. 12.15 **a**, **b** Graph a shows changes during heart rate variability training or coherence training, namely changes in breathing (respiration), heart rate variability and in the blood pressure rhythm. Specific training helps to quickly get from a strained to a harmonious, coherent state. All three rhythms are synchronized. To the left of the marker all rhythms are unsynchronized as they occur in stress situations. To the right of the marking line one can see how coherently and synchronously the rhythms appear in a balanced state. The aim of heart rate variability training is to achieve this coherence as often as possible during the day to relieve the body. **b** shows the difference between "relaxation" and "appreciation" in the frequency spectrum. The expression of the vagal tone (expressed by the RSA, is usually in the high frequency range (HF) (between 0.15 and 0.4 Hz) slips into the "low frequency" range during this breathing training in conjunction with heart rate variability training. *Image source* By courtesy of HeartMath Institute (www.heartmath.com)

12.6 Awareness and Consciousness Training

Awareness and consciousness training is done using multimodal biofeedback training. Thereby the change of the individual parameters is observed and practiced in small steps. The Life Script Analysis and Work Script Analysis provide preliminary data, also combined with 24-h heart rate variability measurement and a consultation. It is of fundamental importance to clarify with the trainee before the start of the training the contents and connections between physical, psychological and mental condition and to define the goal for change, whether it be anger or emotion management, learning concentrated serenity, mindfulness, distancing from what is going on or the reduction of muscle tension. Every training step has a relationship as its goal, especially for letting go of inner pressure:

- Respiratory training: general oscillation ability, inner peace, and precursor to HRV training
- EMG training = perception of tension and reduction of muscle tension
- Hand warming = general relaxation and uncramping
- RSA training: harmonization, strengthening the parasympathetic system
- Skin conductance: reduction of mental tension, reduction of a sympathetic over excitation
- Combination with HEG-training and neurofeedback for special issues

Helpful strategies for self-control are supported by biofeedback training (Pirker-Binder 2008) (Fig. 12.16a, b).

In awareness and consciousness training the learning content is intensified self-awareness, a balance between brain and heart and body-mind balance (psychosomatic competence), the return to one's own needs, support in the processing of old conflicts and, above all, letting go of inner pressure in the workplace.

- **Heightened self-awareness in the sense of psychosomatic competence increases responsibility for one's own health. Biofeedback shows the way to self-help**.

Control of one's individual life energy can be named as the paramount goal, i.e. realizing how much energy is necessary for what task and life situation as well as avoiding long-term tension and stress.

- **Dysponesis—protective function of the body**

Whatmore and Kohli (1974, 1979) coined the term dysponesis in 1974, which still is not represented in the health literature and German-language research. Dysponesis ("dys": bad, faulty, false, "ponos": effort, work, energy) is a reversible pathological condition due to errors in energy consumption, which is disadvantageous on the nervous system and the control of the organ functions.

> As unhealthy strain, the effort to give even more or to grit the teeth, triggers functional disorders in the organism. It is often unclear whether we are dealing with inherited, constitutional characteristics or effort patterns acquired in the course of life. Dysponesis is related to physical, emotional and mental reactions. Unhealthy, i.e. wrong, efforts then exist

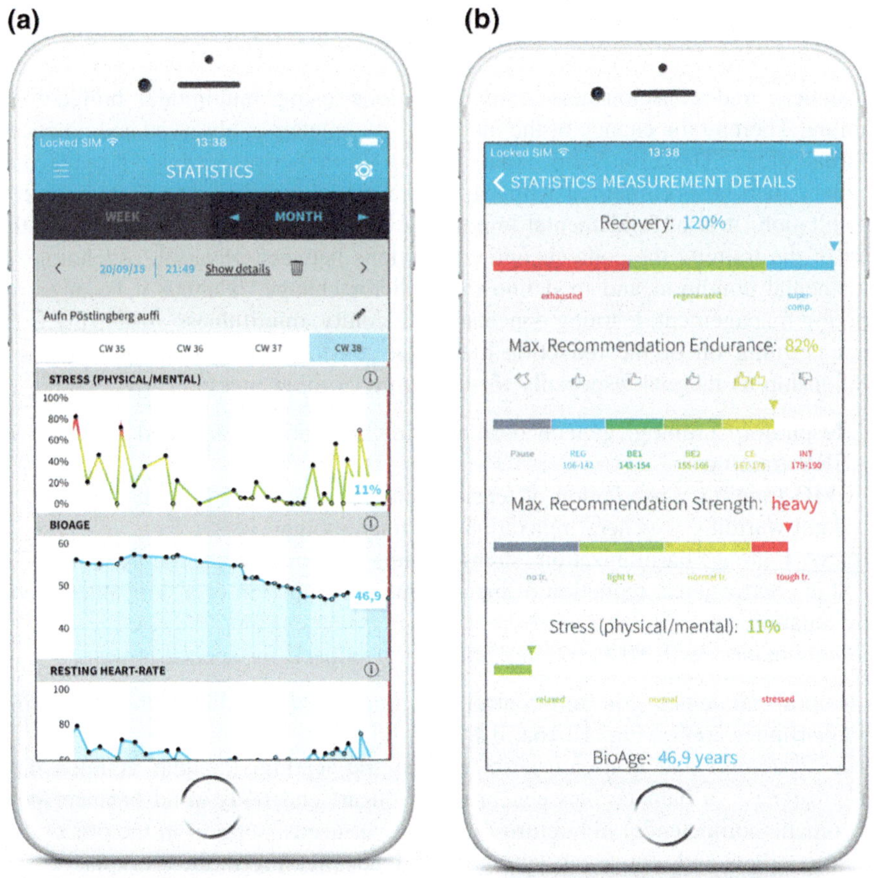

Fig. 12.16 **a**, **b** Based on the progressive graph the daily stress and regeneration factor can be read. Calculating the biological age is particularly exciting. *Source of image* By courtesy of Pulse7 GmbH

> mainly from errors in nerve impulses (action potentials) in nerve tracts, which include motor and premotor cortex neurons, pyramidal and extrapyramidal strands up to the peripheral musculature. These nerve pathways are involved in all conscious motor activities. (Whatmore and Kohli 1974).

Whatmore could prove that on the one hand dysponesis represents a safety mechanism, namely at the beginning of the so-called fight/flight mechanism, but also develops from itself by means of hereditary disposition as a reaction against stress, through illness and/or pain or it accompanies these. Muscular dysfunction has many different sources, be it pathology of the muscle tissue, dreams or injury, accompanied by a wrong muscle strain or poor posture. All this leads to physical symptoms that are often mistakenly regarded as anatomically or biochemically pathological and become evident through trembling, sweating, respiratory problems, palpitations, stomach problems and more. Dysponesis affects the entire organism and affects the respiratory function, gastrointestinal activity, cardio-vascular activity and the movement pattern. It produces states of exhaustion, insomnia, headaches, back pain, hyperventilation, anxiety, depression and indigestion. Dysponesis can stand alone or be embedded into a disease or the course of a disease.

The importance of dysponesis in health prevention is obvious. Chronic muscular tension causes pain, which in turn entails a poor posture and/or further tension. Just think of a dental appointment: once the drill is in action, approximately 95% of patients tense up in order to better endure the coming pain. Often this tension also causes the sensation of pain even though none is present yet—tension increases the pain (Pirker-Binder 2008)

- **Dysponesis builds a bridge to corporate culture and shows the relationship between an unsuitable reaction on stress and anxiety and high muscle tension. Biofeedback measurement and training can give an answer to that.**

12.7 Biofeedback and Ergonomics at the Workplace

In the field of ergonomics, the focus is not on the attitude to work or work experience, but the body posture, which is adopted during work, such as tense, pulled-up shoulders, neck, forehead, cramped breathing, twisted sitting position, incorrectly adjusted office furniture or screens, which can cause eye problems or headaches. It is about resource-oriented work with the right body posture and micro-breaks for the prevention of chronic tension, but also about restoring healthy awareness of the needs of the body and preventing pain through disuse. To measure the influence of psychological and physical stress on the body, HRV measurement during working hours, shift work etc. seems to be useful.

The analysis gives an insight into how the organism copes with strain, or whether it still has a good regeneration capacity. By recording the daily routine in the activity record, the different stress peaks can be seen. Information about the muscular tension is provided by biofeedback measurement at the workplace, during lectures or a meeting, which can also be combined with video recording.

With the increasing number of computers and workstations with screens the related stress problem was understood in the 1990s and regulated in the EU directive 90/70/EEC Council Directive regarding the minimum safety and health requirements for work with display screen equipment.

> In Austria the implementation was carried out in §§ 67.68 ASchG (Employee Protection Act), Federal Gazette no. 450/94 and in the BS-V (Ordinance for Work with Visual Display Units). § 67 (2) ASchG states that employers are obliged to design ergonomic screen workstations. (Wichtl 2007)

Compliance with the regulations is a prerequisite for complaint-free work. The complaints through screen workstations include:

- Shoulder-neck complaints 49.2%
- Back and low back pain 37.3%
- Headaches 35.4%
- Eyestrain 29.8%
- **Despite good workplace equipment, stress and tense muscles may occur—namely because of sitting in the wring position or for too long and/or unhealthy tension during work**.

Apart from a bad posture, high internal pressure, deadlines, tight time windows and high work requirements are frequently to blame for physical tension despite good workplace equipment. High muscle tension is often accompanied unconsciously and unnecessarily by high concentration.

Biofeedback measurements of muscle tension at the workplace can provide initial insight into self-inflicted complaints. Figures 12.17, 12.18, 12.19, 12.20 and 12.21, show how muscle tension and breathing change while working on the PC, depending on how much tension work causes or in how far concentration can be represented through muscle tension.

Concentration often entails muscle tension in the forehead and neck. If one is not aware of this, it is often the pain that makes the concentrated, working people take a short break or change the posture.

Biofeedback measurement makes this unconscious tension during concentration or work under pressure visible. During the training, relaxed concentration is practiced, as well as working without too much muscle tension. The goal is to use only as much muscle tension as necessary.

When writing on a computer short micro-breaks should be taken, i.e. a short release of tension to allow the muscle(s) brief relief (Fig. 12.18). In Fig. 12.17 the short relief of the muscle while writing can be seen very well. With regard to working on a PC, it is about the flow, the alternating play between adequate tension and short phases of letting go, when not writing but thinking or when the computer is processing information and one has to wait anyway. Figures 12.18, 12.19 and 12.20 show relaxed concentrated working on a PC with micro-breaks.

Biofeedback supported awareness training increases the sensitivity to the body, one begins to feel like oneself again and listens to the needs of the body. Pain is like a bomb: there is a long fuse, a long time of not realizing or suppressing, until the bomb bursts and the pain hits. Also, it is not just about working on the PC. Being aware of muscle tension is useful wherever people are at work, especially in professions that typically involve bad posture, such as musicians or dentists. Without a more sensitive awareness and feeling there will not be any change; those who are not aware of themselves, quickly fall back into old patterns of tension after a relaxing massage or physiotherapeutic treatment (Fig. 12.21).

The aim of biofeedback measurement or biofeedback training in ergonomics is perception training of the physical and psychological strain during working, making people aware of unconscious tension and tenseness and learning a

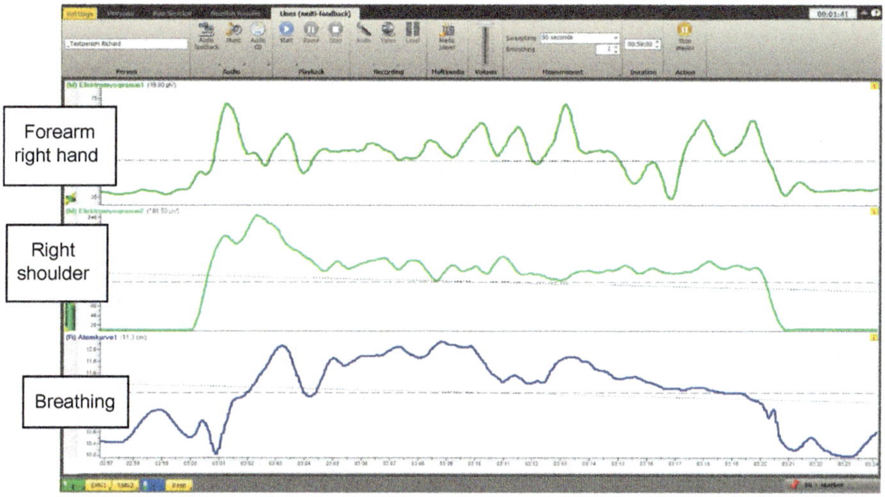

Fig. 12.17 Muscle tension measurement of the forearm of the right hand, right shoulder and breathing during writing on the computer. When typing starts, muscle tension increases and breathing becomes unrhythmical. Upper line: forearm, medium line: shoulder, lower line: breathing. *Image source* By courtesy of Schuhfried GmbH

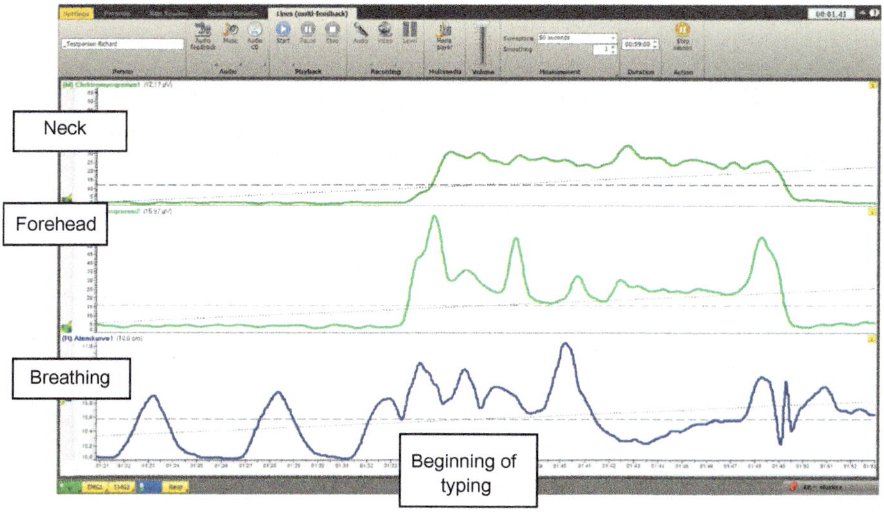

Fig. 12.18 Muscle tension in neck and forehead during concentrated typing on the PC. Breathing is unrhythmical. Upper line: neck, middle line: forehead, lower line: breathing. Image source by courtesy of Schuhfried GmbH

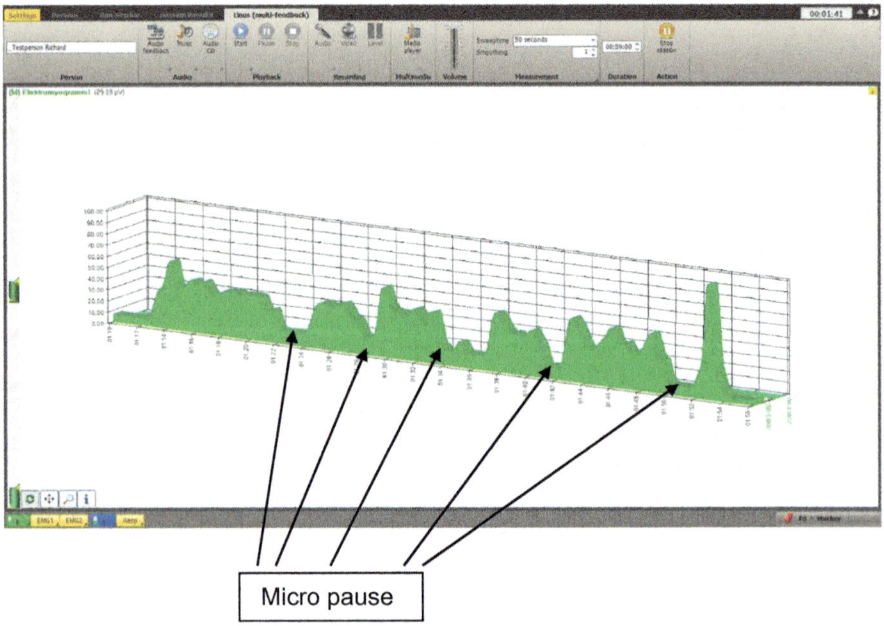

Fig. 12.19 Writing on the PC with micro-breaks; muscle tension is measured. At the low points of the graph small breaks were taken. *Image source* By courtesy of Schuhfried GmbH

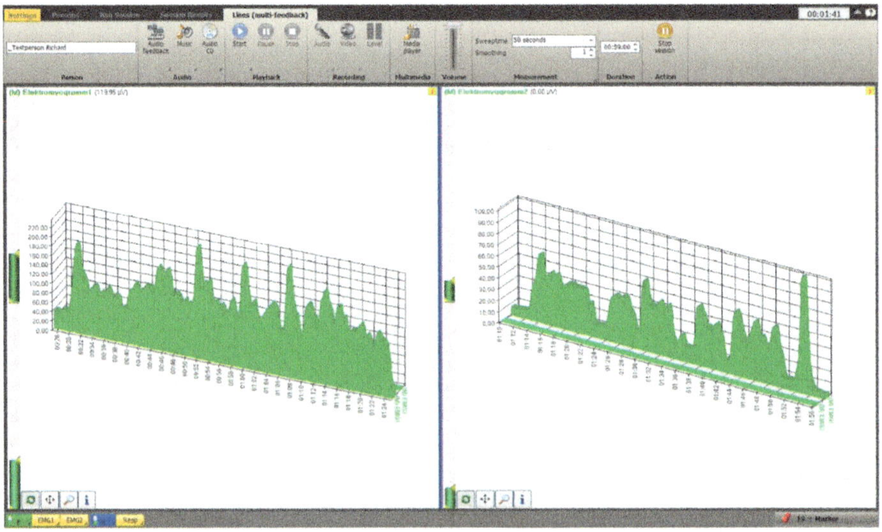

Fig. 12.20 A comparison: left—working on the PC with a lot of tension; right—working on the PC with micro-breaks. *Image source* By courtesy of Schuhfried GmbH

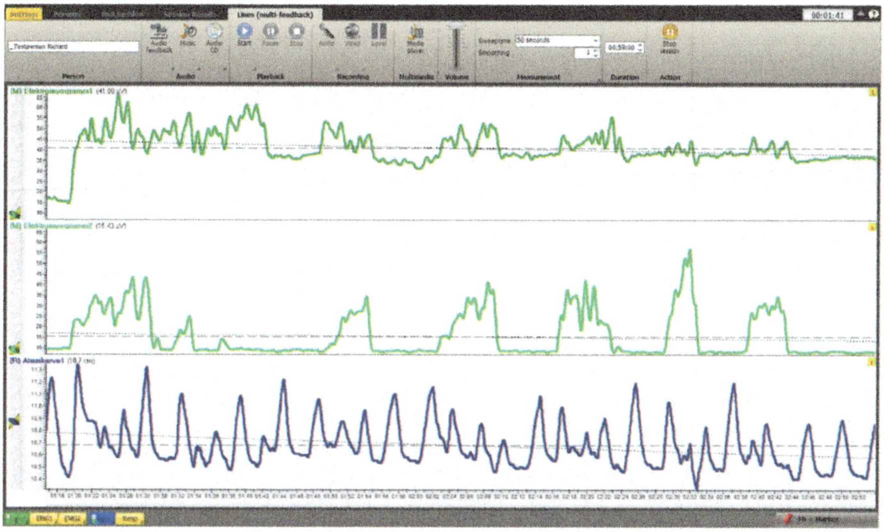

Fig. 12.21 Working on a pic with micro-breaks and regular breathing. *Image source* By courtesy of Schuhfried GmbH

resource-oriented attitude. Even the best office chair can cause discomfort if one is either sitting too long on it or with too much tension.

Aims of Working with Biofeedback in Ergonomics

- Making conscious and creating awareness of the transformation of performance pressure and/or concentration into muscle tension.
- Recognizing how inner pressure leads to tense muscles and changes in breathing, which consequently may cause stress- and workplace-related pain, respectively chronic tension.
- Learning a mindful attitude towards work with micro-breaks.
- Resource-oriented work means tension adapted to the situation with integrated micro-breaks, during which the tension is loosened rather than rigid persistence in a specific work posture.
- People at work have to learn to feel themselves again in order to establish contact to their resources.

However, not only screen workstations require special attention. Work on the assembly line, at changing workplaces (the traveling manager) or shift work need good energy management of the affected people, so that they do not become exhausted. This necessitates a high degree of sensitivity to the needs of the body and its performance capacity. Biofeedback measurements reveal tension and strain on the screen and thus provide information about different kinds of physical and psychological strain and relief.

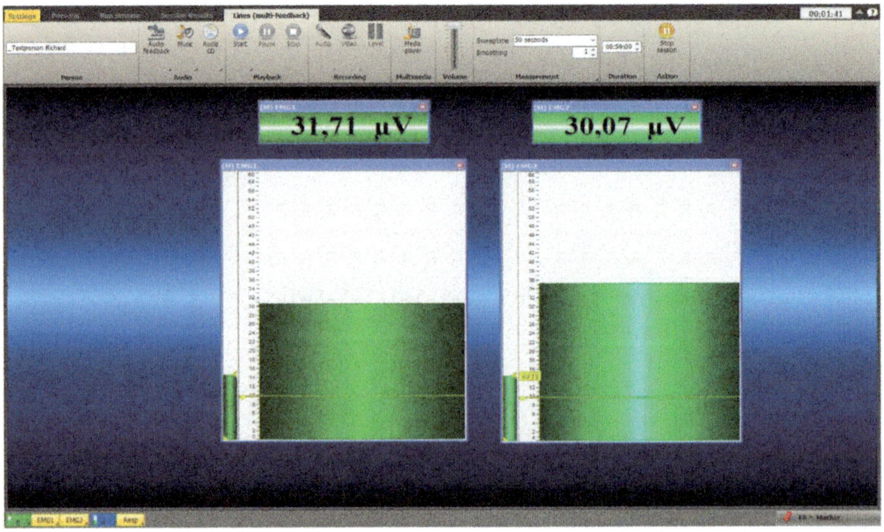

Fig. 12.22 Training screen, right and left Trapezius *Image source* By courtesy of Schuhfried GmbH

- **Relaxation is not synonymous with regeneration, but only a preliminary stage**.

One of the most important learning steps is learning regeneration. Relaxation is not regeneration, but only a preliminary stage. The term regeneration includes "to generate", i.e. one would like to generate energy again, to refuel, so to speak. Regeneration and recreation are both active processes of the passive will, that is, allowing the regeneration mechanisms of the body to happen. Small children are not yet aware of this. When they are tired, they sleep as long as they need to. Unfortunately, we unlearn these mechanisms, this feeling for what the body needs, with everyday life.

People who travel a lot and those doing shift work must comply with active and passive regeneration times. Active regeneration time may be a break; passive regeneration time is restful sleep.

- **The quality of the regeneration is determined by the ability of the respective person to go into inner stillness, to make body, mind and soul coherent.**

Biofeedback in ergonomics deals with

- Raising awareness of the body, breathing, muscle tension, regeneration mechanisms,
- Reduction of unnecessary tension, use of adequate energy,
- Healthy breathing also during work,
- adequate energy use, i.e. suitable for given task,
- Learning of micro-breaks for regeneration,
- Sleep quality.

12.8 The Process Model of the Life Energy Analysis (LEA)

The goal of a Life-Energy Analysis is to provide awareness about the use of life energy, the individual activation level, the process of activation and deactivation, and to learn self-awareness and self-control of energy use—so as to facilitate work without energy loss and the adequate use of individual resources in the work process. The Life-Energy-Analysis builds on information gained through Life Script Analysis and Work Script Analysis and supplements this subjective information with biofeedback measurement data and additional holistic measurement methods for the analysis of the stress level.

The Life Energy Analysis prepares the ground for targeted biofeedback and neurofeedback training as well as a holistic process of change. Relationships between activation and work situations or stress and psychosomatic complaints in professional and private life can be recognized and understood. If mental relaxation is very difficult, complementary neurofeedback training is recommended. It works like biofeedback training—the client learns to influence his/her brainwaves, i.e. to make them rest. Neurofeedback alone without previous biofeedback or heart rate variability training is not advisable, since only conscious awareness of the body and learning regeneration mechanisms can lead to the desired success in the long run, that is, work and life in flow.

A 24-h heart rate variability measurement as vegetative functional diagnostics represents the current use of energy. It indicates whether a specific state of activation is already exaggerated and poses a risk to health. It is also possible to determine whether sleep is restful and whether sufficient regeneration is available. This measurement provides information on the autonomous vegetative balance.

The Life Energy Analysis (Table 12.2) is considered to be a template for biofeedback consciousness and awareness training. Information from the Life Script Analysis and Work Script Analysis (Sect. 12.1) run together here. By means of biofeedback the individual can recognize the impact of negative thoughts and feelings on the activation in the body. With training supported by biofeedback new behavior, inner peace and self-control can be learned. In particular, it is learned to use activation carefully and in relation to the tasks and situations at hand, and to return to a phase of rest and regeneration in due time.

Changes in the workplace and permanent availability psychologically and physically demand a lot from people. Unfortunately, more and more people are unlearning the feeling for the needs of their body and for their physical resources. They do not get in touch with themselves any more.

Body awareness, mindfulness and consciousness exercises are an integral part of effective prevention. The so-called relaxation, which people want to turn into regeneration in the evening or on holiday, is not enough. What sport is beneficial for what people at what time is dependent on the energetic condition of their organism. It is the task of the occupational and business psychotherapist to

Table 12.2 Life Energy Analysis® (Pirker-Binder)

Test type	Content	Why?
Biofeedback test procedure		
Biofeedback HRV	24 h vegetative function diagnostics	– Strain/relief during 24-h period – Regeneration capacity during sleep, sleep diagnostics – Breaks
Multimodal biofeedback	Base line measurable parameter	Insight into psychophysiological connections, initial information
Biofeedback test procedures	Passive/active/ combined tests	– Understanding connections – Expectations – System most sensitive to stress – Stress, workplace induced and psychosomatic complaints
Biofeedback—consciousness and awareness process		
Multimodal BF	Sensitizing awareness	Self-control of activation and deactivation
RSA-biofeedback training	Coherence between breathing and heart rate	Strengthening parasympathetic nerve in the HF range
HRV-biofeedback training	Increasing coherence between – Breathing – Heart rate – Baroreflex system	– Increasing HRV = preservation of health – Learning regeneration – Serenity and mindfulness – Easing complaints
Neurofeedback		
EEG neurofeedback	Improving brain function	– Self-regulation – Improving performance – Diverse applications (ADS, ADHS, peace of mind and focusing, tics etc.)
HEG-neurofeedback	Blood circulation in the frontalis	– Direction of attention – Peace of mind
SCP-neurofeedback	Training slow potentials	Learning activation/deactivation
Complementary measurement methods		
Cortisol	Saliva test	Measurement of cortisol to determine stress level, adrenal gland fatigue
FRAS-test or others (Free Radical Analytical System Test)	– Analysis of free radicals – Antioxidative capacity	Analysis of the body's capacity to deal with oxidative stress
Complementary questionnaires/ conversations /findings	e.g. Blood count	Micronutrient requirement, allergies, other strain
Collecting data on mental states, pain symptoms, sleep quality	Questionnaires Life-script analysis Work-script analysis Mental stress and energy profile (MSEP)	Determining internal triggers Inner balance

holistically treat the people and to show them ways to concentrated serenity and resource-oriented work.

The biofeedback technology and the possibilities of heart rate variability analysis are adequate tools for the prevention of exhaustion in the workplace and complement the Life Script Analysis and Work Script Analysis. The Life-Energy Analysis provides an overview of the application of biofeedback in the work and economic world, and is complemented by alternative methods of stress measurement in the organism.

References

Aapb (2011) About biofeedback. Association of applied psychophysiology and biofeedback. Wheat Ridge, CO. URL: http://www.aapb.org/i4a/pages/index.cfm?pageid=3441. Last access: 12.1.2016

Amerikanische Gesellschaft für Psychophysiologie und Biofeedback, available at: http://www.aapb.org

Deutsche Gesellschaft für Biofeedback, available at: http://www.dgbfb.de

Eller-Berndl D (2010) Herzratenvariabilität. 1. Aufl, Verlagshaus der Ärzte, Wien

European Heart Journal (1996) Heart rate variability. Standards of measurement, physiological interpretation, and clinical use. Euro Heart J 17: 354–381. URL: http://www.ncbi.nlm.nih.gov/pubmed/8598068. Last access:12.1.2016

European Society of Cardiology (1996) Heart rate variability Standards of measurement, physiological interpretation, and clinical use. URL: http://www.escardio.org/guidelines-surveys/esc-guidelines/scientific_statements/documents/guidelines-heart-rate-variability-ft-1996.pdf. Last access: 5.7.1996

Gevirtz R, Teacher L (2003) Resonant frequency heart rate biofeedback. In Schwartz MS, Andrasik F (Hrsg) Biofeedback: a practitioners guide 3rd edn. Guilford Press, NY, S 212-244

Green E, Green A (1999) Biofeedback, eine neue Möglichkeit zu heilen. 2. Aufl Hermann Bauer, Breisgau

Haus KM, Kowalski A. Krombholz A, Nowak, Schneider, Strauß, Wiedemann (2013) Praxisbuch Biofeedback und Neurofeedback, Springer Wien Heidelberg

Harvard Business Review (2015) How to be productive without burning out. Harv Bus Rev 02/17

Johnson RW, Piscataway NJ (2000) Resonant frequency biofeedback training to increase cardiac variability: Rationale and manual for training. Appl Psychophysiol Biofeedback, 25, 177-191. URL: http://www.ncbi.nlm.nih.gov/pubmed/10999236. Last access: 25.1.2016

Lehrer PM et al (2000) Resonant frequency biofeedback training to increase cardiac variability: Rationale and manual for training. Appl Psychophysiol Biofeedback 25:177–191

Lehrer PM et al (2003) Heart rate variability biofeedback increases baroreflex gain and peak expiratory flow. Psychosom Med 65:796–805

Lehrer PM et al (Hrsg) (2007) Principles and practice of stress management, vol 3. Aufl Guilford Press, NY

Mück H Was bedeuten die gemessenen Daten? URL: http://www.dr-mueck.de/HM_HRV/HM_HRV-Bedeutung.htm. Last access 4.11.2015

Myers CW et al (2001) A model for the genesis of arterial pressure Mayer waves from heart rate and sympathetic activity. Auton Neurosci Basic Clin 91:62–75

Pirker-Binder I (2008) Biofeedback in der Praxis, Bd II Erwachsene. Springer, Wien, Heidelberg

Pirker-Binder I (2014) Biofeedback-Neurofeedback. URL: http://www.pirker-binder.at/heg-konzentrationstraining/biofeedback-neurofeedback. Last access: 5.5.2014

Pirker-Binder I (2015) Prävention von Erschöpfung am Arbeitsplatz aus Sicht der Existenzanalyse und Logotherapie nach Frankl. Dissertation SFU 2015
Porges SW (1995) Cardial vagal tone: a physiological index of stress. Neurosci Biobehav Rev 19:225–233
Porges SW (2010) Die Polyvagal-Theorie. Neurophysiologische Grundlagen der Therapie. Emotion, Bindung, Kommunikation und ihre Entstehung. Junfermann, Paderborn
Roth G (1996) Das Gehirn und seine Wirklichkeit, kognitive Neurobiologie und ihre philosophischen Konsequenzen. Suhrkamp, Frankfurt
Roth G (2009) Persönlichkeit, Entscheidung und Verhalten, warum es so schwierig ist, sich und andere zu ändern, Klett-Cotta, Stuttgart, 5. Auflage
Scharmer CO (2009) Theorie U – von der Zukunft her führen. Carl-Auer, Heidelberg
Schwartz MS, Andrasik F (2003) Biofeedback, a practitioner's guide, vol 3. Aufl. Guilford Press NY
Simonton C, Matthews Simonton S (2005) Wieder gesund werden. Eine Anleitung zur Aktivierung der Selbstheilungskräfte für Krebspatienten und ihr Angehörigen, vol 4. Aufl, Rowohlt Reinbeck
Sroka K (2002) Herzinfarkt vermeiden; neue Wege zur Vorbeugung und Heilung. Psychosozial Gießen
Vaschillo EG et al (1983) Research of the resonance characteristics for cardiovascular system. Human Physiol 257–265
Vaschillo E et al (2002) Heart rate variability biofeedback as a method for assessing baroreflex function: a preliminary study of resonance in the cardiovascular system. Appl Psychophysiol Biofeedback 27:1–27
Vaschillo E et al (2004) Heartbeat synchronizes with respiratory rhythm only under specific circumstances. Chest 126:1385–1386
Whatmore G, Kohli Dl (1974) The physiopathology and treatment of functional disorders. Grune and Stratton NY
Whatmore G, Kohli D (1979) Dysponesis. a neurophysiologic factor in functional disorders in Peper et al (Hrsg) Mind/body integration. Essential readings in biofeedback lenum Press NY
Weippert M (2009) Frequenzanalyse der Herzratenvariabilität in der Präventivmedizin. Dissertation Rostock. URL: http://d-nb.info/1000905411/34. Last access: 31.1.2015
Wichtl M (2007) Ergonomische Gestaltung von Büroarbeitsplätzen.Bundesministerium für Wirtschaft und Arbeit. URL: http://www.arbeitsinspektion.gv.at/ew07/artikel/artikel03-04.htm. Last access: 5.11.2015
Yang A (2006) Poincaré plots: a mini review. URL: http://www.physionet.org/events/hrv-2006/yang.pdf. Last access: 9.8.2014

Chapter 13
Health in the 21st Century

Ingrid Pirker-Binder

Contents

This is a time of reflection, rethinking and a new beginning. The human beings and their resources are at the center of attention, as the speed of time and the dynamism of technological development take their toll. The amount of psychological illnesses explodes and the health costs are no longer financially viable. The living conditions of the people have changed drastically. This development is creating a new awareness of human resources. The responsibility for one's health can no longer exclusively be delegated to the health system, but rather lies in the individual's own hands. Thereby people are supported by new digital technology.

Performance pressure and pressure to succeed, existential fears, multiple burdens of work and raising children, multiple jobs and performance demands in the leisure area, divorce (patchwork families), poor nutrition, environmental pollution such as contaminated water, air pollution and electrosmog, and many more affect the body, mind and soul of the people. It is not only high time, but already 10 past 12, to reflect on our values, needs and resources, if we do not want to perish despite technological top performances and significant research results.

For a long time, western health care has only concentrated on combating symptoms and diseases. The question "how does the individual human being stay healthy?" has not been asked. Performance mentality and the pursuit of ever more success, power and development has long been the prevailing goal in private life and the economic environment. The education system can be taken as an indicator of this zeitgeist.

I. Pirker-Binder (✉)
Saileräckergasse 43/26, 1190 Vienna, Austria
e-mail: office@pirker-binder.at

I. Pirker-Binder (ed.), *Mindful Prevention of Burnout in Workplace Health Management*, https://doi.org/10.1007/978-3-319-61337-6_13

Here, the foundations for the future should be laid with the children. What catches our eyes in this respect? Healthy nutrition is considered a project and not daily learning, the issue of a daily gym class at school is merely a political discussion, and much more.

In the age of resource scarcity, more mindfulness of nature, life and people is called for. Our body is a marvel of nature, a finely tuned chemical plant; the only thing it needs is air, water, food and MINDFULNESS. This means that one must not interfere in its processes and workflow; it must be given rest and regeneration, necessary nutrients and understanding. An active mind and a happy soul can only live in a healthy, balanced body. This, however, is the prerequisite for motivation, performance and work capability.

Responsibility for one's own health is first and foremost in the hands of every human being. The future goal must therefore be mindfully dealing with one's life and physical resources, so that the human being does not have to become ill to learn to appreciate health and its preservation.

Salutogenesis—preservation of health—replaces pathogenesis (healing of disease).

This leads to questions such as:

- What do people need to stay healthy?
- How can they better recognize the needs of their body?
- How do they keep body-psyche-brain healthy, active and powerful into old age?

Two pathways result from this:

1. Back to nature, to Mother Earth, to reflection, to more mindfulness and care of resources: one's own and those of the environment.
2. Taking advantage of the growing digitalization of the world and cloud communication.

13.1 Back to Nature

Great progress has been made in understanding health and the relationship between body-psyche-brain through psychosomatics, psychoneurology, neuropsychology, neurosciences, psychotherapies, etc. These scientific fields explain how psychosocial and psychological factors affect the nervous, hormonal and immune system. In psychotherapy, especially in occupational and business psychotherapy, the psychiatrist and pioneer of logotherapy and existential analysis Dr. Viktor Frankl made a great contribution. The orientation towards meaning and values has entered the economy (see Chap. 1, Sects. 1.1, 1.2, 1.4 and 1.5).

In the field of psychoneuroimmunology, cPNI, i.e. clinical psychoneuroimmunology has emerged. The significance of this still young science is the support of self-healing powers by means of active substances that the body desperately needs, such as certain herbs, supplements, etc. (see Chaps. 7, 9). They must be supplemented when a person is exhausted, or does not absorb them due to poor nutrition; abandoning the path of exclusively combating symptoms in favor of healing the causes of illnesses.[1]

Psychotherapeutic diagnosis, counseling and treatment will increasingly come to the fore, because every affect status determines the immune status (Lukas, Elisabeth 1998, Lehrbuch der Logotherapie, Profil Verlag München, Wien). Occupational and business psychotherapy particularly deals with psychological problems at the workplace. Management consulting, training, preventive measures, acute counseling, quick preventive intervention and short-term therapy are its main focus.

13.2 E-health: Digitialization and Cloud Communication

"My health is my responsibility, it lies in my hands" is the new slogan. Health cannot be handed over to doctors in general. "The doctor will put it right" is no longer universally valid. Digitization and technology are not only making working life easier, they also help interested people in staying healthy. This trend has long been visible in sports. Fitness bracelets, heart rate monitors, step counters, breathing trainers, computers attached to the fitness machines, etc. shape sports in everyday life.

What is new now is that one can keep records on one's health via PC or smartphone and APP (Fig. 13.1). If you are interested, you can enter your sleeping habits, your diet, blood values, blood pressure, heart rate variability and your training intensity into your smartphone or PC, or directly transfer them from measuring instruments. Not only that, also the transfer of the data directly to the doctor, therapist, fitness trainer or coach is now possible without sitting in the waiting room for hours. Webinars, online and Skype coaching are new ways of communication, counseling and therapy.

13.3 Outlook

New measurement and training methods are an integral part of good diagnostics and are indispensable in occupational and business psychotherapy. It somewhat relieves the strict schedule of time and space of practice-based consultation by facilitating measurement and interdisciplinary intervention at any place and at any time. Health is becoming visible and is thus increasingly moving into people's awareness and responsibility. Also, the concept of psychological health is becoming more and more understandable and is gradually losing its often negative connotation. Psychological health includes the whole human being, i.e. the harmonious interplay

[1]For more information about seminars, workshops, retreat-week mail to office@pirker-binder.at.

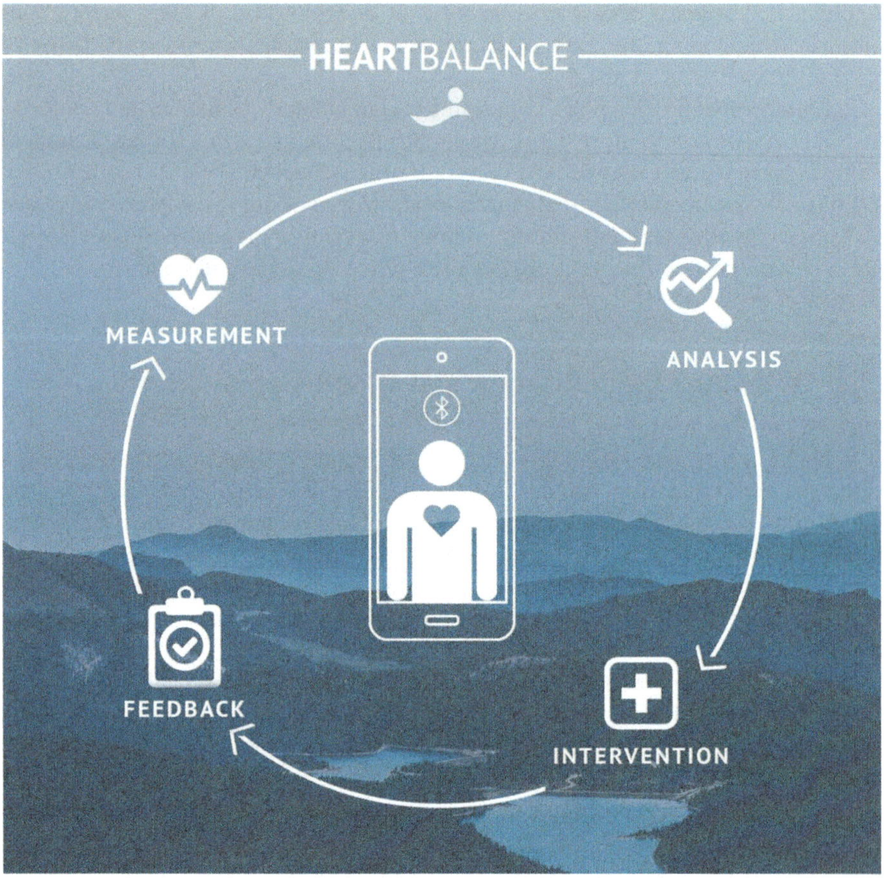

Fig. 13.1 Intervention cycle via PC, smartphone, App; provided by www.heartbalance.org

of body, brain and psyche, because "every affect status influences the immune status" (Viktor Frankl). Psychological health includes MINDFULNESS; **meaning-centered occupational and business psychotherapy integrates it into the working life. It combines economic knowledge with psychotherapeutic knowledge about psychological health. Occupational and business psychotherapy is dedicated to prevention, personality training, short-term therapy and counseling**. It is concerned with interventions in the economic context. As a new special psychotherapeutic area, it will increasingly be recognized and become a link between workplace and people with their resources.

Printed by Printforce, the Netherlands